THE
REPUBLICAN PARTY
IN GEORGIA

OLIVE HALL SHADGETT

THE REPUBLICAN PARTY IN GEORGIA

From Reconstruction through 1900

UNIVERSITY OF GEORGIA PRESS Athens

Paperback edition, 2010
© 1964 by the University of Georgia Press
Athens, Georgia 30602
www.ugapress.org
All rights reserved
Printed digitally in the United States of America

The Library of Congress has cataloged the hardcover edition of this
book as follows:

Library of Congress Cataloging-in-Publication Data

Shadgett, Olive Hall.
The Republican Party in Georgia, from Reconstruction through 1900.
ix, 210 p. 24 cm.
Bibliographical references included in "Notes" (p. 175-193)
Bibliography: p. 194-202.
1. Republican Party (Ga.) I. Title.
LC Classification: JK2358 .G4   1964
329.609758   64-22781

Paperback ISBN-13: 978-0-8203-3482-0
ISBN-10: 0-8203-3482-0

Contents

	PREFACE	vii
I	RADICALS IN RECONSTRUCTION	1
II	THE FALL FROM POWER	21
III	THE LIBERAL REPUBLICAN SPLIT IN 1872	33
IV	FACTIONALISM, FEDERALITIS, AND THE FINAL RACE FOR GOVERNOR	49
V	COOPERATION WITH THE INDEPENDENTS	61
VI	LILY-WHITE VERSUS BLACK-AND-TAN	76
VII	THE SYNDICATE	90
VIII	FUSION WITH THE POPULISTS	105
IX	TRIUMPH WITH MCKINLEY	122
X	THE NATIONAL PARTY AND THE SOUTH	137
XI	CONCLUSION: ECLIPSE ON THE GEORGIA SCENE	152
	APPENDICES	162
	NOTES	175
	BIBLIOGRAPHY	194
	INDEX	203

Preface

THIS IS the story of a fight which was lost almost before it began. The very conditions that gave rise to the Republican party in Georgia after the Civil War made almost inevitable its downfall. And the party's brief moment of power during Reconstruction only hastened its collapse as an effective political force in Georgia.

Without question, there was place for a second party in the state after the war. Georgia had not always been a one-party state. On three occasions—in 1836, 1840, and 1848—the state's electoral votes had gone to the Whig candidates for president, and during the 1830's and 1840's the Whigs frequently elected the governor and controlled the legislature.

When the national Whig party broke up during the 1850's, most of its members in Georgia turned to the Democracy because there was nowhere else to go, but many former Whigs were unhappy in the Democratic party and would have welcomed an alternative. In addition, there were many Unionists in Georgia, especially in the mountainous areas of the northern part of the state, who had opposed secession and had had little enthusiasm for the war. After the fighting was over, many of these were ready to support the Reconstruction measures as a matter of principle. These two groups formed a nucleus around which, under happier circumstances, an effective second party might have been formed.

Unfortunately, however, for the future of the Republican party in Georgia, it was from the beginning identified with the extremes of Radical Reconstruction, with bayonet rule and the Negro voter. Add to this the onus of the corrupt administration of Rufus Bullock, Georgia's only elected Republican governor, and it is easy to see why the party did not prosper in the state. After the Conservatives regained control of Georgia, most of the "better elements" of the Republican party fell away and it became more and more the party of the Negro and of the federal officeholder and office seeker. During the last two decades of the nineteenth century the state party's chief functions were to dispense the federal patronage when a Republican was in the White House and to aid in the nomination of some favorite candidate at the Republican national conventions. The last Republican candidate for governor in Georgia was nominated in 1876 and there was never any real chance of winning the presidential vote after 1868.

The role of the "Radical" (Republican) party in Georgia government before the fall of the Bullock administration is an essential part of the story of Reconstruction in Georgia and has been dealt with by many writers on that subject. In the present study this phase of the party's history is presented as an introduction. The material is taken largely from secondary sources and summarized, except in instances pertaining primarily to party activities as distinguished from the general history of the period.

There are no official party records from which to abstract this story of Republicanism in Georgia. The internal conflicts and cleavages recorded in these pages have continued almost to the present. The frequent existence of rival factions, each claiming to be the *real* Republican party in Georgia, has made it all the more difficult to find reliable accounts of party history.

Nothing included in this account is intended to reflect in any way upon the present-day Republican party in Georgia. The party in the late nineteenth century was a product of its age, and that age is gone. Just as the South of today still bears scars of the Reconstruction experience, however, so does the Republican party of the mid-twentieth century still labor to some extent under the shadow of the post-war years.

Since the Republican party was never in power in Georgia after 1872, official state records after that date include little of value on the subject. Some federal documents are helpful, but the various reports on conditions in the South during the post-war period tend to be biased and contradictory. It has been necessary to lean heavily upon accounts in contemporary newspapers, which admittedly are not always reliable, but these have been substantiated and elaborated wherever possible by information from other sources, including manuscript collections in the University of Georgia Library, the Atlanta Historical Society, and the Library of Congress.

During the several years in which this study was in progress, the author incurred a debt of gratitude to many associates who gave aid

• *Preface* ix

and comfort along the way, especially to her professors and former colleagues on the faculty of the University of Georgia. Special thanks are due to Professor Horace Montgomery of the History Department, to Regents' Professor Emeritus E. Merton Coulter, and to Albert B. Saye, Alumni Foundation Distinguished Professor of Political Science, whose assistance and encouragement were invaluable. Members of the staffs of several libraries cooperated in assembling material. Especially helpful in this respect were John Bonner, Mrs. Susan B. Tate and Mrs. Alice Willard Power of the Division of Special Collections of the Library of the University of Georgia.

The author would be ungrateful indeed if she did not include a tribute to her husband, Laurence Moss Shadgett, whose patience and forbearance made possible the preparation of this work and whose gentle but persistent prodding hastened its completion.

To these and many others the author gives credit for any merit this volume may claim to possess, while reserving for herself alone all responsibility for its deficiencies, for omissions and errors which almost certainly have been made. This story of the Republican party in Georgia is submitted not as a definitive history but as a beginning which may well be amplified at some future date.

O. H. S.

Georgia State College
Atlanta, Georgia

I

Radicals in Reconstruction

THE YEAR 1877 is generally recognized as marking the end of Reconstruction in the South, but in Georgia the downfall of Radical rule had come sooner. On January 12, 1872, amid general rejoicing, a Democratic governor was inaugurated. Both houses of the state legislature were already controlled by the conservative whites (i.e., the Democratic party). The reign of the carpetbagger and the scalawag was over.

Georgia had been "reconstructed" three times between April, 1865, and July 15, 1870. The first reconstruction had come under President Andrew Johnson. The state had complied promptly with the presidential terms: the secession ordinance had been nullified, the state's war debt repudiated, and the Thirteenth Amendment ratified. A new constitution had been written, incorporating these provisions. When all requirements had been met to the satisfaction of the President, Provisional Governor James Johnson of Columbus was relieved from office and the newly elected governor, Charles J. Jenkins, was inaugurated on December 14, 1865.[1]

This first reconstruction of Georgia was accomplished quickly and with very little bitterness or division among the people of the state. Stunned by the outcome of the war and devastated by the ravages of an invading army, most of the people of Georgia asked nothing more than to be permitted to live in peace and to retrieve their own fortunes. For the most part, politics was laid aside. Some of the leading pre-war and wartime leaders were still laboring under the disabilities imposed by the presidential plan, and there was little opposition to the candidacy of Charles J. Jenkins.

Jenkins, a Whig leader in the 1830's and 40's and author of the Georgia Platform of 1850, had opposed secession but had "gone

1

with the state." From 1860 until his inauguration as governor in 1865, he had served as a justice of the Georgia Supreme Court and had removed himself from partisan politics. Under his leadership as governor, the economy of the state was fast being restored and there was relative calm on the political front.[2]

Already there were some Republican sympathizers in the state but they were few in number and had neither the occasion nor the opportunity to make themselves felt as a political force. The first Republican candidate for president had been put forward in 1856, but neither in 1856 nor in 1860 had there been Republican electors on the ballot in Georgia. The election of a "Black Republican" in 1860 had been the trigger that set off the first wave of secession in the South. During the war there were many "Unionists" in Georgia, but at that time even the most ardent anti-secessionist would have hesitated to take the name of "Republican."

The second reconstruction of Georgia was under the Sherman Act, the general Reconstruction Act passed in March, 1867, when the radical Republicans in Congress seized control from the hands of Andrew Johnson. The Southern states were divided into five military districts; more stringent disabilities were laid upon the former leaders, and the Negroes *en masse* were given the vote. New requirements were imposed, including the ratification of the Fourteenth Amendment, and the state was ordered to draw up a new constitution embodying these additional demands.

The Reconstruction Acts of 1867 were received in Georgia with dismay and there was a great conflict of opinion regarding the course that should be followed. Paradoxically, Governor Jenkins, the old Unionist, advised the Georgia legislature to reject the Fourteenth Amendment and hastened to Washington in an unsuccessful attempt to test the constitutionality of the acts in the United States Supreme Court, while former Governor Joseph E. Brown, arch-secessionist and wartime leader, urged the people of Georgia to yield promptly to the demands of Congress. In a famous letter, dated February 23, 1867, and widely circulated, Brown expressed his views on the situation. For this he was hailed by many as a Radical sympathizer, a traitor to the Southern cause.[3]

A few months later Brown declared, "I belong to no party organization of any character, except the reconstruction party of Georgia. . . . My platform is the Sherman Act, with the Wilson supplement. . . ."[4]

It is beyond the scope of this study to probe the motives of Joseph Emerson Brown. Probably no point in Georgia history has aroused more curiosity and more controversy than this phase of Brown's career. His own explanation, then and later, was that it would be better for the state to yield quickly to the demands of Congress rather than to prolong the agony of reconstruction by defiance. He predicted that Georgia must eventually submit and that the requirements would grow more stringent rather than less. History would seem to support him on that score.

Brown and others of that ilk preferred to call themselves "Reconstructionists" rather than Republicans. The Democratic press commonly used the term *"Radicals"*—an epithet flung with scorn and fury both at the Republicans in Congress and the Reconstructionists at home. "No greater insult could be offered to a decent white man than to call him a Radical," declared the editor of the Savannah *Morning News*.[5] During this period the term "Conservatives" was often applied to the Democrats. This was done to encourage the adherence of former Whigs and others who might find the Democratic label unpalatable but who were opposed to the Reconstruction policies of Congress.

While Brown was the first top-level Democrat in Georgia to come out in open support of Republican policies, foundations for state Republican parties were being laid all over the South in the Union Leagues, or "Loyal Leagues," as they were called. The Union League of America, pledged to unconditional loyalty to the Union, had its origin in the North early in the Civil War. As the federal forces penetrated the South, the League sent its agents to organize those Southerners who showed signs of disaffection. The first members were white men, loyalists of the hill and mountain country, some old line Whigs who still hated and resented the Democrats, and others who, for personal reasons, chose to align themselves with the victors.

Working with the Freedmen's Bureau, the Northern promoters began to enroll Negroes into the League and, as the blacks became more numerous, the native whites began to withdraw. By 1868 the Union League had become predominantly a Negro movement, controlled by Radical whites who saw the opportunity to organize the freedmen for their own political gain. Appealing to the blacks by mysterious secret meetings, by ritual and regalia and fearsome oaths, the League organizers, often unscrupulous adventurers from the North, bound the freedmen into a cohesive bloc to vote the Radical ticket. The Negroes were told that Democratic victories would mean re-enslavement, and, through persuasion and intimidation, they were held in line for the Republican party.[6]

The political functions of the Union League were well recognized by Republican leaders. At the Republican national convention of 1868, reference was made to the Union League of America, "to which is due the first Republican ascendancy in the South, and upon whose efficiency depends in a great measure the success of the Republican party in the South in the coming election."[7]

The Union League became prominent in Georgia politics in 1867. It had been introduced into north Georgia in the summer of 1866, but it was not until after the passage of the Sherman Act (which extended the suffrage to the freedmen) that it assumed the character of a political agency. By the autumn of 1867 the organization had spread into 117 of the 132 counties of Georgia. At the time of the election for the constitutional convention, late in October, there were said to be 253 councils with a white membership of 27,830 and more than 300 councils with a colored membership of about 53,000.[8]

As early as May of 1867 the Augusta *Daily Chronicle* referred to a procession of some twelve hundred members of "the colored Republican Union Club" in connection with a visit to Atlanta of Henry Wilson, United States Senator from Massachusetts. Henry P. Farrow, grand secretary of the Union League in Georgia, introduced the Senator, whose address was directed chiefly to the newly franchised Negroes.[9] Early in 1868 Farrow became state president of the League, succeeding William Markham. Both Farrow and Markham were Republicans by conviction and for many years were among the top leaders of the party in Georgia.

In the registration of voters under the congressional acts of 1867, Negroes were assisted in registering by Republican managers as well as by agents of the Freedmen's Bureau. The first election in which they participated was the five-day balloting on the dual question of calling a constitutional convention and choosing delegates therefor. This election was ignored by most of the Conservatives of the state. In general the Conservatives were opposed to calling a convention and in some cases were ineligible to vote had they wished to do so. The Reconstructionists were successful in securing the convention and in electing most of the delegates. A few days after the election, a circular from the Union League headquarters in Atlanta congratulated the members upon the "brilliant triumph" that had been achieved.[10]

Of the 169 delegates to the convention, thirty-seven were Negroes and nine were white carpetbaggers, Northern men who had come to Georgia after the war to seek their political fortunes. The great majority of delegates were white men who had either been born in the South or had come to Georgia from other sections of the country before the beginning of the war. Only about a dozen of these were

Conservatives. The majority of delegates, even among the Southern-born whites, advocated the acceptance of the congressional program of Reconstruction and thus were termed, derisively, "scalawags." Some, however, were more moderate in their views than others.

The Augusta delegation furnished the heads of the Radical wing of the convention and some of the strongest Republican leaders in the state. Among members of the "Augusta Ring" were: Rufus Bullock, the only Republican ever to be elected governor of Georgia; Benjamin Conley, who succeeded Bullock as governor after his resignation; Foster Blodgett, chairman of the Republican state central committee; and John E. Bryant, secretary of the committee, a former agent of the Freedmen's Bureau, who was known as a skillful manipulator of the Negro vote.[11]

The first convention of the Republican party of Georgia and its formal organization on a statewide basis had taken place in Atlanta on July 4, 1867, with Foster Blodgett presiding. Blodgett was a native Georgian, had lived in Augusta for many years, and in 1860 had been mayor of that city. A vigorous and vocal anti-secessionist at that time, he was among the first to join the Reconstructionists after the war and in 1865 was appointed postmaster of Augusta. He prided himself on having presided at "the *last* Union meeting held in Georgia" before secession and at "the *first* Republican convention ever held in the State."[12]

The call for the convention, to be on the Fourth of July, had been issued in the name of the "Executive Committee of the Union Republican Party in Georgia" and signed by William Markham, chairman, and Henry P. Farrow, secretary.[13] It is not clear how this "executive committee" had been constituted or by what authority Markham and Farrow had called the meeting, but the use of their names indicates the close link between the Union League and the Republican party, as the two men were serving at that time as president and secretary respectively of the Grand Council of the Union League of Georgia.

Henry Farrow was a Southerner, born in South Carolina and educated at the University of Virginia, but his opposition to ideas of disunion was so intense that he had left South Carolina in 1856 "in disgust." Starting the practice of law in Cass County (later named Bartow County) in Georgia, he soon found himself again battling in a minority against sectionalism and secession. During the war Farrow was conscripted against his will but rose to the rank of captain and served as superintendent of the Georgia district of the Confederate Nitre and Mining Bureau. At the close of the war he was only thirty-one, capable, energetic, highly articulate, and still passionately opposed to disunion. He was a natural leader for the forces of Reconstruction, and as early as June, 1865, was actively promoting a meeting in Cassville of citizens ready to return to the support of the United States government. His prominence in the Union League and later in the Republican party represented the convictions of a lifetime.[14]

William Markham was also a Unionist and Republican by conviction but of very different antecedents. Born in Connecticut, he came to Georgia in 1835 and became one of the pioneer builders of Atlanta, establishing the first rolling mill in the South and amassing great wealth in real estate. In 1854 he was elected mayor of Atlanta on the Whig ticket. After the war he was one of the leading figures in the rebuilding of the city and was highly respected as a businessman and civic leader in spite of his unpopular political beliefs which led him into the Republican party.[15]

At the state convention, held in Atlanta, delegates officially adopted the name, Union Republican Party of Georgia, and Farrow headed a committee of fifteen who drew up a platform of principles for the party. Foster Blodgett, seated as president of the convention, was authorized to appoint members of a state central committee to serve with him as the governing body of the party.[16] Later in the summer meetings were held at various points in the state to ratify the action of the convention and to build support for the party. Farrow, Markham, and others spoke at these meetings, and resolutions of varying degrees of vigor were adopted.[17]

The first reference to Republicans in Georgia in Avery's *History of the State of Georgia from 1850 to 1881* is found in connection with the constitutional convention which convened in Atlanta on December 9, 1867. Isaac Avery, a contemporary historian well versed in the politics of the day, was himself an active and highly partisan Democrat but he was acquainted with leaders in both parties. In writing of the convention he listed a number of delegates as Republicans, classifying some as sincere in their politics and enjoying "personal esteem," and dismissing others simply as "others who have been prominent in the republican party."[18]

The constitutional convention, highly unpopular with Georgia Conservatives, remained in session until the middle of March, 1868. During that time Governor Charles Jenkins and State Treasurer John Jones were removed from office by General George G. Meade, commander of the Third Military District, for their refusal to draw funds from the state treasury to finance the convention. They and other statehouse officials were replaced by army officers. On March 10 the convention adopted an ordinance providing for the election of civil officers to the state, to be held over a period of four days beginning April 20. At this same election the new constitution would be presented to the voters for ratification.[19]

It was recognized that the Republican candidate for governor would probably be elected, and before the close of the convention there developed in the Republican ranks a great rivalry for the nomination. One of the leading candidates was Henry Farrow. Farrow had a strong following in the Union League and among the Unionists of north Georgia, but Radical leaders of the convention were determined to nominate Rufus Bullock.

The Farrow boom had started even before the opening of the convention and had gathered momentum during the winter months. In November a letter signed by eleven men in Dalton urged Farrow to become a candidate. Early in 1868, a circular from Union League headquarters placed his name in the running. The Griffin *American Union* printed below its masthead "For Governor of Georgia, HENRY P. FARROW." Mass meetings endorsed his candidacy in widely separated parts of the state. By the middle of February public meetings in thirty-two counties had declared in favor of Farrow.[20] A letter signed by thirty-one members of the constitutional convention, including its president, J. R. Parrott, invited him to address them in the convention hall. [21] It seemed that Farrow was well in the lead for the nomination. Backed by the League, his strength was impressive.

The "Augusta Ring," however, and other Bullock supporters in the convention were not easily deterred. Moreover, with Foster Blodgett as chairman and J. E. Bryant secretary of the Republican state central committee, this group controlled the nominating machinery. On January 22 a nominating convention was called for February 19, but on January 31 the call was cancelled and the convention suspended. Finally, after some prodding to set another date, the central committee announced on March 2 that delegates to the constitutional convention would themselves act as a nominating body and would meet for this purpose at noon on March 7.[22] Farrow and his friends charged that this maneuver was a deliberate plot to rob him of the nomination.*

*A scrap of paper in the Farrow collection bears the following statement in Farrow's handwriting, dated August 16, 1883, and initialed "H.P.F.": "The call for State Convention in 1868 as issued by Committee—when Blodgett saw that I would get the nomination over Bullock he withdrew the call and resolved the constitutional convention into a nominating body."

On the night before the nominating session, a caucus was held to protest the Blodgett-Bullock scheme. More than a hundred persons were in attendance and a strongly worded protest was adopted, together with a resolution calling for a special state convention to be held in Atlanta on March 24. In spite of this, however, the meeting for nomination was held as scheduled on the following day.[23]

At this "nominating convention," which was really a star-chamber session of Bullock's friends and supporters, the Augustan was nominated by acclamation, and the newly drafted constitution was presented as a platform, with the urgent recommendation that it be ratified. Blodgett was renamed chairman of the state central committee and delegates to the Republican national convention were appointed and instructed to vote as a unit for General Ulysses S. Grant. While all delegates to the constitutional convention were eligible to participate if they favored Reconstruction and agreed to support the new constitution, only ninety-two members were present, representing thirty-five of the state's forty-four senatorial districts.[24]

Among those present was Joseph E. Brown, who supported a move to require a two-thirds vote for nomination. Brown, allegedly, hoped thus to defeat both Bullock and Farrow and to make way for his own candidate, Judge Dawson A. Walker, member of the state supreme court. In this he was unsuccessful.[25] (As Brown was not a member of the constitutional convention, his presence at the meeting seems somewhat anomalous, but the former Governor's name—and his influence—appear time after time in the chronicles of the period.)

On the evening of the same day, a meeting was held at the city hall in Atlanta to ratify the nomination of Bullock. There were several speakers, headed by Brown, who spoke in favor of Bullock and tried to conciliate the disgruntled supporters of Farrow. Brown declared that his own choice for the nomination had been his old friend, Judge Walker, but that he would yield to the popular will and support Bullock. Supporters of the various candidates had used caucuses and other tactics, said he. "Colonel Farrow's friends used the *Leagues;* some of us used other methods. We all did the best we could. Colonel Bullock's friends outplayed us a little, and I think we should all acquiesce with a good grace, and give him our active support."[26]

A few days later Farrow addressed the members of the constitutional convention, announcing his support for the candidate and promising to campaign in his behalf. In a circular letter, also, he urged all friends of Reconstruction to unite in support of Bullock and of the new constitution.[27] At the four-day election in April, Bullock was duly elected governor of Georgia, by a majority of 7,171.[28] The Democratic candidate was General John B. Gordon, who had been nominated after two previously named candidates had been declared ineligible by General Meade.

Rufus Brown Bullock was not, strictly speaking, a carpetbagger, although that term was often applied to him. Born in New York in 1834, he came South before the war, settling in Augusta in 1859 as an agent for the Southern Express Company. Bullock opposed secession but served the Confederate cause as a special assistant to the quartermaster general. After the war he returned to Augusta, where he organized the First National Bank and was elected president of the Macon and Augusta Railroad. He was characterized by Joseph E. Brown in 1868 as "a first rate business man and a first rate manager of finances." Bullock had taken no part in state politics before the constitutional convention of 1867. He was generally regarded as an affable, likable, and capable man at that time. Avery describes him as "a large, handsome, social specimen of a man, pleasant-mannered and well-liked." While the Democrats opposed him on general principles, there was apparently no indication at the time of his election of the corruption which would mark his administration.[29]

The legislature elected at the same time as Bullock showed a clear majority for the Republicans in the Senate, while in the House of Representatives the Democrats seemed to have the edge, although the situation was somewhat confused. It is not possible to determine the exact political alignment of the two houses. Political affiliation is not recorded in the House and Senate journals, and lists in the various newspapers of the day were not always in agreement. The official list from Headquarters of the Third Military District was without party designation. Parties were not yet definitely crystallized and in some cases individuals were not consistent in their attachment to one party or the other. In one newspaper story, members were listed variously as: Negro, Radical, Democrat, Independent, and Doubtful. Avery gives the composition of the Senate as twenty-six Republicans and eighteen Democrats but says "the complexion of the House was in doubt."[30]

More accurate perhaps is the classification given by Mildred Thompson, who makes a distinction between Radical Republicans and Moderate Republicans. In both houses the Moderate Republicans held a key position, opposing Bullock on many issues and eventually leading to his downfall. At the beginning, however, the cleavage between the two wings of the party was not as pronounced as it later became. Both houses elected Republicans as their presiding officers—in the Senate, Benjamin Conley of Augusta, and in the House, R. L. McWhorter of Greene County.[31]

The new regime took office on July 4, 1868, with Bullock classified as provisional governor until July 22. The legislature ratified the Fourteenth Amendment on July 21, and Georgia was restored to the Union a second time.

One of the first actions of the new government was the election of United States senators. As those chosen by the Jenkins legislature in 1866 had never been seated, Georgia had been without representation in the Senate since secession. Both seats were now to be filled, one term to expire in March, 1871, the other in March, 1873. It was generally accepted that Bullock's candidates would be Joseph E. Brown for the long term and Foster Blodgett for the short. As early as February, even before Bullock's election, this combination had been freely predicted.[32] True to expectations the two men were nominated in a Radical caucus late in July, but Conservatives and Moderate Republicans formed a coalition to defeat the Radical ticket. Joshua Hill, a Republican, was elected for the long term and H.V.M. Miller, a Democrat, for the short.

The Democrats, who had vehemently opposed both Brown and Blodgett, were overjoyed at their defeat. While they disliked and distrusted Blodgett, they hated Brown with the intensity reserved for a friend or kinsman turned traitor. A spontaneous celebration was held at his defeat. Robert Toombs, writing of the election to Alexander H. Stephens (who had been the first choice of the Conservatives for the long-term senatorship) found a peculiar satisfaction in the fact that Brown had been beaten by Joshua Hill, a man who, in 1863, had run against Brown for the governorship on a platform of opposition to the war. "[T]here was political justice in making the earliest traitor defeat the worst one and break down his party," declared Toombs.[33]

Joshua Hill was an example of the old line Whig who had never allied himself with the Democratic party. Born in South Carolina, he had been in Georgia since early manhood, practicing law and politics. When the Whig party fell to pieces in the 1850's, Hill did not follow Toombs, Stephens, and Jenkins into the Democratic fold but became an ardent Know-Nothing and was elected to Congress on the American party platform in 1857 and again in 1859. He vigorously opposed secession and refused to acknowledge the validity of the secession ordinance. When the other Georgia representatives withdrew from Congress, Hill made quite a point of resigning instead of withdrawing.

Near the end of the war, Hill had tried unsuccessfully to persuade the Georgia legislature to make a separate peace, after spending two days in conference with General W. T. Sherman behind the Union lines. When the war was over he had hoped to be named provisional governor by President Andrew Johnson, but, failing in that, had been appointed as collector of customs at the port of Savannah. Now, as an avowed Republican, he was to take the seat in the United States Senate left vacant in 1861 by Robert Toombs himself.[34]

Georgia's members of the lower house of Congress had been elected in April, along with the governor and the members of the state legislature and had taken their seats on July 25, 1868, just three days after the official recognition of the state's return to the Union. The delegation of seven members included four Republicans and two Democrats. The other seat (that of the Sixth District) was claimed by John H. Christy, Democrat, and John A. Wimpy, Republican. Neither was seated.

Of the four Georgia Republicans in the Fortieth Congress, two were carpetbaggers. Joseph Wales Clift, of Savannah, was born in Massachusetts, had graduated from the Harvard medical school in 1862, and had acted as a surgeon in the Union army. Moving to Savannah, he practiced medicine and dabbled in politics, being appointed registrar of the city of Savannah by General John Pope under the Reconstruction Acts.

Charles Henry Prince, also a veteran of the Union army, was a native of Maine. He attended the common schools there, engaged in mercantile pursuits, and was appointed postmaster in 1861. When he settled in Georgia in 1866, he became cashier of a bank in Augusta. He served as a delegate to the state constitutional convention of 1867-68.

Another of the Georgia congressmen, Samuel Francis Gove, was born in Massachusetts but had moved to Georgia as a boy with his parents. He was a farmer and a merchant in Twiggs County, and later became an ordained Baptist minister and a traveling missionary. The fourth Republican member of the Georgia delegation, William Posey Edwards, was the only native-born Georgian in the group. A lawyer, practicing in the town of Butler, he had served during the war in the Georgia Volunteer Infantry and was a delegate to the constitutional convention of 1867-68.[35]

The Georgia members of the House of Representatives were seated just two days before the adjournment of the session of Congress. The Georgia senators were elected by the legislature two days after the adjournment of Congress and thus could not present themselves for admission until the December session. By December events had taken place in Georgia which had again placed a cloud over its status in the Union, and the admission of Hill and Miller was deferred.

From the time that the General Assembly of Georgia had convened on July 4, a controversy had raged regarding the eligibility of some of its members. The quarrel was twofold. Bullock and the Radical Republicans charged that a number of members were ineligible under the provisions of Section 2 of the Fourteenth Amendment and had not had their disabilities removed by Congress as required. The Conservatives on the other hand declared that all the Negro members of the body were ineligible, on the ground that the right of Negroes to vote did not carry with it the right to hold office. There were thirty-two Negroes in the General Assembly, three in the Senate, and twenty-nine in the House. At this juncture, a colored politician was assumed *ipso facto* to be a Radical Republican and was so classified.

Investigating committees in both houses had declared that all members were eligible to serve, and General Meade had accepted their findings and refused to go along with Bullock and the Radicals in their demands that certain members be disqualified. He saw that the dispute was personal, centering in the struggle to control the election of the two senators, and Meade was not in sympathy with the Radical group.

The most significant conflict in the legislature was between the Bullock Republicans and the anti-Bullock Republicans. The anti-Bullock, or Moderate, Republicans joined with the Democrats to elect the Moderate instead of the Radical candidates for the Senate, as related above. This victory of the Moderate-Conservative coalition, and others that followed, eventually provoked Bullock and other Radical leaders to complain in Congress that the General Assembly was not constituted in accordance with congressional requirements, and their complaint was one factor which led to the third reconstruction of Georgia.[36]

A second factor, and one which placed Georgia in an untenable position in the eyes of the nation, was the expulsion of most of the Negro members of the General Assembly. Many of those who had aligned themselves with the Republican party and acquiesced in the Reconstruction Acts, including the requirement of Negro suffrage, had never subscribed to the doctrine that suffrage gave the Negro full political equality and the right to hold office.

Finding themselves holding the balance of power in the legislature, the Moderate Republicans united with the Democrats in

September, 1868, and expelled all but two of the Negro members over the outraged protests of Bullock and the Radicals.* The vacancies left in the two houses were filled in each case by the defeated candidate who had received the next largest number of votes in the April election. This gave the Conservatives a clear majority in the lower house and cut down the Radical lead in the Senate.

The question of the expulsion of the Negro legislators never came directly before the Supreme Court of Georgia, but a test case involving the same principle was decided in June, 1869. In August, 1868, the court had been reorganized under the provisions of the new constitution, and Bullock had appointed Joseph E. Brown chief justice. The other two members were Henry K. McCay, Republican, and Hiram Warner, Democrat. Warner had been demoted from the office of chief justice to make way for Brown. The ruling of the court was strictly along party lines, Brown and McCay affirming the right of Negroes to hold office, Warner vigorously dissenting. The Chief Justice was denounced vehemently for his part in this decision, as he had asserted at an earlier date that the granting of the suffrage to Negroes would *not* give them the right to hold office. McCay, while nominally a Republican, was never active in partisan politics and drew less fire than Brown for his vote. A native of Pennsylvania, he had come to Georgia in 1839 and during the war had served under Stonewall Jackson and later as a brigadier general in the Georgia state troops. He was credited with being one of the more moderate members of the constitutional convention of 1867-68 and later was respected by all parties as judge of the United States District Court for the northern district of Georgia.[37]

The controversy over the right of Negroes to hold office continued in the General Assembly and played a key role in March, 1869, in

---

*Only twenty-five of the twenty-nine Negroes in the House of Representatives were expelled by the action of September 3. A committee was appointed to investigate the racial status of the remaining four, and two additional members were expelled when the committee reported them to have more than one-eighth Negro blood. However, Madison Davis of Clarke County and Edwin Belcher of Wilkes County continued to serve throughout the sessions of 1868 and 1869, although they were recognized as Negroes and were always referred to as such in newspaper accounts of their activities in the Republican party. In the Senate one of the Negro members, the notorious agitator Aaron Alpeoria Bradley, had already been excluded because of evidence of his conviction of a felony in New York in 1851. The two remaining senators were expelled in the action of September 3. *Journal of the House of Representatives of the State of Georgia, . . . 1868* (Atlanta, 1868), 222, 229, 242-43, 248, 336, 507; *Journal of the House of Representatives of the State of Georgia, . . . 1869* (Atlanta, 1869), *passim; Journal of the Senate of the State of Georgia, . . . 1868* (Atlanta, 1868), 137-38.

that body's rejection of the Fifteenth Amendment. This rejection was another cause that led to Georgia's third reconstruction, and Bullock's enemies charged that he himself deliberately brought about the defeat of the amendment in the hope of bringing the state back under military rule in order to strengthen his own worsening position. The facts of the case seem to support this contention. The amendment was rejected by the Radical-dominated Senate after passage in the House, where the Conservatives were in control.

When the Negro suffrage amendment was submitted to the General Assembly, the question arose as to whether it included the right to hold office, and the Governor sent a message to the legislature giving his opinion that the right of the Negro to vote did necessarily include the right to hold office. This, according to Bullock's critics, was designed to drive the Democrats from the support of the amendment. However, many moderate members, Conservatives and Republicans alike, had determined to vote for the amendment, since Negro suffrage had already been imposed on the South by the congressional Reconstruction Acts. The proposal passed the House and was defeated in the Senate only because some of Bullock's supporters absented themselves from the Senate chamber rather than take an open stand on the issue.[38] Regardless of how the action came about, the defeat of the amendment placed yet another black mark against Georgia in the eyes of the Radical Republicans who controlled Congress.

The rejection of the Fifteenth Amendment, the expulsion of the Negroes, and the alleged irregularities in the composition of the General Assembly all contributed to the third reconstruction of the state, but the event which most effectively alerted Congress to the realization that the Radicals were losing ground in Georgia and that the state might need further discipline was the vote in the presidential election in November, 1868. The Democratic electors polled almost double the number of votes given to the Republicans—over sixty-four per cent of the total.[39]

This was an amazing reversal since the election held in April, less than seven months earlier, and, in the eyes of the Radicals in Congress, must certainly indicate some skullduggery, or, more specifically, some very sharp and forceful tactics on the part of the Ku Klux Klan. More incriminating even than the total figures were comparative voting records in certain Georgia counties, where the Negro vote dropped off to a startling degree. For instance, in April the vote for Bullock in Oglethorpe County was 1,144, while in November Grant received only 116. In Columbia County, the Republican vote dropped from 1,222 in April to one lone vote in November. In eleven counties, no Republican votes were reported.⁴⁰

Aside from tactics of intimidation there were logical, legitimate reasons for the upsurge of Democratic strength and a falling off of the Republican vote. The April election had marked the peak of activity of the Union League in Georgia, while apathy and disability had taken a heavy toll of the Conservative vote. By November the Democrats were aroused to the danger of the situation, were better organized, and were ready to make a fight to regain control of the state. By this time also some of the Reconstructionists, Moderate Republicans, were beginning to fall away from Bullock and the Radicals. Moreover, the November election was held in the traditional manner of American elections, on a single day. The April balloting, extended over a period of four days, had encouraged multiple voting and other corrupt practices on the part of the Radical leaders with their large and mobile battalions of Negro voters.

Even so, it is generally recognized that the Conservatives used a great variety of questionable tactics to lessen the Republican vote. By November, aroused white men were meeting fire with fire, threat with counterthreat, and intimidation with forms of coercion more effective than the Union League could afford. A modern historian writes: "The Klan's most spectacular work was done in convincing the Negroes that politics was a game reserved exclusively for the white man."⁴¹

The poor showing of the Republicans in Georgia was all the more disappointing to national party leaders in light of the bold promises made by Joseph E. Brown at the Republican national convention in Chicago in May. Brown had led a delegation of Georgia Republicans to the convention, where they participated in the nomination of Ulysses Grant and Schuyler Colfax.⁴²

There is no indication in the official report of the convention that Brown had been slated to take a conspicuous part in the proceedings, but the former Governor was a marked man wherever he went. At a slack moment in the program, when the assembly was awaiting the report of the credentials committee, a delegate from Louisiana called attention to the presence of a former governor of "one of the rebellious states who has since become reconstructed," and Brown was called upon for a speech. After a few perfunctory protests, he took the floor. As he warmed to his subject, he made a truly remarkable speech, punctuated frequently by cheers, applause, and cries of "Good!" "Good!" He justified his own stand in becoming a Republican and, in the course of his talk, made some observations on the principles of the Democratic party for which, in some quarters, he was never forgiven.

In conclusion, Brown promised to carry Georgia for the Republican nominees if he and his colleagues were given the fruits of their victory in the recent state election and were permitted promptly to take over the control of the state government and its patronage.[43] It should be remembered that this address was made in May, 1868, one month after the election of Bullock and the Radical legislature but before the new officials had been allowed to take office. At this point, Brown had every reason to believe that he himself would be one of those elected to the Senate, and his speech at Chicago might well have insured him a cordial reception in that body.

The Conservative press in Georgia flayed Brown unmercifully for his part in the Chicago convention. He was condemned especially for misrepresenting the Democratic party in order to ingratiate himself with his new friends. There seems no question but that, at this juncture, the former Governor had allied himself openly with the Republican party on the national as well as the state level. On his return to Georgia, Brown was active in organizing the state for Grant and Colfax. He was appointed chairman of the executive committee of the Central Grant Club of Georgia and, late in June, issued a call for rallies to be held throughout the state on July 4 in support of the Republican candidates.[44]

Late in August Brown published a long and scathing attack on the leadership of the Democratic party, once again justifying his own course and urging strong, open support for the Republican ticket. He exhorted his fellow Republicans to labor earnestly, to form clubs in every county and district, to see that every Republican enroll his name, attend meetings, and vote on election day. In conclusion, he admonished them to "rally, rally to the rescue, and bear aloft your proud banners, with Grant, Colfax, and Peace, inscribed in burning letters of living light, high upon their sacred folds."[45] Strange words indeed to flow from the pen of Georgia's wartime governor!

For the first time in Georgia, Republican electors appeared on the ballot in 1868. The list was headed by Henry P. Farrow and Amos T. Akerman as electors-at-large.[46] Farrow canvassed in person thirty-six counties, embracing all of north Georgia. In this section of the state, then as later the stronghold of white Republicanism in Georgia, the party vote held up well in comparison with the April election. In the state as a whole, however, as related above, the Republican vote dropped almost unbelievably.[47]

The result of the election, while not surprising to many in Georgia, came as a stunning blow to Radical leaders in Congress. Charges of intimidation were promptly made (and no doubt with reason) but the accusations were discounted by the Conservative press. "Their party is dead in this State," declared the Atlanta *Constitution,* "and no human power can ever even so much as galvanize it into life again."[48]

When Congress opened the electoral votes in February, 1869, there was a question as to whether the Georgia vote should be counted because of the widespread charges of intimidation of the Negro vote. After a disagreement between the two houses in the matter, it was decided to announce the tally both with and without the Georgia vote. In the meanwhile, at the opening of the session of Congress in December, 1868, the senators from Georgia had been refused admission, and the status of Georgia became uncertain again. The members of the lower house had been seated during the preceding summer, but when the Forty-first Congress convened in special session in March, 1869, and the same Georgia representatives presented themselves for admission, they were refused seats on the technical ground that their credentials did not specify that they were to serve in the Forty-first Congress as well as the Fortieth. The wording of the ordinance providing for the election of these representatives in April, 1868, would seem to leave no doubt that they were expected to serve through the Forty-first Congress, but Congress, dubious about the state of affairs in Georgia, apparently took advantage of the technical flaw in their credentials to bar their admission. The question was raised, also, as to the legality of electing members for more than one term at a single election. At any event, Georgia was left again without representation in either house of Congress.[49]

On March 5, 1869, a Republican convention was held in Atlanta, with 238 delegates representing 104 counties. Led by Foster Blodgett, state party chairman, the delegates adopted harsh resolutions condemning the state's failure to comply with the Reconstruction Acts of Congress in the organization of the General Assembly, and requesting Congress to reorganize the legislature, reseat the colored members, and establish a "loyal government." A committee was appointed to go to Washington to urge Congress to take action. On November 24, at a secret meeting of the Republican state executive committee, Blodgett, Bullock, and Benjamin Conley forced through a recommendation that the state be reconstructed for the third time. Armed with this document, Bullock proceeded to Washington to complete his scheme to return Georgia to military rule.[50]

Two days before the Forty-first Congress convened for its second session, in December, 1869, the New York *Times* published a letter from Bullock, including a copy of the resolutions adopted by the state committee. Bullock and the committee blamed all the difficulties in Georgia on the fact that persons disqualified by the Fourteenth Amendment were permitted to take seats as members of the legislature, from which vantage point they had been able "practically to nullify the whole reconstruction policy."[51]

Editorials in Northern papers denouncing alleged atrocities in Georgia, and testimony by Georgia Radicals helped to influence Congress in its view of the situation. Bullock himself was present on the floor of Congress in what was said to be "about the boldest piece of lobbying ever witnessed in Congress."[52] It was not surprising that that body, on December 22, 1869, passed an act remanding the state to military jurisdiction and requiring that the Negro members of the legislature be reseated. The act required, also, that the Fifteenth Amendment be ratified as a further condition for readmission. Thus began the state's third period of military rule and reconstruction. Backed by the United States Army and working hand in hand with General Alfred E. Terry, Bullock, again termed "provisional governor," now proceeded to do by force the things that he had not been able to accomplish by normal legislative action.

First came the reorganization of the legislature, beginning on January 10, 1870, and directed by appointees of the Governor, J. T. W. Mills in the Senate and A. L. (Fatty) Harris in the House.[53] In accordance with the special act of Congress, Bullock summoned all persons elected to the General Assembly whose names had appeared on the official list proclaimed by General Meade on June 25, 1868. These must individually take one of two oaths, either that they were not disqualified under Section 2 of the Fourteenth Amendment or that their disability had been removed by act of Congress. Eligibility in contested cases was decided by a military board appointed by General Terry. As a result of the reorganization, commonly known as "Terry's Purge," twenty-two Conservatives were declared ineligible, and the complexion of the legislature was greatly altered. One Republican replaced a Conservative member of the Senate, and twenty-one new Republican members were seated in the House. In addition, the Negroes expelled in 1868 were back. Both houses were now strongly Republican with the Radical wing in control, ready to do the bidding of Bullock and his friends.[54]

What followed is a matter of history which has been recounted many times. The scandals of the Bullock administration, the waste, the extravagance, the corruption, are not properly a part of this study. Although they took place under a Republican administration, they were aided and abetted by men who later stood high in the Democratic party of Georgia. It was a corrupt age on the national as well as on the state scene, and the corruption was by no means an exclusive attribute of the Republican party.

In February, 1870, the legislature ratified the Fifteenth Amendment and re-ratified the Fourteenth, on the ground that the 1868 legislature had not been properly constituted and therefore its actions were not legal. On this same pretext the body elected new United States senators—*three* senators, in fact. These were all Radical Republicans, the Conservative members of the legislature (with a few exceptions) refusing to vote. The "senators," none of whom were ever seated, were: Henry P. Farrow, in place of Joshua Hill for the term ending March, 1873; Richard H. Whiteley, in place of H. V. M. Miller for the term ending March, 1871; and Foster Blodgett for the next *full* term, March, 1871-March, 1877.* Under no type of reasoning should the election for the full term have taken place at this time, but the General Assembly was acting while it had the votes—and the backing of the United States Army.[55]

The third restoration of Georgia was legally completed by the Act of Congress of July 15, 1870, which declared that Georgia was once again entitled to representation in Congress. A determined effort was made in Congress to prolong the power of the Radicals in Georgia by postponing the election of a new legislature for two years. A bill to this effect was introduced by Benjamin F. Butler, but Congress would not go along. The prevailing sentiment was that Bullock had overplayed his hand in the matter and that the state had had enough reconstruction from the national legislature. The Georgia Act, as finally passed, upheld specifically the right of the people of the state to elect their legislature as provided in the Georgia Constitution.[56]

In spite of the express provisions of the act, Radicals in the

---

*Each of the three men waged a vigorous contest for the seat that he had been elected to fill. In Farrow's case the contest lasted for almost a year and while it was pending he was paid a senator's salary, from February 16, 1870, until January 30, 1871, when the decision was made in favor of Joshua Hill. This salary, with mileage for 1,662 miles of travel, totaled $5,420.56. During this period he spent much time in Washington pressing his case, although he was serving at the same time as attorney general for Georgia and as special counsel for the state railroad. Farrow's commission as senator, bearing the Governor's seal, and information regarding his contest are found in the correspondence folders in the Farrow Collection.

Georgia General Assembly, realizing that their power could not be sustained for long after the end of military rule, made a desperate effort to keep themselves in office for two additional years by doing away with the 1870 elections. Termed "the crowning act of infamy" by the Milledgeville *Federal Union*,[57] the prolongation plot was finally defeated in the legislature, and elections were assured in accordance with state law. This was the beginning of the end of Radical rule in Georgia.

II

The Fall from Power

THE MOVE to do away with elections in 1870 did not affect directly the term of the governor. Rufus Bullock had been elected in 1868 for a four-year term but he had good reason to suspect that he could not maintain himself in power for long if confronted with an unfriendly legislature. If the General Assembly should be dominated by the Democrats, or even by Moderate Republicans, his freedom of action would be seriously curtailed. Moreover, Bullock must have been aware of the financial irregularities of his administration and of the probable consequences. Some of the questionable transactions had already come to light, and others would inevitably be exposed.

The prolongation dispute demonstrated the cleavage in the Republican ranks and the falling away from Bullock of many who had formerly supported him. Attorney General Henry Farrow, usually classed as a Radical, published a letter opposing the proposal to postpone the election of a new legislature, and Chief Justice Brown resisted the idea vigorously. Amos T. Akerman, who had in June been appointed by Grant as attorney general of the United States, wrote a powerful opinion against prolongation.[1] Akerman, the only Georgia Republican ever to hold a cabinet post, was a native of New Hampshire who had come South long before the war. His vigor in supporting the Reconstruction Acts made him an unpopular figure among Georgia Conservatives, but his Puritan conscience and integrity often set him at odds with the Radicals of his own party. He had withdrawn from the constitutional convention of 1867-68 because of its enactment of the "relief laws" and now he spared no words in denouncing the prolongation scheme.[2]

The night before the final vote on the measure a Republican mass meeting of protest was held at the city hall in Atlanta. In spite of attempts to disrupt the session, vigorous resolutions against prolongation were adopted. Among the speakers was Henry Farrow, who denounced Bullock and urged Republicans to stand by the right and not forsake the true principles of Republicanism.[3] The bill to defer elections had already been passed by the Senate but it was defeated in the House of Representatives on August 11 by a margin of ten votes, with twelve Republicans joining with the Democrats to kill the proposal.[4]

Although elections were now assured for 1870, the Radicals still used their power to defer as long as possible the day of reckoning. First, they postponed the date of the balloting until December 20 and adopted an election law designed to favor the Radical candidates. Second, they put off convening the new legislature for almost a year, setting the date as November 1, 1871, instead of the customary second Wednesday in January. This action was made possible by the fact that the Georgia constitution of 1868 gave the General Assembly some discretion in changing the dates specified by that document.[5]

The special election law removed all right to challenge would-be voters. A majority of the election managers in each county (three out of five) were to be chosen by the Governor, and they were instructed not to refuse or question the ballot of any male person "of apparent full age," a resident of the county, who had not previously voted at the election. The measure provided for a three-day balloting, seeking no doubt to recapture the magic formula that had brought victory to the Radicals in two previous extended elections. The act was generally ascribed to the authorship of Amos Akerman and was commonly referred to by the press as the "Akerman Election Law." The Attorney General had been widely acclaimed for his stand on prolongation, but his alleged connection with the election law plunged him into new disrepute in Conservative eyes.[6]

Farrow, opposing some provisions of the law as unconstitutional, published an opinion in which he stated that the election managers had a right before receiving the ballot of any suspected illegal voter to require him to take an oath that he had all the qualifications prescribed for voters by the Georgia constitution. Chief Justice Brown was said to entertain the same opinion.[7]

Plans for the election proceeded in both parties. District nominating conventions of the Republican party were held over the state on October 5 to name candidates for Congress. Because of the fact that no Georgia representatives had been accredited specifically to the Forty-first Congress and the hold-overs from the previous Congress had been refused seats, each district must now name two candidates, one for the short remainder of the current Congress and one for the full term of the Forty-second Congress.

The Democrats in five of the seven districts nominated the same candidates for the short and long terms, but the Republicans in most cases named two separate candidates. The nominee for the short term, which was only for a few weeks, was in several instances a Negro, while the candidate for the full term was a white man. The Milledgeville *Federal Union,* commenting cynically upon the Republican candidates for the Fourth District, Jefferson Franklin Long, a Negro, and Thomas Jefferson Speer, declared that "the colored men who constitute more than nine-tenths of the party are put off with the chaff, whilst the White trash get the wheat."[8]

In spite of the election act which permitted Bullock to supervise the balloting in every county, the Democrats gained a clear majority in each house of the state legislature and four of the seven seats in the national House of Representatives. The new legislature, which was to put an end to Radical rule in Georgia, would not convene for almost a year, but the knowledge of changes to come still further divided and demoralized the Republican party.

At the third session of the Forty-first Congress, convening in December, 1870, the Georgia members were admitted without delay to the House of Representatives. There was some question as to who were the properly elected Senators, but the claims of Joshua Hill and H.V.M. Miller were upheld over those of Farrow and Whiteley. By a special resolution, Congress suspended the test oath for Miller, and in February, 1871, he and Hill took their seats, thus giving Georgia full representation in the United States Congress for the first time in ten years.[9]

The three Republican Congressmen from Georgia were Richard Henry Whiteley from Bainbridge, Marion Bethune, Talbotton, and Jefferson Franklin Long, Macon. Bethune and Long were native Georgians, while Whiteley was born in Ireland and had immigrated to Georgia as a child. Whiteley was the only Georgia Republican who served more than one term in Congress. He was a member of the Forty-first, Forty-second, and Forty-third Congresses, and was defeated for the Forty-fourth and Forty-fifth. Admitted to the bar in Georgia in 1860, Whiteley had opposed secession but had served in the Confederate army throughout the war. He was a member of the 1867-68 constitutional convention. In 1870, he was in the peculiar position of having been elected by his district to the House of

Representatives for the Forty-first and Forty-second Congresses and having been named, in addition, to the United States Senate by the Georgia legislature. As recorded above, his claim to the Senate seat was not recognized.

Bethune also was a lawyer and had served as probate judge of Talbot County, a member of the state legislature, and a member of the convention of 1865 which repealed the ordinance of secession. Long was the only Negro ever to represent Georgia in the United States Congress, the second Negro to serve in Congress, and the first to speak on the floor of Congress. (He opposed a bill to modify the test oath.) Born a slave, he was self-educated and became a merchant-tailor in Macon. Jeff Long was active as a leader of the Negroes in the Republican party of Georgia for many years after his brief service in Congress.[10]

Though the service of the Georgia members of the Forty-first Congress was brief (until its adjournment, March 3, 1871), their admission was important, as it bore evidence to the fact that the state had once again been accepted into the Union. When the Forty-second Congress assembled in December, 1871, the Georgia members were sworn in as a matter of course, and the state was never again unrepresented. Again there were three Republicans in the House and one in the Senate. Joshua Hill was still a member of the upper house.

In addition to Whiteley, the Georgia congressmen were John S. Bigby, Newnan, and Thomas J. Speer, Barnesville. Speer died before the end of his term and was succeeded by a Democrat. A native Georgian, Speer was a merchant-farmer and had served as justice of the peace, justice of the inferior court of Pike County, delegate to the constitutional convention of 1867-68, and member of the state Senate. During the war he had been appointed collector of Confederate taxes for Pike County. On the death of Speer, one Democratic newspaper admitted grudgingly that the deceased "outside of politics was considered a clever citizen and there were much worse men in the Radical party."[11]

John Bigby was among the more prominent of the state Republicans. Georgia born and educated (Emory College at Oxford), he had been admitted to the bar in 1856 and had served as solicitor general of the Tallapoosa circuit and judge of the superior court of the same circuit before going to Congress. He, too, was a member of the constitutional convention of 1867-68. Defeated for re-election to Congress in 1872, Bigby resumed his practice of law in Atlanta and remained an influential member of the party. In 1876 he became president of the Atlanta and West Point Railroad and in 1880 succeeded Henry Farrow as United States attorney for Georgia.[12]

By the time the members of the Forty-second Congress took their seats in Washington, a sensational development had occurred in Georgia politics. Rufus Bullock had resigned and left the state!

The year 1871 had been a bad one for Bullock. The pillars of his party were crumbling away. His principal confederate in his fiscal operations, Hannibal I. Kimball, had met with reverses in his grandiose business enterprises and had left Georgia under a cloud.[13] Joseph E. Brown, the most prominent Reconstructionist in the state, had cooled off perceptibly toward Bullock and the Radicals. Besides, for the moment, Brown was more interested in business than in politics, and in December, 1870, had resigned his office as chief justice to become president of the corporation which had leased the state railroad. Foster Blodgett was a fugitive from justice, accused of cheating and swindling and suspected of embezzling large sums from the state railroad.

Bullock's own appointee as attorney general, Henry Farrow, had fought him openly on important matters of policy and was soon to repudiate him entirely. The other statehouse officers—David G. Cotting, secretary of state, Nedom L. Angier, state treasurer, and Madison Bell, comptroller general—, elected by the legislature before Terry's purge, had never really been henchmen of Bullock's, although they had been labelled "Radicals" when they were elected. Bell was a native Georgian, a graduate of the University of Georgia law department, and an officer of the Confederate forces during the war. Angier and Cotting were New Englanders, but had both come to Georgia many years before the war. All three had opposed secession and all had been Republican members of the constitutional convention of 1867-68. Bell and Cotting had been delegates to the Republican National Convention in 1868.[14]

Angier had been the first state official to sound the alarm regarding the financial irregularities of the administration, as early as January, 1869, and he and Bullock had engaged in several rounds of mutual recrimination. Efforts to impeach Angier had died in the House of Representatives in September, 1870—"postponed indefinitely."[15] Now it seemed very probable that Bullock himself would face impeachment proceedings when the new legislature should convene.

Bullock had delayed the fateful day by arranging the postponement of the 1871 session of the General Assembly, but he could not silence the hostile press nor stifle his political opponents in both parties. As the months passed the clamor grew, and it became evident that measures would be taken against the Governor as soon as the legislature convened. The General Assembly was scheduled to meet on November 1. On October 23 Bullock resigned and left the state. He left his letter of resignation with the secretary of the executive department, R. H. Atkinson, to be delivered to the secretary of state on October 30 and to take effect on that day, just two days before the meeting of the legislature.

This was a shrewd move on Bullock's part. The Georgia constitution provided that a vacancy in the office of governor should be filled by the president of the state Senate. Benjamin M. Conley, staunch Republican and friend of Bullock, had held that position in the preceding legislature and would still be considered in that capacity until the new legislature should meet and organize. Bullock hoped that Conley could be sworn in as governor and hold the office for the remainder of the unexpired term. Cotting, on receipt of Bullock's resignation, communicated immediately with Conley, and the latter presented himself promptly to be sworn in as governor. O. A. Lochrane, who had succeeded Brown as chief justice, administered the oath. Lochrane, like Brown, had been a Reconstructionist in 1867 and was generally classed as a Republican for a number of years after that, although he eventually found his way back into the Democratic ranks.[16]

Benjamin Conley was no carpetbagger, although he was born in New Jersey. He had come South as a boy, settling in Augusta while still in his teens, and was to spend his entire adult life in the South. Successful in business, Conley was prominent in local politics before the war, serving on the city council of Augusta for twelve successive years, 1845-57. He was elected mayor in 1857 and re-elected without opposition in 1859. A former Whig, Conley had opposed secession and retired to his plantation near Montgomery, Alabama, for the duration of the war. On his return to Georgia after the surrender it was natural for him to join the Republicans and to support the congressional plan for Reconstruction. He was a delegate to the constitutional convention of 1867-68 and in 1868 was elected to the state Senate, becoming its president.[17] Now he became the second Republican governor of Georgia.

In his message to the incoming legislature, Conley declared that, while it was well known to the people of Georgia that he was a consistent and unyielding Republican, he would not, in the discharge of his executive duties, permit politics to have anything to do with his conduct.[18] The tone of his message was conciliatory and its con-

The Fall from Power 27

tent irreproachable, but the legislature was in no mood to accept his leadership.

There were two opinions regarding the succession to office: that the president of the Senate should become governor, in all respects, for the remainder of the term; that he should simply carry out the executive duties as part of his office as president of the Senate. Conley took the former view. It is significant that his message to the General Assembly and all his other official communications were signed "Governor," not "Acting Governor."

The majority of the members of the legislature took the opposite view. In their eyes, the president of the Senate was to act as chief executive only until arrangements could be completed for the election of a new governor. Moreover, since Conley had been replaced as presiding officer at the opening of the session, logic would suggest that the president, L. N. Trammell, a Democrat, should exercise the *ex officio* powers. Resolutions to that effect were promptly introduced into the legislature, but the members moved slowly and warily.

The experience of the third reconstruction of Georgia was fresh in the minds of the people of the state, and there was great anxiety over the outcome of the present situation. If the Republican Conley was ousted from office, would the Republican majority in Congress again reject the Georgia representatives when the Forty-second Congress should assemble one month hence? The majority of members of the legislature determined to compromise: to permit Conley to retain the office for the time but to provide for an election for governor as quickly as possible.

The General Assembly, elected almost a year before it convened, was heavily Democratic, although there were still a goodly number of Republican members. Under the 1868 constitution the Senate term was for four years. Only half the members (those from the odd-numbered districts) were elected in 1870, and of the twenty-two senators then chosen only three were Republicans. Benjamin Conley was one of the eleven Republican senators held over from 1868. In the *Manual and Biographical Register of the State of Georgia for 1871-2*, compiled by Alexander St. Clair-Abrams, the political division of the two houses is given as follows:

Senate—Democrats	29	Republicans	14
Independent	1		
House—Democrats	136	Republicans	29
Independents	9		

There were twenty-three Negroes in the body, five in the Senate and eighteen in the House.[19] In compiling the biographical register, the author went to great pains to secure material for biographical sketches of the white members but simply listed the Negroes. In his preface he calls attention to the "manifest absurdity" of writing the lives of men "who were but yesterday our slaves." St. Clair-Abrams confesses another motive in omitting sketches of the colored members: the satisfaction of knowing that neither Congress, military government, a triple reconstruction, or even another amendment to the Constitution could compel him to publish their biographies![20] Since the colored members composed such a large percentage of the Republicans in the legislature, the *Register* gives little attention to the Republican side of the picture. As events were to prove, the Republican members were to receive little attention from *anyone*—in this and subsequent legislatures.

The session of the General Assembly which began on November 1, 1871, settled down into a fight between the Democratic majority and the Republican Governor. Among the most controversial of the acts passed was the one providing for a special election on December 19 to fill the unexpired term of Rufus Bullock. This and other measures were passed over Conley's veto. A beginning was made in untangling the state's financial snarls by the passage of the "Bond Bill," which required the registration of all outstanding state securities and laid the groundwork for the subsequent repudiation of fraudulent bonds. Several other acts were aimed at ending the waste and extravagance which had characterized Bullock's administration.[21]

After his unsuccessful attempt to forestall the special election for governor, Conley still protested the validity of the election act. There seems to have been general confusion in the ranks of the Republicans as to the course to take in this crisis. Conflicting statements found their way into the newspapers day after day. First it was said that there *would* be a nomination for governor, and the Macon *Union* went so far as to publish a schedule for a series of campaign rallies to be held in principal cities. These were allegedly to be addressed by a list of notables headed by Joseph E. Brown and Senator Joshua Hill. A Washington dispatch to the New York *Herald* on December 8 stated that Grant, Akerman, and other Republican officials endorsed the program. A few days later the Republican state executive committee declared the proposed election void and advised the Republican party to have nothing to do with it. Reports now indicated that Grant, Akerman, and the others approved the policy of ignoring the election.[22] Radical members of the General

Assembly signed a statement concurring with the latter opinion and declaring that Conley was the legal occupant of the executive chair for the remainder of Bullock's term.[23]

The bald truth seems to be that the Republicans had neither a candidate nor a platform on which a candidate could run. To base a campaign on the record of Bullock's administration would have been political suicide. To run a candidate known to have been connected with the Bullock ring would have been disastrous, but it is doubtful whether any man of stature outside the Bullock camp would have been willing to run under the circumstances. There is no indication that Conley ever intended to make the race.

Just before the election the Atlanta *Constitution* raised the cry that the Republicans were planning to run James S. Atkins as a secret candidate and that the colored voters were organized to go to the polls in a surprise move to defeat the Democratic nominee. This proved to be a false alarm.[24] Atkins indignantly denied that he was a candidate, and the Republicans for the most part ignored the election, allowing the Democrat, James M. Smith of Columbus, to win by default in one of the quietest elections ever held in the state.[25]

Two days after the election, the *Constitution* declared that although Atkins had, "over his own signature," stated that he was not the secret Republican candidate for governor, certainly his candidacy had been intended at one time. The Atlanta paper produced two telegrams to prove its point. The first, from Henry Farrow to Dr. Charles Evans of Catoosa County, stated that the national administration desired a candidate to run for governor and that Atkins had been agreed upon. Farrow asked that Evans telegraph immediately a list of names of persons willing to sign a letter to Atkins.

Evans's reply minced no words in giving his opinion of the nomination. "Atkins has no influence, less intellect," he declared. "Bullock stripe, bad egg—won't do at all." The Catoosa Republican suggested that either William Markham or James Dunning be nominated, characterizing both of them as capable and honest.[26]

The publication of these two telegrams drew an angry rejoinder from Farrow in the form of a long "card," in which he completely repudiated the administration of Bullock and explained the stand of the Republican party in regard to the election and to the situation in general.[27]

Said Farrow, at one time there was every indication that there would be a Republican candidate in the field. Early in the session of the legislature, a caucus was held at the Capitol, which had for its object the reorganization of the Republican party and the nomination of a suitable man as a candidate for governor. The meeting was composed of such men as former Governor James Johnson, John S. Bigby, Judge J. R. Parrott, Madison Bell, R. L. Mott, and a number of others who had been in no way connected with the Bullock ring.

A series of such meetings was held, according to Farrow, resulting in the partial reorganization of the party, the resignation of Foster Blodgett as chairman of the state central committee, and the actual nomination at one time of James Atkins for governor. Realizing that "the shameful administration" of Governor Bullock had driven thousands of the best men in the state out of the party, the members of the caucus were determined to go before the people upon the broad proposition that the Republican party, as a party, was not responsible for Bullock's conduct. Desiring to have a candidate against whom no charge could be made of complicity with any of Bullock's schemes, "a man of unimpeachable private character, a Republican and a gentleman," they centered upon Atkins.

However, said Farrow, the short period intervening before the election and the doubt as to the constitutionality of the election law made a "considerable portion" of the party unwilling to enter the canvass; so Atkins declined to run, and all thought of entering a candidate was abandoned. There was never any intention of running him secretly.

James Atkins, born in Georgia and educated at Bethany College in West Virginia, had practiced law in Griffin before the war but had gone to Ohio (his wife's home) at the beginning of the war and allegedly had served in the federal army. He had been active in the Republican party in Georgia since its inception and had been its unsuccessful candidate for Congress from the Seventh District in 1868. He had served in the Georgia General Assembly from 1868 through 1870 as the representative from Oglethorpe County. Judging from the House *Journal,* his record there was undistinguished. His votes were sometimes with the Bullock faction, sometimes against.

The choice of Atkins as candidate for governor seems a questionable one, especially in view of the fact that the Republican party was seeking to rid itself of the stigma of corruption. In 1870 Atkins had narrowly escaped expulsion from the legislature on charges that he had received a bribe for voting against the prolongation measure. An investigation by the House brought to light evidence that he had accepted, also, a bribe of $300 in July, 1868, for voting for Joseph E. Brown for United States senator. A resolution demanding that he be expelled was defeated only because of the fact that a two-thirds vote was required, the vote being sixty-five to forty-five in favor of expulsion. Later, in 1880, charges of corruption caused Atkins's removal as collector of customs for Savannah; and in 1882 his nomination as district judge by President Chester Arthur was opposed vigorously by the Georgia delegation in Congress and rejected by the judiciary committee of the Senate.[28] It seems doubtful that Atkins would have received much support for governor even had he chosen to run in 1871.*

Benjamin Conley was not in office long enough to prove his mettle, and the atmosphere of hostility inherited from the Bullock regime was hardly conducive to accomplishment on his part. However, Avery pronounced his administration a great improvement over that of Governor Bullock and admitted that Conley did some commendable things. "He was game and personally honest, but he was an uncompromising partisan, and struck the democracy every hard blow that he could."[29] Among the actions of Conley that brought forth the most criticism was his last-minute pardoning of Foster Blodgett for all possible charges that might grow out of the latter's administration of the state railroad.[30]

When Conley had been re-elected president of the state Senate in the reorganization proceedings of January, 1870, he had declared in the flush of victory: "The Government has determined that, in this republic—which is not, never was, and never can be a democracy—that, in this republic republicans shall rule."[31] Two years later, in January, 1872, it was clear that the people of Georgia had determined otherwise: that, in Georgia at least, Republicans should *not* rule.

Whether or not Conley would step down from the governorship peaceably was a question up to the very day of Smith's inauguration. The legislature convened on Wednesday, January 10, 1872. On the following day, the Acting Governor sent its members a

---

*Some confusion exists between the names of James Atkins and of Joseph Adkins, senator from the Nineteenth District. Atkins's name is frequently spelled "Adkins" in contemporary newspapers and even at times in the Georgia House *Journal*. Adkins, also a Republican, came to an untimely and violent end in 1869. At the beginning of the 1870 session, Senate President Conley called attention to "the seat of the murdered Adkins." *Journal of the Senate of the State of Georgia, ... 1870* (Atlanta, 1870), 27.

The confusion between these two names illustrates the difficulty encountered throughout this study in listing proper names because of variations in spelling, in initials, and sometimes even in given names. Wherever the error seems obvious, the correction has been made by the author without the formality of calling attention to the fact. Wherever there is doubt regarding the identity of a person or the correct form of his name, the name is given as in the source cited.

written communication along with the sealed packages containing returns of the election for governor held on December 19. Conley still protested the validity of the election and cited the small vote as proof that the people had not wanted a special election for the unexpired term. As a final gesture, he flung the question back to the General Assembly in the hope that it would "correct the error into which, in a heated excitement, it inadvertently fell." However, said he philosophically, if the General Assembly should declare Smith the duly elected governor, "I shall submit to a decision from which I have at present no appeal."[32]

On January 12, at noon, at a joint session in the House of Representatives chamber, the new Governor was inaugurated. The Athens *Southern Watchman* reported that Conley conducted himself "in the true spirit of gentlemanly magnanimity," accompanying Smith down the aisle and to the speaker's desk, where the new Governor was sworn in by Hiram Warner, justice of the Georgia Supreme Court. "It was certainly one act for which all the people will give him [Conley] credit," concluded the Athens paper.[33]

The Liberal Republican Split in 1872

IN MANY respects, 1872 was a year of decision in Georgia politics—and most of the decisions worked to the disadvantage of the Republican party.

When Benjamin Conley stepped down from the governor's chair, the party lost not only the executive control of the state but the great power of state patronage that went with it. The legislative majority was already lost, and, even before that, the support of the military, which had bolstered the party during the periods of reconstruction and had made it possible for the Radicals to gain and maintain their power in Georgia.

Even more serious, in its long-term implications, was the loss of confidence in and respect for the party on the part of a large segment of its own membership. The excesses of the Bullock administration had disgusted and disillusioned many Republicans. Those who had joined the ranks to promote their own good—with an eye to the loaves and fishes—now found themselves on the losing side, with little hope of nurturing their ambitions for political power. Those Reconstructionists who had acquiesced only for the good of the state found their goal had been achieved and saw little use of continuing an unpalatable affiliation. Others, who had believed sincerely in the principles of the Republican party, or who had, at the least, welcomed it as a vehicle of opposition to the Democrats, found their faith shaken by the abuses of Reconstruction. Many began to look with longing upon the greener (and more popular) pastures of the Democracy. Some had already left the Republican party. Others were simply awaiting an opportunity for a graceful exit. That opportunity was not long in coming.

The Liberal Republican movement of 1872 provided the occasion. When the national Democratic convention endorsed the candidate and the platform of the Liberal Republicans, and when the Georgia Democratic party decided to go along, a link was forged between the two parties which must have seemed heaven-sent to dissident Georgia Republicans. Across this bridge Joseph E. Brown and others made a safe passage from the foundering Republican party of Georgia to the Democratic majority.

Even among those who chose to remain in the Republican ranks, there were serious dissensions. Late in 1871, during the session of the legislature, there had been a partial reorganization of the state party, with Foster Blodgett resigning (or, possibly, being removed) from the chairmanship. It is not clear just what happened at this point, but it seems evident that there took place a struggle for power among the party leaders. By summer, Henry P. Farrow had emerged as undisputed chairman of the state central committee, but, judging from the somewhat sketchy accounts in the contemporary press, he was not in control during the early months of 1872.[1]

On January 18, 1872, just six days after the inauguration of the Democratic governor, the Republican state central committee held a meeting in Atlanta and chose delegates to the Republican national convention, not scheduled to meet until June. The greater part of the proposed delegation was composed of members of the committee itself. Other party leaders protested vigorously the precipitate action of the committee and demanded that a state convention be held to elect delegates. So far as can be determined from newspaper accounts of the January meeting, Farrow was not present, nor was his name included in the list of delegates.[2]

The apportionment of delegates to the Republican national convention at that time (and for many years afterward) allowed a state two delegates for each member of Congress. Ordinarily four of these were chosen from the state at large, with two additional representatives from each congressional district. The usual pattern in Georgia was to name state party leaders as delegates-at-large and the places were much sought after. Leaders who had been ignored at the January meeting were determined to nullify the action of the central committee.

It was reported that there would be two contesting delegations to the national convention at Philadelphia. The Atlanta *Constitution* stated that a call was being circulated for a convention to be held in Atlanta to reorganize the party and to appoint a second slate of delegates. Shortly afterward it was reported that Henry Farrow was sending around a printed petition protesting the recent appointment of delegates. The press also reported meetings of Republicans in Augusta and Albany, where resolutions of protest were adopted.[3]

Apparently nothing came of the January move to hold a state convention in Atlanta, but on May 8-9 such a meeting was held in Macon, with eighty-six counties represented by 226 delegates. Here, after much wrangling and confusion, a new delegation was chosen and a state central committee named.[4] Although apparently not yet recognized as the state party head, Henry Farrow was very much in evidence at this meeting and headed a committee to report on delegates and state central committee membership, the two most controversial questions before the convention. Judge Dawson Walker was named chairman of a committee on resolutions and business.

For some unexplained reason the proposed slate of delegates included twelve names from the state at large and three from each district, instead of the customary four and two. Thirteen of those named were federal officeholders. (No alternates were specified, but at the national convention in June some of those elected as delegates were designated as alternates, since the number was too large.)

The membership of the state central committee included eight names from the state at large and four representatives from each of the seven districts. On the state committee, as in the case of convention delegates, state party leaders were usually included among the members-at-large. Those elected at large in May, 1872, were: A. T. Akerman, Benjamin Conley, Dawson A. Walker, William Markham, George Wallace, T. W. Thurman, William Finch, and H. P. Farrow. No chairman was specified but they were listed in this order in every source examined, and the Savannah *Morning News* reported that a state central committee was appointed "headed by" Akerman and Conley.

The fact that Farrow's name was listed last among the members-at-large might be attributed to the circumstance that he was chairman of the committee that brought the report to the convention. Certainly he had no idea of taking a back seat in the party councils. Apparently he was chosen as chairman by the central committee itself shortly after the May meeting, as he is so listed in the official proceedings of the Republican national convention in June. At the next state convention, in August, he was recognized publicly as state chairman. Before that time, however, much was to happen in Republican circles in Georgia and in the nation.

It was not in Georgia alone that there was disenchantment with the Republican regime. The incompetence and corruption of the Grant administration were coming to light and there were rumblings of discontent throughout the country. This discontent crystallized early in 1872 in the Liberal Republican movement, and a convention was called to meet in Cincinnati in May to draft a platform and nominate a candidate in opposition to Grant.

This development was watched with interest by Moderate Republicans in Georgia. On May 1 the Milledgeville *Federal Union* reported that almost the entire mass of native white Republicans of Georgia were behind the movement and favored the convention in Cincinnati. Representatives had been chosen to attend the convention, and on May 2 a dispatch from Cincinnati stated that the Georgia delegation had arrived. The names listed in the press included some of those who had been most prominent in the Georgia party.* The Washington correspondent for the Savannah *News* wrote that the administration was very much astonished to find that Joseph E. Brown, James Johnson, and Thomas P. Saffold were either in favor of or had gone to the Cincinnati convention. These men had been counted on for Grant and were said to be "so pledged" by certain parties who had recently secured federal appointments on their recommendations. Actually, Brown did not attend the Cincinnati convention, as he was, at the time it took place, participating in the Georgia Baptist convention in Macon, but his subsequent actions made it plain that he favored the Liberal Republican movement.[5]

The Georgia delegates to Cincinnati were divided among themselves regarding the nomination for president and for the first five ballots their votes were split among several different candidates. On the fifth ballot, Charles Francis Adams was leading Horace Greeley 309 to 268 and it seemed that he might win on the next ballot. At this point the Georgia delegates agreed to cast all their votes for Greeley on the sixth ballot. It was said that when Georgia, with her twenty-two votes, previously divided, declared for Greeley it flashed over the house like lightning. Other states rapidly followed Georgia's lead and Greeley was nominated. The nomination of B. Gratz Brown for vice-president followed shortly afterward.[6]

One month after the Liberal Republican convention, on June 5, the regular Republican delegation from Georgia attended the official party convention in Philadelphia. John S. Bigby was chairman of the

---

*The list of appointed delegates as given in the *Federal Union* included Thomas P. Saffold, former Governor James Johnson, Edward Hulbert, John D. Pope, J. C. Hendricks, William Gibson, David B. Harrell, J. H. McWhorter, Dr. W. R. Bell, Robert M. Paris, J. W. B. Summers, John Harris, John S. Fain, William F. Bowers, Solomon L. Strickland, and Charles S. Hooks. The Atlanta *Constitution*, May 2, 1872, mentioned also the names of R. L. Mott, R. L. McWhorter, and J. K. Parrott among those who had actually arrived in Cincinnati for the convention.

Georgia delegation, which cast its twenty-two votes for Grant. The official record of the convention shows little participation by the Georgia delegates except for voting and the routine committee assignments. The only speech delivered by a Georgia man was a seconding speech in behalf of Henry Wilson for vice-president, made by J. F. Quarles, a colored delegate from Augusta. The Georgia vote for vice-president was divided—Wilson 16, Colfax 6.[7]

Benjamin Conley was the Georgia representative on the committee named to notify Grant of his nomination. A Washington observer commented on this occurrence with some humor. "Benjamin Conley, of Georgia went it slowly. He spoke with very heavy brakes on, which brought a grin." Conley said, the report continued, " 'We will do the best we can for you, Mr. President. That is as much as Georgia can do!' (Laughter)"[8]

The Democratic national convention, meeting in Baltimore early in July, determined to support Greeley and Brown and to adopt the Cincinnati platform of the Liberal Republicans. In spite of a lively controversy over the matter among the Democrats of Georgia, the party decided to go along with the national stand. On July 24 a Democratic state convention was held in Atlanta to endorse the action of the Baltimore convention and to name a slate of electors.

On the same day, July 24, Georgia Republicans who favored the election of Greeley and Brown held their own convention in Atlanta at the state Capitol, side by side with the Democrats, and there was consultation between the two groups during the day.[9] On motion of Joseph E. Brown, the Republicans appointed a committee of five to prepare a communication to the Democratic convention. The communication was signed by Brown, John Harris, John D. Pope, R. L. McWhorter, and R. L. Mott.

Stating that they represented at least fifteen thousand Republican voters in Georgia, the committee members asked that a similar committee be formed by the Democratic convention to confer with them regarding the possibility of cooperation between the two groups in the election of Horace Greeley and B. Gratz Brown. Convinced that there should be only one electoral ticket in the field for Greeley and Brown, the Liberal Republicans asked that they be allowed representation on the Democratic slate of electors.

Former Governor Brown and his colleagues on the Republican committee deplored the course of the Grant administration. Declaring that the control of the government by the extreme Radical element and the increasing centralization of government threatened the destruction of local state government and constitutional state rights, the Liberal Republicans offered to align themselves with the Democratic party of Georgia to insure victory for the forces of reform in the election of Greeley and Brown. The communication held out an added inducement for Democratic acceptance in the suggestion of a cordial cooperation in state as well as national elections.

When the Republican message was presented to the assembled Democrats it was greeted coolly, but a committee of five, headed by James Gardner of Augusta, editor of the Augusta *Constitutionalist,* was appointed to confer with the five-man Republican committee. The two committees were unable to agree upon a basis of cooperation. The Republicans asked to be treated as equals and to be given representation upon the electoral ticket. The Democratic committee, as Gardner reported to the convention, considered the request intrinsically just and reasonable but was convinced that it would be unacceptable to the convention and so declined to recommend its acceptance.

A second communication was read from the Liberal Republicans, regretting that the Democrats could not agree to cooperate, protesting their "spirit of illiberality," but promising to support the Democratic electoral ticket rather than to imperil the success of Greeley and Brown in the state. However, as to *state* elections, said they, "we hold ourselves at liberty to cast our suffrage in such manner as our self-respect and our sense of duty to the country may dictate."[10]

While the published communications from the Republican committee were not specific on this question, it was said that T. P. Saffold was the man proposed by Brown and his associates for inclusion on the Democratic slate of electors. The editor of the Atlanta *Constitution* conceded that Saffold was in many respects "a clever, worthy gentleman" and that his opposition to Bullock's "thieving administration" was very much to his credit. However, said the editor, the Democratic slate had already been chosen, and, besides, the Liberal Republicans had made no pledges about supporting the Democratic state nominees. Gardner, after his conference with the Brown committee, had said specifically that the Liberal Republicans were desirous of cooperating with the Democratic party both in the state and national elections, "and thus practically be united with the Democracy as an integral part of its organization." The failure to reach an agreement, however, and the reservation as to state elections expressed in the second Republican letter left the matter open.[11]

This uncertainty about the state elections was a source of concern to many. The editor of the Milledgeville *Federal Union* chided the

Democrats for rejecting the Liberals. "It will probably lead to an opposition State ticket," said he, "a warm contest and may possibly endanger some of our members of Congress when all might have been peace and unity."[12]

It was not until late August that the Republican party of Georgia put a candidate into the field in the gubernatorial race. At their convention on July 24 the Democrats had renominated Governor James M. Smith. On August 21, the Republicans held a convention in Atlanta and nominated Dawson A. Walker of Dalton, former justice of the Georgia Supreme Court. The Republicans also named a slate of electors for Grant and Wilson and once again reorganized the state central committee. It is not clear why the committee should have been reorganized at this time, only three months after its election at the convention held in May. Probably this unusual procedure reflects the struggle for power taking place in the party and probably, also, the falling away of some former party leaders who had joined the Liberal Republican movement, with its slant toward the Democrats.

At the August reorganization Henry Farrow was specifically designated as state party chairman. The committee still included four representatives from each district, but the members-at-large now numbered fourteen instead of eight and represented almost a complete turnover from the membership chosen in May. Of the fourteen, only three—Farrow, Akerman, and Conley—were held over from the members-at-large of the former committee. A number of those elected were Negroes. It was reported that the colored delegates were "very largely in the ascendent" at the August convention.[13]

Farrow, Akerman, and Conley had been leaders in the Republican party of Georgia since its origin and had apparently strengthened their hold on the party machinery. Because of opposition from many quarters, Akerman had been forced to resign as attorney general of the United States in December, 1871, and had refused other federal appointments reportedly offered to him by Grant.[14] Conley, ousted from the governor's office, still retained his seat in the Georgia Senate. He and his son, John L. Conley, then United States commissioner, were to hold various federal offices. Farrow had been appointed by Grant as United States district attorney for Georgia in March, 1872, resigning the office of state attorney general at that time.[15] Although Farrow had opposed Bullock for the Republican nomination for governor in 1868, he had been closely identified with the Bullock administration as attorney general. Toward the end of the regime he had fought the Governor on the prolongation issue and other matters of policy, and after the collapse of the administration had been quick to repudiate Bullock and his works.[16]

When Farrow became chairman of the Republican party in Georgia in 1872, the party was undergoing a period of readjustment. With the state patronage lost, more emphasis was placed upon the federal patronage, and the party was to come more and more under the control of the federal officeholders. The great majority of Republican voters were Negroes, but in 1872 the colored members of the party were largely dominated by the white minority. (The clash between the two races came later.) Although large segments of the "better elements" of the party had fallen away or were in process of doing so in 1872, there were still capable, substantial white men in the state who opposed the Democratic party and who had not lost hope of making the Republican party a respected and effective vehicle of opposition. Such a man was Dawson A. Walker, the Republican candidate for governor.

Walker was a native of Tennessee but in 1845 had moved to Murray County, Georgia, where he began the practice of law. Avery describes him as a self-made man, "very plain in manner and habits," but "a lawyer of uncommon ability and energy, and a citizen of integrity and pure character." Walker was a long-time friend of Joseph E. Brown and was appointed by Brown as judge of the Cherokee Circuit in 1860. In January, 1866, he was elected by the legislature to the Georgia Supreme Court, where he served until its reorganization by Bullock in 1868.[17]

After the war, Walker, like Brown, acquiesced in Reconstruction but opposed the extreme, punitive measures. In August, 1866, he was a delegate from Georgia to the National Union Convention held in Philadelphia to protest the rising Radicalism in Congress. Early in 1867, Walker went with Brown to Washington, where they talked with many people of importance. It was just after this trip that Brown published his famous "Views on the Situation," advising the people of Georgia not to resist the congressional edicts. Apparently Brown and Walker were in complete accord in the matter, as Walker immediately became active addressing meetings, writing letters to the papers, and advising all eligible to vote for the constitutional convention.[18] As related above, Walker was Brown's original choice for the Republican nomination for governor in 1868. At the ratification meeting at which Brown endorsed the nomination of Bullock, he spoke warmly of Walker, terming him "a man of sterling worth and tried integrity," and stressing the cordial personal relations between the two and also Walker's capabilities as a lawyer and judge.[19] Four years later, in 1872, when Walker was nominated for governor by the Republicans, the Atlanta *Constitution* termed the candidate their strongest man, "a gentleman of ability, influence in his section, and integrity." The editor warned his readers, however, that "Democracy is pitted against Radical[ism], constitutionalism against centralism—Smith and Greeley, with the Democracy, against Walker and Grant, with the Radicals...."[20]

The newspapers of the day carried very little information on Walker's campaign for the governorship. Whether it was a deliberate omission (a sort of conspiracy of silence) or whether the Republican candidacy was simply not considered important enough or dangerous enough to warrant much comment, it is hard to say.

During September, in the paid advertising columns of the Atlanta *Constitution,* there appeared a series of notices listing the speaking engagements of the Republican candidate. Apparently Walker centered his campaign efforts in north Georgia, his own locality, and the section of the state where, traditionally, Republicanism has had the strongest hold on white voters. His appointments from September 12 through October 2 covered sixteen counties: Greene, Clarke, Jackson, Madison, Hart, Franklin, Banks, Habersham, White, Lumpkin, Dawson, Forsyth, Cherokee, Pickens, Gilmer, and Murray. Walker's advertising card carried an invitation to his Democratic opponent to join in discussion at these appointments with assurances of "a fair and equitable division of time at each of them."[21] There is no evidence that Governor Smith accepted Walker's invitation to join him in the canvass.

While the Democratic press did not dignify Walker's candidacy by covering his campaign, the editors were by no means oblivious to his activities. In mid-September, the Milledgeville *Federal Union* warned its readers that "Dawson Walker like a sly fox is prowling around, and Amos Akerman is going to and fro like his master, the father of lies and liars, seeking whom he may devour." Later the Athens *Southern Watchman* commended Governor Smith for having "set his face against the vile practice of stump-speaking, which did not pay Judge Walker for his time and trouble."[22]

While Walker was stumping north Georgia in his own interest, Akerman, as a presidential elector, was carrying the fight to the rest of the state in behalf of Grant and Wilson. A series of paid advertisements, similar to the Walker cards, appeared in the *Constitution,* beginning on September 13, 1872, listing the Akerman engagements.

His itinerary included Augusta, Waynesboro, Savannah, Thomasville, Albany, Americus, Oglethorpe, Fort Valley, Columbus, Macon, Forsyth, Barnesville, Griffin, McDonough, and Jonesboro.

Since Walker's campaign was necessarily tied in with the candidacies of Grant and Wilson, there was much speculation regarding the stand to be taken in the state election by Georgia Republicans who were supporting Greeley for president. The Liberal Republicans at their convention in July, had pointedly made no commitment in this matter, after their offer of cooperation had been rejected by the Democrats. Walker had never been identified with the discredited Bullock faction of the party. He was known as an upright man and a friend of Governor Brown, and, it would seem, should have commanded the votes of sincere Republicans who wanted to see the position of their party improved in Georgia.

Early in September, a correspondent signing himself "A Liberal Republican" published a communication designed to answer the question, "For whom shall Liberal Republicans vote for governor?" Judge Walker, wrote he, could not expect a Liberal Republican, even though a personal friend, to vote for him. His election would be counted a Grant triumph and an endorsement by Georgia of the blunders and corruption of the Grant administration.[23]

Two weeks later a bombshell dropped on the gubernatorial campaign. Joseph E. Brown came out publicly for Smith and urged Liberal Republicans to vote not only for the Democratic candidate for governor but for other state Democratic candidates as well. Newspapers of the state, with profuse editorial comment, published a long letter from Brown directed to one John I. Hall of Thomaston. Writing in response to an inquiry as to the course Liberal Republicans in Georgia would pursue in the coming elections, and as to his own position in the matter, Brown recounted the history of the Liberal Republican movement and the action of the Democratic national convention in adopting both the candidates and the platform of the Liberal Republicans. "If the Democracy are willing to support our candidates for President and Vice-President," said he, "I think we may, without sacrificing our self-respect, support their candidates for State offices, who are pledged to the support of Greeley and Brown. . . ."[24]

Brown acknowledged his personal regard for the Republican candidate. Their acquaintance had been long and intimate, said he, and he knew Walker to be an honest, capable man, who would fill the position ably and well if elected. "If he were the Liberal candidate, it would afford me great pleasure to support him." Falling back easily into his old Democratic allegiance, the former Governor urged all to give Smith and *"our* State ticket" a great majority in October.

Brown's turning away from the state Republican candidates was a death blow to any hope that he and the Liberal Republicans might stick with the party in state elections, but it could not have come as a surprise to political observers. His opposition to Bullock and the Radical faction had been outspoken for some years. He had opposed the third reconstruction of Georgia, the prolongation proposal, the election law of 1870, and other administration measures. In December, 1871, he had written a sharp reply to a proposal that evidence be manufactured if necessary to prove that Negroes in Georgia were being denied the right to vote. "The Republican party has been constantly weakened," he declared, "until it is almost destroyed in Georgia, by the repeated acts of Congress, during the period of reconstruction, prompted no doubt by unwise counsellors professing to speak for the State. . . ."[25]

Although it is not the purpose of this study to dwell upon the motives of Joseph E. Brown, it seems fitting to observe that he would not long remain active in a party which he considered to have been "almost destroyed" by the irresponsible actions of its leaders. A few more years must pass before he would be welcomed back with full privileges into the Democratic party, but his adherence to the Republican party in Georgia was quite evidently a closed chapter.*

Fighting not only the Democrats but at the same time a sizable portion of his own party, and branded unjustly with the stigma of the Grant and Bullock administrations, the Republican candidate for governor was routed at the polls on October 2. No one was surprised that Smith was reelected, but his majority, nearly 60,000 votes, was larger than most Democrats had dared to predict.[26]

In Baldwin County, where Walker polled 158 votes to Smith's 1,069, the Milledgeville *Federal Union* ridiculed the Republican candidate: "It was all a Joke. *Dawson Walker was not a candidate.* . . . A few of the darkies voted for him just for fun."[27]

Herbert Fielder, a contemporary observer, felt that the public odium that had attached to the Republican party because of Bullock's administration and his sudden departure had completely

---

*Speaking in the United States Senate on March 28, 1881, Brown said, "I returned to the Democracy, or they returned to me, whichever you choose to call it, in 1872, . . . and I have acted steadily with them from that day to this. . . ." Herbert Fielder, *A Sketch of the Life and Times and Speeches of Joseph E. Brown* (Springfield, Mass., 1883), 633.

dispirited the rank and file of the party and many of its leaders. Though he conceded that Judge Walker was himself "an able man of good private character," Fielder was not surprised that Walker was "literally overwhelmed" by Smith, the popular Democratic governor. Writing in 1883, he saw it as "easy, logical, and natural" that Brown and other Reconstructionists had returned to the Democratic party in 1872 by their support of Greeley and Smith.[28]

Not only was the October election a great victory for Smith, but it brought corresponding victories to Democratic candidates for the state legislature. The number of Republican members and the number of Negroes were cut appreciably. In some counties independent candidates split the Democratic vote and permitted the election of Republicans. In other counties there was still a clear Republican majority. On the whole, however, the trend was sharply away from the Republican candidates.[29]

Typical of the reaction in counties where white Democrats had succeeded black Republicans was the rejoicing in Clarke and Baldwin. The Athens *Southern Watchman* heralded the new day with joy: "Old Clarke 'Redeemed, Regenerated and Disenthralled!' " The Athens *North-East Georgian* came out with an eleven-deck head to proclaim that "Old Clarke" was herself again: "Negro Representation is a Thing of the Past." For the first time since the adoption of the constitution of 1868, the county had elected two white representatives to the legislature. Madison Davis and Alfred Richardson, both Negroes, had been elected in 1868 and again in 1870. In Baldwin, the colored incumbent, George Wallace, was defeated by a landslide, 144 votes to 1,072 for his opponent, and the colored voters were praised for helping to elect a white Democrat.[30]

In numerous places throughout the state there were disorders on election day, and both sides leapt into action with charges and counter-charges. The Democrats accused the Radicals of stirring up strife at the polls in order to intimidate the white voters and to provide a pretext for interfering with the result after the election. The Republicans charged the Democrats with preventing persons from voting for Walker by the use of intimidation and also by unreasonable challenges for non-payment of taxes. During the Bullock administration the payment of the poll tax as a requirement for voting had been suspended, although it was a provision of the 1868 constitution. One of the first acts of the Democratic legislature in the fall of 1871, over the veto of Benjamin Conley, had been to restore the operation of the poll tax requirement. This was a source of much irritation and was one of the main points involved in the series of arrests and trials that occurred following the October election.

One of the most serious riots in the state on election day took place in Macon and was led by Republican Jeff Long, the former Congressman from the Fourth District. It was said that the Negroes had been organized into companies and drilled for weeks in anticipation of the election day march to the polls. As the solid phalanx of colored Republicans approached the polls, trouble broke out between white and Negro voters. Brickbats were hurled; shots were fired; and the Negroes marched back to the city hall, where the mayor tried to persuade them to return in an orderly way to vote. This they refused to do, and thus laid grounds for the claim that they had been prevented from voting by violence at the polls.[31]

In Savannah white Republican leader J. E. Bryant, deputy collector of customs, allegedly attempted to create a riot at the polls. Ordered off by a deputy sheriff, Bryant attempted to draw his pistol and was struck over the head with a club by the officer and taken to jail. In Bryan County a Negro attempted to vote without having paid his poll tax. A sheriff ordered him to leave, and a crowd of Negroes rushed upon the sheriff and beat him badly.[32]

In many other cases tempers soared and fists flew, and members of both parties were prevented from casting their ballots. The Democrats were in control of the state machinery and of most local law enforcement agencies, but the federal officers were Republicans. Operating under the Ku Klux acts, John L. Conley, United States commissioner, made arrests and Henry Farrow, United States district attorney, prepared with vigor to prosecute cases against white citizens who had allegedly interfered with the voting of Negroes. These incidents provoked some of the most bitter resentment manifested during the entire post-war period.[33] The fact that Farrow was the Republican state chairman and Conley the son of a former Republican governor gave a partisan flavor to the entire proceedings and operated to discredit the party still further in the eyes of most white Georgians.

Badly beaten in the state election in October, the Republicans now turned their faces toward the November election. At the August convention a slate of eleven electors had been named to carry the banner of Grant and Wilson (Georgia's electoral vote having been increased from nine to eleven as a result of the 1870 census).[34] Serving as an elector in 1872 was not an empty honor. The electors were chosen well in advance of the election and were expected to campaign for the party ticket. In the Democratic party, each district elector had several "sub-electors" to assist in the canvass. On the Republican side, Amos Akerman, one of the electors-at-large, had been stumping the state. Presumably the others had been active, also, but the lack of newspaper coverage of Republican activities leaves much to speculation.

Republican papers of the period were usually short-lived and obscure. At their convention in August, 1872, the Republicans had designated as official organs three papers—the Atlanta *Whig,* the Savannah *Journal,* and the *Southwest Georgian.*[35] The Atlanta *Daily New Era,* one of the best of the so-called "Radical" papers during Reconstruction, had suspended publication in March, 1872, unable to continue after the patronage of the Bullock administration was no longer available. The paper had changed hands in 1870. Under the proprietorship of Samuel Bard, it had been an ably-edited, strong mouthpiece for the Republican party. Bard, however, turned against Bullock and his wing of the party and was forced out in January, 1870. The *Era* was sold to Bullock supporters, with much speculation as to where the money came from. Later it was charged that $25,000 of the state railroad money was used to buy the paper from Bard. At the time of its suspension in March, 1872, it was the only Republican daily paper in the state.[36]

In spite of the lack of newspaper support, however, in spite of the split in the Republican party, and in spite of the disillusionment with the Grant administration, the Republican ticket in the November election polled a larger percentage of votes in Georgia than at any other presidential election in history, either before or after 1872. The Democrats won in the state, but the Republican candidates received forty-five per cent of the votes. The official tally was 76,356 for Greeley and Brown, and 62,550 for Grant and Wilson, much closer than in 1868. The Democrats carried ninety-five counties, the Republicans forty-one, with one county equally divided. In 1868 the Republicans had carried only eighteen counties.[37]

The Republican vote in Georgia in November, 1872, was larger than in 1868 numerically, percentage-wise, and in counties carried. At first glance, this seems almost incredible, in view of the great deterioration in the Republican ranks in Georgia and the tremendous Democratic majority in the state election just one month before. Several explanations suggest themselves.

First, there was the obvious fact of Greeley's unpopularity and the incongruity of his running on the Democratic ticket when he had spent most of his life as a newspaperman seeking to discredit the Democratic party. Greeley was popular neither with Democrats nor with the Liberal Republicans. Many of the latter, while agreeing with his politics, considered him too erratic and unpredictable to make an effective candidate. The rise in Republican votes in Georgia was part of a nationwide trend, and it reflected not so much an enthusiasm for Grant and the Republican party as a decided lack of enthusiasm for his opponent.

A second explanation of the increase in Republican ballots in Georgia in 1872 might be found in a lessening of intimidation of the colored voters, as compared with 1868. The tremendous Democratic victory in November, 1868, had admittedly been gained, at least in part, by discouraging large numbers of Negroes from voting. In 1872, however, during the month that elapsed between the state and national elections, vigorous efforts were being made in the federal district court to prosecute persons accused of preventing Negroes from voting in October. No doubt this served as a deterrent in November. Moreover, some Democratic leaders were beginning to see possibilities in the colored vote. Colored "Greeley Clubs" had been formed around the state, and the Negroes were encouraged to vote the Democratic ticket. While most Negro voters were still Republicans, the realization was dawning that perhaps they were not irrevocably so and that it might be better to cultivate their vote for the Democracy than to suppress it entirely.

Still another factor was the relaxing of tension after the Conservatives had regained control of the state government. In 1868, under Radical rule, Conservative leaders were almost in a frenzy to defeat the Republican ticket in the November election. By November, 1872, the danger had receded. The Democrats were firmly back in the saddle in Georgia, the Republican party in the state seemed no longer a threat, and there was a decided moderation of the vehemence of 1868.

In the congressional elections the Republicans held their own numerically, winning again in three districts, although not the same three. Since there were now nine districts instead of seven, the party distribution was six Democrats and three Republicans, a loss percentage-wise for the latter. At first it seemed that there would be only two Republicans, Whiteley re-elected in the Second District, and James C. Freeman victorious in the Fifth. In the First District, however, Andrew Sloan, the Republican candidate, contested the election of Morgan Rawls and unseated him in March, 1874.

Freeman and Sloan were both native Georgians. Freeman, then living in Griffin (later in Atlanta), was a farmer-merchant-banker, educated in the common schools of Georgia. Sloan, a Savannah lawyer, had attended Bethany College in West Virginia and had served in both the state and federal court systems in minor capacities. He had acted also as a local counsel for the United States in regard to cotton claims and with a mixed commission on British and American claims.[38]

These Republican members of Congress elected in 1872 were the last Republicans to represent Georgia in the United States Congress (as of 1963). Joshua Hill, the only Republican Senator from Georgia, had completed his term with the end of the Forty-second Congress and was succeeded in March, 1873, by John B. Gordon, Democrat.

In January, 1873, James M. Smith, the Democratic Governor, was installed for a full four-year term, and the remaining Republican statehouse officers—N. L. Angier, Madison Bell, and David Cotting—were replaced by Democrats. Tribute was paid by the Democratic press to Angier and Bell, who had refused to join in Bullock's schemes, although, in their offices of treasurer and comptroller general, they would have been in position to enrich themselves at the expense of the state. In spite of the admitted capabilities of these officers, they were *Republicans*; they had been identified with the hated Bullock administration, and it was inconceivable that they would have been elected for another term by the Democratic legislature. The Conservatives of the state rejoiced to see them go.[39] Somehow the state seemed safer and Reconstruction more and more like a bad dream, now that Democrats had moved back into the key positions of the government.

IV

Factionalism, Federalitis, and the Final Race for Governor

AS THE TERM of the governor under the 1868 constitution was for four years, the Republican party in Georgia would not be faced with another gubernatorial campaign until 1876. In the meanwhile the party had the urgent need to strengthen its organization and to consolidate its forces if it hoped to remain as a serious factor in Georgia politics. Instead, its position continued to deteriorate.

From the beginning the party had been ridden with factional strife. Even at the peak of its power there had been the Radical and Moderate wings, and Bullock's inability to control the Moderates was one of the primary causes leading to his downfall. After his resignation and exit from the state the party was reduced for a time to a condition of chaos, with rival leaders fighting for control. The lines were not clearly drawn. There were antagonisms between the carpetbaggers and the native whites, antagonisms between the whites and the Negroes, between officeholders and office seekers. Perhaps the greatest divisive force following the fall of the Bullock administration was the mad scramble for federal office, which was intensified after the party's loss of power in the state government. With all chance of state patronage gone and little hope of elective office remaining, the only recourse of the perennial office seeker was to the federal government.

So long as there was a Republican in the White House, the cause was not completely lost and all roads led to Washington in the eyes of ambitious party leaders. There, in person or by proxy, many tried to gain the ear of the President or of those who controlled the appointments. Postmasterships, internal revenue and custom house jobs, and posts in the federal courts were plums assiduously cultivated and greedily grasped by Southern Republicans—and those from Georgia were no exception. From 1872 the preoccupation with federal patronage became more pronounced and was inseparably interwoven with the party's chronic factional strife. It was an infection in the body politic—a sort of *federalitis*—to which few were immune, and it spread its way through the party leadership and affected even the rank and file.

A Republican in Augusta writing to Benjamin Conley in August, 1872, complained of the fact that in many sections of the state the party interests were being "entirely grabbed up and controlled by Federal Office Holders" who were "now filling every Committee, becoming delegates to every Convention, and shaping every party movement."[1] Frequent references to the "Revenue Clique" and the "Custom House Ring" are found in the personal correspondence and the public utterances of Republicans of the day. The fact that some of the most coveted offices were held by men from the North who had come to Georgia after the war caused much bitterness. Another of Conley's correspondents wrote with feeling of "these hungry, never-satisfied carpet-baggers, who are held in their places by the present administration."[2]

Conley, ousted from the governor's chair by the Democratic majority, remained an influential figure in the Republican party in Georgia for many years. Although he never served as its state chairman he was active as head of the Fifth District executive committee and in other positions of leadership. He was able to satisfy many of the requests he received from Republicans around the state for aid in getting federal appointments but he found great difficulty in satisfying his own ambition for office. His experience in this respect affords a good example of conditions prevalent in the Georgia Republican party during the 1870's.[3]

Conley tried unsuccessfully in 1873 and 1874 to get the appointment as postmaster in Augusta, an office held by C. H. Prince, carpetbagger from Maine, who had served briefly in the Fortieth Congress. Prince was supported by members of the "Custom House Ring," including J. E. Bryant and James S. Atkins, who held a series of federal appointments during their respective careers. Henry Farrow, chairman of the state central committee and United States district attorney for Georgia, wrote to Conley from Washington declaring his own obligation as chairman to remain neutral in the matter of appointments and advising Conley not to come upon the field.[4] A few days later, Benjamin Conley's son, John (himself an officeholder), wrote to his father warning him that Farrow was advising him to stay away in order that he might work against him. "Go to Washington," he urged. "If you stand high away you will stand high there."[5]

On the following day, John Conley wrote again to his father, and his concluding paragraph shows the intensity with which the quest for office was pursued. "Press your claims with the utmost vigor until the fight is ended and if you are defeated at Augusta *go for anything else in sight*."[6]

Particularly significant was a letter to Conley from Rufus Bullock in New York—from one Republican governor of Georgia to the only other Republican governor of the state. Bullock mentioned the fact that the entire Georgia Republican delegation in Congress was united in recommending "the Carpet Bagger [Prince]." He assured Conley of his willingness to go to Washington in his behalf but felt that this would hurt rather than help his cause, that "Bryant & Co." would use the opportunity to get at Conley through Bullock. "Of course the Georgia correspondents would fill the papers with the howl that Bullock was there *spending millions* to insure the appointment of Conley, etc., etc."[7]

In February Conley went to Washington to press his suit in person but in March his bid was rejected and Prince was reappointed. Early in 1875, however, the former Governor was again on the patronage trail, this time seeking appointment to the collectorship in Atlanta. One of his supporters, who had approached Bryant in the matter, reported to Conley that Bryant would not oppose the appointment although he did not feel at liberty to give Conley active support. Apparently, though, the bid was too late. An influential friend in Washington wrote Conley that he and others were already committed, not having known that Conley wanted the job. He suggested that Conley apply instead for the postmastership in Atlanta to replace Sam Bard, who he believed was about to be replaced. Bard, former editor of the Republican *Daily New Era* in Atlanta, had secured his own appointment only the year before, after months of hard campaigning in Washington.[8]

This latter office Conley did obtain, although the official confirmation by the Senate was not forthcoming until February 15, 1876, and then in the face of vigorous opposition from one faction of disgruntled Republicans in Fulton County. A delegation and a petition were sent to Washington protesting the appointment. But the Atlanta *Constitution's* Washington correspondent reported that the Georgians in Congress regarded Conley as "infinitely preferable" to any one of those who were desirous of stepping into his shoes. "Whatever may be his political opinions," wrote Thomas Hauck, "his integrity is undoubted, which is an excellent recommendation in these days."⁹ "These Radicals are queer folks," commented Hauck on another occasion. "They war on each other like Kilkenny cats."¹⁰

During the course of Benjamin Conley's campaigns for appointment, after his failure to obtain the postmastership in Augusta, his son had referred critically to the Georgia Republican delegation in Congress. "For myself I do not care a cent whether any of the present members are re-elected or not. I believe if they are all defeated it will tend more to break up the Ring of which Bryant is the moving power than anything else. I do not expect either to spend my time or money on any of them."¹¹

With the party leaders so lacking in harmony and cooperation and so immersed in their own personal ambitions and animosities, it was not surprising that Republicans in Georgia continued to lose strength during the period between 1872 and 1876. This was reflected without question in the results of the midterm elections of 1874. With neither a president nor a governor to be elected, there was little public interest in the campaigns, but the results showed clearly that the party had reached a new low in voting strength. In the state election in October the Republican membership in the General Assembly was drastically reduced, and in the congressional elections in November the Georgia Republican delegation in Congress was completely wiped out.

According to accounts of the October election in contemporary newspapers, there was scarcely any opposition to the Democratic candidates except in a few counties. The Republican party elected only one man to the state Senate and seven to the lower house, four whites and three Negroes. In Fulton County three Republican candidates, two white and one colored, nominated at the eleventh hour, were listed as receiving four votes each, while Jonathan Norcross, Atlanta businessman who was not a candidate, had one vote.¹²

In some counties where Republicans had formerly been in the majority, the election of Democratic candidates to the legislature was hailed with a fervid enthusiasm which showed the depth of public feeling in the matter. From Madison came a special dispatch to the Atlanta *Constitution*: "Morgan County is ablaze with a delirium of joy. . . . The odds were fearful—1300 colored, to 600 whites—but the gallant democracy of old Morgan were determined to have victory." From Bainbridge in Decatur County, a stronghold of Republicanism, came the word: "Glory to God! Decatur redeemed by 23 majority. Let the state of Georgia rejoice with us." The story from Bainbridge predicted that the work would not cease until "so help us God, Smith is elected to the next Congress, and Whitely [sic] consigned to oblivion."[13]

Richard H. Whiteley of Bainbridge was the only Georgia Republican who had served more than one term in the United States Congress. So firmly was he entrenched after three terms in the House of Representatives that the Democrats put on a special campaign to defeat him in the 1874 election, sending such influential leaders as Senator John B. Gordon and Benjamin H. Hill into southwest Georgia to speak in favor of W. E. Smith, his Democratic opponent. In the election in November, Smith won by a majority of 2,309.[14]

The other two Republican incumbents in the House, Andrew Sloan in the First District and James C. Freeman in the Fifth, were not candidates for re-election. J. E. Bryant, one of the most powerful figures in the state Republican organization, ran in the First District but was defeated by more than four thousand votes. Two Republican members of Congress from earlier years, Marion Bethune and Samuel F. Gove, were candidates in the Fourth and Sixth districts respectively, but both were defeated by large majorities.[15]

Unaffected apparently by these reverses, the factional strife within the party went on apace and party leaders continued to undermine each other in their quest for lucrative federal posts. In Atlanta in 1876 Jesse W. Jackson, leader of the *outs* in the Fulton County party organization—"ex-chairman of the ex-county republican committee"—was working against the reappointment of Henry Farrow as United States District Attorney and against the confirmation of Benjamin and John Conley for federal appointments. Republicans Sion A. Darnell, John A. Wimpy, and W. P. Pierce were rumored to be aspirants for Farrow's job, although Darnell denied the rumor and denounced the reporter who wrote the story. Farrow was still chairman of the state central committee but his influence was said to be waning.[16] James Atkins, long a target of Republicans and Democrats as well, had been forced out of at least two federal offices under a cloud, but was soon to receive another appointment. Practically every account of Republican activities in the state revealed evidences of friction and controversy.

The charge was often made (and has continued to be made until very recent years) that the leaders of the Republican party in Georgia, as in most other Southern states, were not really interested in building a large and effective party but found it to their advantage to keep the party small and more easily controlled. As early as 1872 the Atlanta *Whig* had made such charges openly, attacking "the Ring" and stating that Republican leaders in Georgia had been interested in keeping the party "as select as possible. . . . They feared the accession of new and able men as the devil fears holy water; all this that a division of offices might be made satisfactory to the few who assumed leadership."[17]

Such was the condition of the Republican party in Georgia at the beginning of 1876, a year of elections. With both president and governor to be chosen, the quadrennial election years were filled with political activity. There were delegates to the national convention to be selected and also presidential electors for the November ballot. And there was the great question of whether to nominate candidates for governor and for other statehouse offices—all this in addition to the usual biennial contests for Congress and the state legislature. Usually in presidential years the Republican party in Georgia held two state conventions, the first in the spring to name delegates to the national convention and to set up new party machinery, and the second in the summer to choose electors and to consider a state ticket. This was the procedure in 1876.

On May 3 a large and rather unruly group convened in Atlanta for a two-day meeting. The press reported an attendance of over two hundred delegates, about three-fourths of whom were Negroes. The meeting was slow in getting under way because of several vigorous contests among delegations (notably the ones from Fulton County under rival leaders, William Markham and Jesse W. Jackson), and the controversies were carried over to the floor of the convention. The temper of the meeting was described as "highly explosive." Apparently there were at least three factions, divided upon almost every question. J. E. Bryant, just reaching the peak of his influence in the party, was successful in naming C. H. Prince, Augusta postmaster, as permanent chairman. Prince and Bryant were both carpetbaggers, said to be from the same town in Maine.

Less successful was the attempt to pack the delegation to the national convention by having its members appointed by a committee named by the chair. This was beaten down after a heated argument, with Farrow and former Congressman Jeff Long, Macon Negro, supporting the right of district delegations to name their own representatives to the Cincinnati convention. The delegation, as named on May 4, included thirteen white and nine colored members and was headed by Farrow, James Atkins, George Wallace, and H. M.

Turner, as the four members-at-large. Wallace and Turner were Negroes. The delegation was almost evenly divided among supporters of the leading candidates for the presidential nomination, votes being reported for Oliver P. Morton, Benjamin H. Bristow, Roscoe Conkling, and James G. Blaine. The scramble for the votes of Southern delegates to the national conventions, which was to become a Republican party scandal in later years, had already begun, and many of the factional fights in the Georgia party can be attributed to such pressures from the outside.

Although Bryant failed in his attempt to control the delegation, he was elected chairman of the state central committee for the next four years. A large state committee was appointed, from which a smaller executive committee would be chosen. The total list included seventy names, thirty-four from the state at large and four from each of the nine congressional districts. Farrow's record as chairman was endorsed. The question of nominating a candidate for governor was deferred, and it was evident that many of those present were opposed to such a nomination. It was decided to reopen the matter at another convention in the late summer, at which time the presidential electors would also be named.[18]

The new chairman, John E. Bryant, had come to Georgia after the war as an agent of the Freedmen's Bureau and had become known as a leader of the colored men and a shrewd manipulator of the Negro vote. Soon, however, he had been barred from appearing as an attorney before the Freedmen's Court by order of General Davis Tillson, assistant commander of the bureau in Georgia, on charges that he was fomenting trouble among the colored people and taking pay from both sides to settle the difficulty. Bryant was a delegate from Richmond County to the constitutional convention of 1867-68 and the first secretary of the Union Republican central committee of Georgia. Closely associated with Bullock at first and a leader of the Radical wing of the party, he fell out with the Governor and, at the reorganization of the General Assembly in January, 1870, he collaborated with the Democrats and became the candidate of the anti-Bullock forces for speaker of the House.*
Although defeated, he continued to fight Bullock in Georgia and in

---

*Bryant's candidacy for speaker of the House was supported by many Democrats both in and out of the legislature. Robert Toombs wrote to A. H. Stephens: "... I and Joe Brown are trying to elect him! Rather a strange conjunction is it not? But you know my rule is to use the devil if I can do better to save the country." Phillips, ed., *Correspondence of Toombs, Stephens and Cobb*, 707-708.

Washington and was the author of several letters and memorials to the United States Senate exposing the "Bullock-Blodgett Ring" and opposing the admission of Foster Blodgett to the Senate in 1871.

At the time of his election in 1876 as chairman of the state central committee, Bryant was a special deputy collector of customs in Savannah and was often spoken of as the leader of the "Custom House Ring." Although he was a prominent figure in the party for many years, both before and after his term as chairman, he was cordially hated by many Georgia Republicans. In a letter written to President Rutherford Hayes early in 1877 by ten members of the party and endorsed by a number of others, Bryant was termed "the most obnoxious carpet-bagger the fortunes of a cruel war ever imposed upon our people . . . a disorganizer of the most pestilential type."[19]

Evidently the new chairman found the going rough. In July, 1876, he wrote to Henry Farrow appealing for his support and reminding the former chairman that he had stood by him for the past four years. Bryant predicted that a desperate fight would be made to remove him from the chairmanship at a convention to be held in Macon the following month. "I rely on you!" he concluded urgently.[20]

Nothing came of the attempt to remove Bryant from the chairmanship, and the convention held in Macon on August 16 was a very tame affair. Only a small group gathered for the purpose of naming presidential electors and considering the question of a candidate for governor. Two weeks previously the Georgia Democrats, in convention in Atlanta, had chosen their standard bearer, the popular Alfred H. Colquitt. To put up a man against Colquitt seemed sheer folly to many Republicans, especially since the idea of a gubernatorial candidate had had little support from the beginning.

Benjamin Conley, however, reporting for the nominating committee, recommended that a candidate be named. His report brought forth quick opposition. The most articulate speaker on the other side was William A. Pledger, a young Negro from Clarke County, editor of the Athens *Blade,* who was just coming into prominence as a party leader. Pledger took the occasion to deliver a blistering speech in criticism of the past failures and bad management of the heads of the Republican party in Georgia, blaming them for the loss of some of the best men in the party. Bryant hotly denied that the party leaders were responsible for the deterioration of Republicanism in Georgia, declaring that the party had been overthrown by the Ku Klux Klan and by fraud. There was more than one Republican, said he, who would grace the governor's chair and who was willing for his name to be used.

The report of the committee was adopted and Conley put forward the name of Jonathan Norcross, prominent Atlanta businessman who had served many years previously as mayor of Atlanta. Conley described Norcross as an old time Whig who would stump the state against Colquitt. Pledger then proposed James Atkins, who had recently been appointed collector of customs at Savannah, and Jeff Long nominated Amos Akerman, former attorney general of the United States. There was great confusion during the voting and Norcross was declared nominated "unanimously by acclamation," although little enthusiasm was reported. A Macon newspaper insisted that the candidate was nominated "by a vote of *three ayes* and *one* negative voice." "This was all the enthusiasm that could be evoked on the gubernatorial question," declared the paper, a staunch Democratic organ.[21]

Jonathan Norcross was one of the few white leaders of the Republican party in Georgia in 1876 who was not concerned with the federal patronage. Wealthy in his own right and considered one of the leading citizens of Atlanta, he was a Republican from conviction, not from expediency. He was one of the pioneer settlers in Atlanta, having come to the little village, then called Marthasville, in 1844. He was born in Orono, Maine, in 1808, the son of a clergyman, and was educated as a machinist and millwright. Before coming to Atlanta he had taught school in North Carolina and Augusta. He established a horse-operated sawmill in Atlanta and later a general store. He became one of the town's most prosperous and prominent citizens and in 1850 he was elected mayor of Atlanta on a reform ticket, running as the candidate of the "Moral Party" against the "Rowdy Party."

At that time the rowdy element was in control in the city and Norcross had his hands full maintaining order. When he began to put pressure on gamblers and other law breakers and troublemakers, he was met with violent opposition. On one occasion the "Rowdies" warned him that he must resign and leave town or else they would blow up his store. But Norcross stood his ground, organized a vigilance committee, and that night descended upon the rendezvous places of the trouble-makers and arrested the leaders.[22]

Such was the mettle of the Republican candidate for governor in 1876! By that time, however, Jonathan Norcross was sixty-eight years old, and although he had a distinguished record in business and civic affairs he had little popular appeal as a candidate and was no match for the brilliant Colquitt. Norcross had been a staunch Whig until the break-up of that party and a strong Unionist who had opposed secession. After the close of the war he cast his lot with the Republican party and supported the Reconstruction measures. He was a man of strong opinions—a stern prohibitionist, straitlaced and unyielding in his views, and vigorously opposed not only to the Democratic party but to the entire concept of democracy, which he considered to be the rule of the lawless and radical elements of society throughout history. In support of his views he wrote two books, *History of Democracy* and *Democracy Examined.*

Avery describes Norcross as "an odd, grizzly person, an intense double-dyed Republican, unskilled in party management, regarded as possessing very cranky political theories." He hastens to add, however, that Norcross enjoyed the respect of all who knew "his undoubted personal worth."[23]

A week after the Macon convention, on August 22, the Republican candidate fired the opening shot of his campaign at a ratification meeting held at the city hall in Atlanta. His speech was a thoughtful one but not designed to arouse popular enthusiasm. Norcross was not a colorful leader. As might be expected, he attacked the Democratic party on both the national and local levels. He declared that the Republican party was in the majority in Georgia but that its prospect of success was not very encouraging, because of defective election laws and the control of the polls by the Democrats. In answer to the question of what he would do in case he was elected, he said that first he would stop the plunder of the state treasury "or die in the attempt."[24]

The attack on state Democratic financial policies was a keynote of the Norcross campaign. In mid-September the candidate elaborated his theme in a two-hour speech in front of the courthouse in Macon, hammering out charges of inefficiency and corruption. According to the *Weekly Telegraph,* Norcross freely admitted in his speech and in private conversation that he had not the remotest chance of being elected, but he declared that there were some things he wanted to say to the people of Georgia and his candidacy gave him the opportunity to do so. Blaming the Democratic administrations of Governors Charles J. Jenkins and James M. Smith for an increase in the state debt of about eight million dollars since 1865, the speaker urged his listeners to instruct their members of the General Assembly to pass a law "to hang each and every man who shall propose to increase the State debt for any cause or pretense whatever."[25]

• *Factionalism, Federalitis* 59

The Atlanta *Constitution* quickly took issue with Norcross and challenged the accuracy of his figures on the public debt. To charges made by the paper regarding the corruption of the Bullock regime, Norcross answered that it was not his province or his duty to defend Bullock. "I never had anything to do with the Bullock administration, nor am I sorry. If his management was bad, that is no reason why we shall continue to have bad management." The *Constitution* countered: "Mr. Norcross is conducting an extraordinary canvass. He claims to be a republican, and yet he tries to repudiate the entire record of his party in Georgia."[26]

It was evident that Norcross found himself in a difficult position in his campaign. Conservative, shrewd, and upright in financial affairs, he could not be expected to condone or defend the Republican reconstruction in Georgia. Nor did he yield to demands made upon him by party leaders. The *Constitution* pointed out the fact that Norcross was a wealthy man and stated cynically that the party had put him up as a candidate in order to plunder him, expecting him to scatter his money freely in order to secure a large vote for himself. But, concluded the paper, "He doesn't milk worth a cent."[27]

It has been said that Norcross was hostile to the Negroes and that his attitude alienated a large section of the Republican party in Georgia. Contemporary accounts do not seem to bear this out—at least for the 1876 election. Newspaper stories of his nomination and campaign indicate strong Negro support. The reputation for hostility and race prejudice probably developed from his later attempts in 1880 and 1884 to set up a separate white Republican party. Even then he emphasized the fact that his movement was not intended to trespass upon the rights of the colored man but simply to provide for the separate exercise of political privileges. (His plan for separate political conventions for white and colored members of the party with conferences between the two groups is described below, in Chapter VI.)*

There are numerous indications that Norcross stood well with Negro members of the party in 1876. In fact, one Negro who op-

---

*The idea of Norcross's hostility to the Negro, encountered in several secondary sources but not in any contemporary newspaper stories, may stem from a misinterpretation of a statement in Avery, *History of Georgia*, 519, where the author describes Norcross's policy of establishing a white man's Republican party as a "maneuver of his in the last campaign." Since Avery's history was written in 1881, the "last" campaign here mentioned would probably have been that of 1880, when Norcross did propose such a plan. This point may easily have been overlooked by subsequent historians who assumed that Avery was referring to the campaign of 1876, as the statement quoted is part of the paragraph about Norcross's candidacy.

posed him at a mass meeting in Atlanta the night before the election was set upon by the other Negroes and had to be escorted away by a guard of police and other white men. At the state convention in May, Norcross was a member of the delegation of the Markham faction, usually considered the more nearly white wing of the party in Fulton County, but, in speaking for his delegation, he emphasized his love and efforts for the "colored population." A month earlier, at a stormy county convention, he had been nominated as permanent chairman by Jesse Jackson, leader of the colored faction, and had pled for harmony in the selection of delegates. At two mass meetings held at the city hall in Atlanta during the campaign, the large number of Negroes in attendance was particularly stressed.[28]

In 1876, apparently, Norcross made no proposals for a segregated Republican party, but it seems evident that his personality and his dull, rather pedantic speeches would not inspire much enthusiasm in voters of the colored race. As a matter of record, it happened that Alfred Colquitt, Norcross's opponent, was extremely popular with the Negroes of the state and a concerted effort was made by the Democratic party to woo the colored vote. Many Negroes did vote for Colquitt in 1876 and again in 1880.

Actually there was little interest shown in the Norcross campaign by any class of voters, colored *or* white. The chief interest in most quarters lay in the selection of the Democratic candidate at the party convention held in Atlanta in August, and Colquitt was assumed by most people to be the governor-elect before the Republican candidate was even nominated. Few persons were surprised at the result of the election on October 4, but the enormity of the defeat—111,297 to 33,443—was a deadly blow to Republican prospects for the future. The magnitude of the Democratic victory surpassed the expectations of even the most partisan. In the words of a contemporary observer: "The Republican party was crushed as by the hand of a giant."[29]

V

Cooperation with the Independents

EVEN BEFORE the disastrous defeat in the governor's race in 1876, some Republicans in Georgia were making tentative moves in a new direction—toward cooperation with Independent candidates here and there in the state. The Independent Movement in Georgia politics was a natural outcome of the single-party control of the state which had developed early in the 1870's. Since 1868 the Democratic party had considered itself the white man's party in Georgia, and by the end of 1872 most of the responsible white voters who had acted with the Republicans had switched over to the Democrats. The party's boast that it had redeemed the state from Radical rule and the Negro made it almost impregnable. To depart from it, in the eyes of most Georgians, constituted a slap at the traditions of the Old South, if not a downright act of treason. Yet all who called themselves Democrats did not by any means agree with the so-called "Bourbon" leadership of the party.* At times they revolted vigorously against the organization but they usually chose to do so under the label of "Independent Democrats" rather than to leave the party.

It was not strange that the revolt should have centered in the mountainous areas of north Georgia, arising first in the Seventh Congressional District and proceeding from there into the Ninth District. The membership of the Democratic party in Georgia was highly heterogeneous, and the small farmers of the upland slopes

---

*"Bourbon," used in this connotation, was a term of reproach, intended to designate a ruling class that held obstinately to ideas adapted to a former era. The post-war leaders of the Democratic party in Georgia, however, while essentially conservative, were interested primarily in the development of industry and commerce rather than in the old agrarian tradition.

felt little kinship with the more prosperous lowland planters. Nor did they feel kindly disposed toward the new emphasis on business and industry that had captured the interest of the party leadership. The mountainous counties had comparatively few Negroes and it was hard for the party leaders to whip their white voters into line with the old threat of Negro domination that worked so well in other parts of the state. Moreover, the area had been the stronghold of Unionism before the war and even then there had been sharp controversies with the States Righters and secessionists who had made up the majority of the Democratic party in Georgia.[1] It was no accident that this same area should embrace the bulk of the white membership of the Republican party in the state.

The Independent Movement was not peculiar to Georgia. It was in progress in some form all over the South, where circumstances had forced into a mold of solidarity elements that did not by nature belong together. In Georgia, as in other states, the earliest manifestations of independence were usually local revolts against county courthouse rings in the interest of candidates for the state legislature or for county offices. As early as 1874 the Macon *Telegraph* complained of "a rank crop of 'independent' candidates, so-called, for the legislature."[2]

In 1874, fourteen Independent candidates were elected to the General Assembly while the Republican total was reduced to eight. In several counties the Independents were elected by a direct combination of Republicans and disaffected Democrats.[3] During the next few years there were many such candidates but there was no Independent organization. The only bond that united them was the common spirit of revolt against the leadership of the Democratic party. For the most part, such candidates as individuals posed no great threat to the Democracy. But there was always the possibility that the local factions might coalesce into an effective opposition party or that they might form a general coalition with the Republicans.

The first outstanding Independent candidate in Georgia was William H. Felton of Bartow County. A graduate of the University of Georgia and of the State Medical College, Felton was a country doctor, an ordained Methodist minister, and a farmer of some note. Always an advocate of reform, he had great appeal for the small farmers of the Seventh District. He was married, moreover, to one of the most astute politicians ever to appear on the Georgia scene, Rebecca Latimer Felton, who was to make her own mark in Georgia politics.* The Felton team ranged far and wide in the district and their vehement attacks on the courthouse rings and the Bourbon leadership of the state party found a ready response.

One of the main grievances of the Independent Democrats against the party heads was that the state executive committee, and especially the "Atlanta Ring," was prone to interfere in local issues. In 1874 it was charged that the state committee was dictating the choice of the district's candidate for Congress, and a number of discontented Democrats persuaded Dr. Felton to run as an Independent against the party nominee. With the aid of many Republican votes, Felton defeated the convention candidate.[4] He was re-elected in 1876 and again in 1878. In 1878, Felton was joined by a second Independent congressman from Georgia, Emory Speer, who was elected in the Ninth District, also with Republican aid.

It was recognized, even in his early races for Congress, that Dr. Felton had a great deal of Republican support. Six weeks before the 1874 election, a friend wrote Felton of rumors that he had been "caught" in private meetings with the Republican party of the district and that he had been corresponding with Samuel Bard, Republican postmaster in Atlanta, who allegedly had agreed that the Republican party would not put a candidate in the field if Felton would run. Mrs. Felton promptly wrote to Bard asking whether he had made the statement attributed to him and Bard promptly replied that he had never corresponded with Dr. Felton on any subject and had never mentioned his name at any time in connection with politics.[5]

It was reported that Negroes of the district were being rallied to the support of Felton and that Republican leaders had endorsed him even though a Republican, N. P. Harbin, was also a candidate. Harbin himself was quoted as saying in Rome that Felton had "ousted him of the vote of his own party."[6] After the election, former Governor Joseph E. Brown referred to the outcome as a Radical triumph. It could not be denied, said he, that Felton had been elected by the almost solid vote of the Radical party, including the united Negro vote of his district. He predicted that the Democratic party had not seen the last of this combination of Democratic bolters and Radicals.[7]

*Mrs. Felton, at the age of eighty-seven, became Georgia's first and to date only woman member of the United States Senate, when she succeeded Thomas E. Watson upon his death in 1922. She served only a brief interval. Her colorful career is described in Talmadge, *Rebecca Latimer Felton, Nine Stormy Decades* (Athens, 1960), one of the best sources also for her husband's story.

In 1876 and 1878 the story was the same. Felton was elected over the regular Democratic candidates, and Republican support was given to him both openly and secretly. Whether this support helped him or hurt him in the long run would be hard to say. Open support by the Republicans was feared by the Independents, as it made them extremely vulnerable to attack and provided a natural target for the partisan press. On the other hand, Republican votes were needed to defeat the Democrats. During the 1876 campaign, Senator Benjamin H. Hill had warned Felton of seeming to seek Radical votes.[8] Hill, who was one of the Doctor's closest friends from their student days at the University of Georgia, had tried in vain to persuade him to go before the Democratic district convention and seek nomination in the accepted way. Hill sympathized with Felton's attack on corrupt elements in the Democratic party leadership but felt that he made a great mistake in opposing the party itself. He realized, if Felton did not, that his self-imposed exclusion from the party organization would almost inevitably throw him into the arms of the Republicans.

After the election of 1878, in answer to criticism, Felton found it necessary to obtain a written statement from the secretary of the Republican executive committee in Washington that he had not been supplied financial assistance by the national organization. George C. Gorham replied emphatically that he knew of no pecuniary aid rendered to Felton or in his behalf by any Republican individually or collectively.[9]

Perhaps Felton had not received financial aid from party coffers, but there was no denying the fact that Republican speakers were utilized in the campaign. One of them was Jeff Long, former Negro congressman from Macon, who was offered fifty dollars expense money by friends of Felton to come into the district and canvass for the Independent Democrat.[10] From the Ninth District came General James Longstreet, a Republican officeholder in Gainesville, who reported later that he had made a point of being in the neighboring district during the election to use his influence for Felton.[11] Longstreet was an ambitious newcomer to Georgia politics and was to take a prominent part in state Republican party affairs during the next few years.

In Rome, Republican Postmaster Z. B. Hargrove campaigned so vigorously for Felton that (according to his own account) Senator John B. Gordon offered to support his renomination as postmaster if he would stop opposing the "organized Democracy."[12] W. L. Clark, editor of the Atlanta *Republican,* urged Republicans to support Felton, but J. E. Bryant, chairman of the Republican state central committee and editor of the rival *Georgia Republican,* supported the candidacy of J. A. Holtzclaw, a Republican, and stumped the district for him.[13] Republican leaders were divided in their own councils as to the course to pursue, and Republican cooperation with the Independents was never wholehearted.[14]

In 1880 Felton was defeated by Judson C. Clements, a comparative unknown in Georgia politics. It seems evident that many Independents left the Felton camp in this election because of his growing attachment to the Republicans. The latter, declining to nominate a candidate in their own district convention, had become bolder and more aggressive in their support, and such an attitude alarmed the organized Democrats, who in some instances resorted to tactics like those of Reconstruction days. One incident, reported in separate letters to Felton by two of his supporters, indicates that the situation had gotten out of hand in both camps.

In Rome, where the fight was especially bitter, the regular Democrats had succeeded in placing their own officials exclusively at the ballot box, and fraudulent ballots, stalling tactics, confusion, and intimidation of the Negro voters were the order of the day. Major Hargrove, the Republican postmaster, stood at one side with a roll of bank checks prepared to pay the taxes of all Negroes wanting to vote for Garfield and Felton. Finally the Democratic leaders spirited away the tax collector so that no more taxes could be paid. Every colored voter was challenged and those who had paid their poll tax but had lost their receipts either voted under threat of arrest or were frightened into leaving without voting. The most flagrant of the fraudulent ballots read exactly like the genuine Independent tickets except the listing for congressman, which was printed "FOR ELECTOR—47th Congress: William H. Felton." Many such ballots were voted and were thrown out. A supporter of Felton pronounced the election in Floyd County "the most stupendous fraud imaginable." Feeling ran high in the town. On the night of the election Hargrove had an altercation with a Clements supporter, jerked out a knife, and cut him in the abdomen.[15]

The Feltons may or may not have solicited Republican aid but certainly they did not discourage it. Mrs. Felton, evincing a lively curiosity about the possibility of a Republican candidate for 1880, wrote to J. R. Wikle of Cartersville for information. Wikle, in response, agreed with her that an "organized" Bourbon would certainly be elected if Dr. Felton was not. He had used that argument with Republicans at each canvass since 1874, said he, and that was the argument that influenced Republicans to vote for an Independent. He assured Mrs. Felton that he would use his influence against the nomination of a Republican candidate in 1880.[16]

Having been defeated in 1880, in spite of the absence of a Republican candidate, Dr. Felton was apparently ready for cooperation with the Republicans on a broader and more effective scale. Late in 1881 he turned a receptive ear to overtures from Republican leaders. At the time, the Republican party organization was in a state of disunion and confusion. At the state convention in April, 1880, the Negro members had gained control of the party machinery, electing the state chairman and three-fourths of the state central committee. The situation was wholly unacceptable to the white members of the party, and the little group of officeholders who dominated the organization were plotting with and against each other for control of the party. J. E. Bryant had lost the party leadership and there were several aspirants eager to succeed him. Without waiting for the inevitable overthrow of the colored regime they were jockeying for position, each in his own way. This was the situation in July, 1881, when General James Longstreet came to Atlanta as United States marshal for the northern district of Georgia. Longstreet's first bid for power in the Republican party in Georgia was a move to form a coalition with the Independents of the state.

James Longstreet was a controversial figure even before the end of the war. One of Lee's chief lieutenants, he was considered by many as one of the most capable generals of the Confederacy. Others blamed him for the costly defeat at Gettysburg. Even so, his position in Southern history would have been more secure if he had stuck to soldiering and had left politics to others. His readiness to collaborate with the Radicals after the war and the eagerness with which he sought and accepted federal office shocked and alienated many. In New Orleans, where he held several lucrative federal and state appointments, he became involved with some of the most notorious political adventurers in Louisiana.

During the late 1870's Longstreet made repeated attempts to secure a federal appointment in Georgia, where he had spent much of his boyhood. Finally, in September, 1878, he was appointed deputy collector of internal revenue in the state and in January, 1879, he became postmaster at Gainesville for a short period. After a brief absence as United States Minister to Turkey, he returned to Georgia in June, 1881, to accept the appointment as United States marshal. He took up the duties of his new assignment in Atlanta on July 1, 1881.¹⁷ Because of his high position in the Confederate army and his native Southern background, he was considered a valuable recruit.*

As early as 1878 Longstreet had advocated a coalition between Independent Democrats and Republicans in Georgia. He felt that the only way to make the Republican party practical and successful in the state was to adopt some plan to secure cooperation from a large part of the best citizens of the section. He believed that the Independent move offered an opportunity that should not be overlooked.¹⁸ Longstreet had some correspondence with the Feltons while he was located in Gainesville, but it was not until after his move to Atlanta that he took steps to effect a combination with the Independents. These steps led to the Markham House conference of December 29, 1881.

Early in December Longstreet wrote to Dr. Felton telling him that he had tried to see him on a recent visit of the latter to Atlanta. "My special purpose," said he, "was to talk politics. . . . It is my opinion that a combination may be made, by which ideas may be so modified as to be acceptable to all."¹⁹ It is not clear whether Longstreet or Felton initiated the plan for the conference at the Markham House. If it was the General's proposal, Felton evidently fell into step with alacrity. Having been defeated in his most recent race, he was leaving no stone unturned to strengthen the Independent cause for 1882.

In several subsequent letters to Felton and to others, Longstreet referred to plans to visit the Doctor in Cartersville on December 20, to a projected call for a convention to organize an Independent party, and to the great importance of getting Alexander H. Stephens lined up from the beginning with "our plans for rehabilitating the state." Longstreet proposed to have the call for a convention signed by Stephens, Felton, John S. Bigby, and himself, and to have the delegates divided equally between Independents and Republicans. He suggested that Felton prepare an address to issue with the call for the convention and thought it might be well for the former Congressman to get some of his influential friends to speak to the Presi-

---

*In view of Longstreet's undistinguished record in his various federal offices, both in Louisiana and Georgia, it is difficult to understand his ability to secure one appointment after another and the great power that he wielded over patronage for a few years after his arrival in Georgia. This power probably stemmed originally from his long-time friendship with Ulysses S. Grant, who nominated Longstreet for a federal post only six days after his inauguration. The party heads in Georgia, however, always accepted him with reservations. They never seemed greatly impressed by his abilities and were no doubt jealous of him.

dent about the matter.[20] That Felton also was busy making plans for the conference is evident from letters received by him from members of both contingents. Apparently he issued the invitations to the Independents, while Longstreet invited the Republicans to the meeting.

On the eve of the conference Henry P. Farrow wrote a long letter to Felton expressing his chagrin at not being invited to attend and included a few candid remarks which showed his opinion of Longstreet as a political leader. While he felt sure that it was "a mere inadvertance [sic]" that he had not been included, Farrow warned the Doctor that he had never said that he would work in the new movement if he was "discarded" at its inception. "The Genl. is not versed in politics . . . and will make blunders unless closely watched," said he. "It's too late in life for him to learn politics. . . . Politics has been reduced to a science and men who know nothing of the science of politics can't run politics." Farrow, himself an old hand at "running politics," urged Felton to see that he was made a part of the conference.[21] The following morning Longstreet called at Farrow's office to say that he would be pleased to have him at the meeting. Failing to find Farrow, the General dispatched a hasty note to him later in the day, and Farrow was among those present at the Markham House that evening.[22] Unfortunately, however, Longstreet had been over-optimistic in his hope that Stephens could be included in the movement from its beginning. There is no evidence that he was invited to the conference.

The Markham House conference was supposedly a secret one, but the story leaked out shortly after its conclusion. Since it was never adequately reported it is difficult to say exactly what did happen. The source most often cited is Mrs. Felton's own account in her *Memoirs,* but this was not written until many years later, is somewhat vague and biased, and contains obvious inaccuracies. The *Constitution* got the story by way of the Chicago *Tribune,* reprinting on January 3, 1882, the *Tribune's* story, which was dated December 29. A correspondent for the Chicago paper was at the Markham House on the day of the meeting and saw the parties go upstairs to Felton's room and later come down together. Afterward he interviewed one of the conferees, Alexander N. Wilson, who was representing James Atkins, former collector of the port of Savannah.[23]

Seven men attended the meeting, four Republicans and three Independent Democrats. The Republicans were Longstreet, Farrow,

Wilson, and John S. Bigby, who had succeeded Farrow as United States district attorney and who was a former Republican congressman from Georgia. Independents were Felton, Judge James S. Hook of Augusta, and Dr. H. V. M. Miller, former United States senator from Georgia. The discussion was based mainly on an interview with Felton published a short time before in the Republican Chicago *Tribune*. At the request of a *Tribune* reporter Felton had formulated a platform embracing principles and political ideas which in his judgment could be agreed upon by men of all parties. The Republican representatives at the conference declared that "fair and just-minded" Republicans of Georgia could vote for Felton or any other Democrat on that platform. Felton was urged to become a candidate for governor, but he declined, wishing to run again for Congress. Since the two groups in the coalition would maintain their separate identities, no convention would be held. Another conference would be held at the proper time for nominating candidates acceptable to both groups and this ticket would be endorsed at a mass meeting to be held in Atlanta on June 1, 1882. Henry Farrow and Dr. Miller were appointed as a committee representing the two groups to confer with other Independents and Republicans and to organize them for joint action.*

What is usually known as the "Markham House Platform" or "Document" was simply a restatement of the eleven planks formulated by Felton in the *Tribune* interview, with an introduction and conclusion and a call to a mass meeting to be held on June 1, 1882. It was issued after the conference and signed by a committee of seven men, all Independents, only two of whom, Felton and Hook, had been present at the Markham House meeting. The platform was a rather strange combination of Republican and liberal doctrines, evidently tailored to appeal to both groups.[24]

No sooner was the proposed coalition made public than repercussions were heard in both camps. A number of Independent Democrats approached by a reporter for the Atlanta *Constitution* disclaimed knowledge of the meeting and said they would not support any scheme originated in this way. "No Independent movement inaugurated and backed from the republican camp can win in

---

*This statement was made by the *Tribune* correspondent to a reporter for the Atlanta *Constitution*. Dr. Miller had denied all knowledge of the conference and had told the reporter that he had simply made a casual social call on Dr. Felton and had left when the other men came in. The *Tribune* correspondent insisted that he saw Miller come downstairs with Longstreet and others after the meeting and that he and Farrow had been named to the committee to act together.

Georgia," declared one. Another expressed his conviction that while it was honorable to be an Independent it would be infamous to sell that independence to the purposes of the Radicals. "I would rather, ten times over, be a Bourbon than a radical!" said he.[25]

The Republican state central committee met on January 2 and passed a resolution endorsing the coalition movement, but it weakened its action to a great extent by saying that the Republicans would not support any man or set of men for office, state or national, who in any way antagonized the Republican organization. Farrow protested that this might be understood as a refusal to cooperate with the Independents, but the resolution was not revised. The Republicans were never unanimous in their attempts at cooperation with Independent or third-party candidates, and Farrow was opposed in this instance by Colonel Alfred E. Buck, who was soon to become the state party chairman and who was much stronger than Farrow or Longstreet with the colored elements of the party —the bulk of Republican voters.[26] Buck, referred to as "a bitter enemy to the Independents," was named chairman of a reorganized executive committee, which supposedly would cooperate with the new movement. His selection was looked upon as a poor omen for the success of any Independent or liberal move.[27]

The most highly publicized opposition to the "New Movement," as it was called, was Senator Ben Hill's blast at Felton's program, which he termed a second attempt to "Africanize" the South. The two men, formerly friends, engaged in a vicious exchange of personalities in a series of published interviews, letters, and speeches. The initial attack by Hill was in the form of an interview with Henry W. Grady, denouncing Felton's program and platform as given in the *Tribune* interview.[28] While Felton and Hill were fighting it out in full view of the public, Longstreet was in Washington working behind the scenes to manipulate the federal patronage in Georgia in such a way as to win the support of key men in the state. With a Republican in the White House, this was an interesting possibility.

Late in January Longstreet wrote Felton that he thought it important for him to come to Washington and talk with President Arthur about his policy in Georgia. Arthur, agreeing wholeheartedly with the idea of cooperating with the Independents as a means of building up the Republican party in the South, was evidently disposed to make some changes that Longstreet felt would damage rather than help the cause. A week later the General wrote Felton again, reporting encouraging conferences with the President. In both communications he stressed the fact that the prevailing feeling was that the organization of the two groups should be kept separate and distinct. "We have so arranged to give the independents our free and full vote, without any semblance of coalition. . . . So you will not be embarrassed by complications, but supported by our votes."[29]

As the months wore on, Dr. Felton continued to write and speak and organize the Independents, and Longstreet and Farrow continued to work with the Republican forces, though sometimes at cross purposes. Early in May Farrow wrote Felton a twelve-page letter urging action to prepare for the mass meeting scheduled for June 1. He felt that proper plans were not being made and he complained that he could get little help from the Republican officeholders. Some were actively opposing the coalition and others had little influence or capability, said he.[30] Farrow had written a lengthy letter to Longstreet a few weeks before, proposing plans for organization, but had received no satisfactory response. Longstreet was ill in Gainesville and expressed doubt as to when he would be able to return to his post in Atlanta and whether he would be in condition even then to undertake any serious business.[31]

The feeling was general that the movement had lost momentum. For one thing, no suitable candidate for governor had appeared. From the beginning, Longstreet and Felton had seen the importance of getting the support of Alexander H. Stephens, and probably they had always cherished the hope that he might be persuaded to become the coalition candidate for governor. Stephens had originally been a Whig and he had never felt any great affection for the leadership of the Democratic party. He was considered a liberal in his views but, on the other hand, he had never broken with the party organization. His good friends the Feltons had made overtures to him and he had expressed sympathy with the coalition cause but had been evasive about committing himself.

It became apparent in March that both the Independents and the organized Democrats were after Stephens as a candidate. For a while it seemed that he might be nominated by both groups. This would apparently have been acceptable to the coalition and to the candidate, but the Bourbons would have none of it. After Stephens was recommended as the Independent candidate at a second conference at the Markham House on May 15, the Democratic executive committee forced him to make a public choice, and Stephens, pushed into a corner, renounced the Independent candidacy as a price for receiving the nomination of the organized Democracy.*

Dr. and Mrs. Felton, who had thought they had his positive assurance that he would not reject the Independent nomination, were bitter at Stephens's desertion, but there was no time now to consider another candidate. At the meeting on May 15 the conferees had announced that the scheduled mass meeting would not be held on June 1. Two reasons were given. First, rumors of a smallpox epidemic in Atlanta might keep people from attending. Second, one of the desired results of the proposed meeting had already been accomplished in the unanimous recommendation of that "incorruptible statesman, Hon. Alexander H. Stephens for the next governor of Georgia." The announcement was signed by nine men, all Independents. No Republican names were included, but Longstreet presumably was present at the meeting, as he was registered at the Markham House and had been seen in earnest conversation with Felton.[32] Letters from Felton to Farrow shortly before the meeting indicate that Farrow also was expected to be present.[33]

On May 23 the Atlanta *Constitution* published a letter from Stephens in which he made it plain that he would not be the Independent candidate but would be available for the party nomination if it was the will of the people. Two days later, Dr. Felton wrote an angry, indignant letter to Henry Farrow in which he assailed Stephens's "duplicity" and spoke of having been "sold out by an egotistical and infirm old man." (The letter was marked "Private" and bore the added injunction, "Please destroy this letter—W.H.F.") Felton declared that he would use every power within his reach to defeat Stephens in his aspirations for the governorship. "I feel inclined to announce myself an Independent candidate for Governor," he wrote. "I would like to discuss with Mr. S. and his 'henchmen' the issues of the day."[34]

Felton, however, did not enter the governor's race. Early in March Mrs. Felton had reminded Farrow that her husband had been the choice of the Markham House conferees for governor but that he had made no pledges and they asked for none.[35] The Doctor had indicated then that he would prefer to run again for Congress and

*The developments leading up to the gubernatorial campaign of 1882 and especially the maneuvers relating to Stephens' candidacy are recorded in more detail and with thorough documentation in John E. Talmadge, "The Death Blow to Independentism in Georgia," *Southern Historical Quarterly*, XXXIX (December, 1955), 37-47. The incident is handled here rather briefly, since this study is concerned primarily with the Republican party in Georgia and not the Independent Movement.

• *Cooperation with the Independents* 73

he adhered to this decision even after it became evident that Stephens was not available.

The coalition could not get the candidate it wanted, but there was already an Independent Democrat in the race for governor. General Lucius J. Gartrell had announced his own candidacy late in February. Gartrell was not considered a strong candidate and the Independents had not wanted him. In fact, Dr. Felton had tried, through a common friend, to persuade him to defer his announcement, and, even after Stephens's defection, had asked Farrow if he could obtain Gartrell's consent to retire.[36] Evidently the rank and file Republicans were not so discriminating. Judging from remarks made at their state convention in August, many of them preferred Gartrell to Stephens and they voted an official endorsement of his candidacy.[37] Actually there were *two* Republican state conventions in August, 1882, held simultaneously and in competition with each other. Both endorsed Gartrell.

Although it was reported that the Republicans had taken complete charge of the Gartrell campaign and had organized the Negroes in every county of Georgia, election day found an unusually light vote and little excitement over the governor's race.[38] Gartrell carried only six counties in the entire state. Moreover, in the congressional elections in November, the Bourbons regained complete control of the congressional delegation. Emory Speer lost his seat in the Ninth District and Dr. Felton was beaten in the Seventh after a hard and bitter campaign. In each case, the most damaging thing charged against the Independent candidate was his connection with the Republicans—"*Radicalism*," the Democratic press termed it.

Gartrell could hardly have hoped to win against Stephens, but even without Stephens the organized Democracy would probably have defeated any other candidate that the coalition could have put up. The movement was doomed by its very nature. It is a tragic commentary on the position of the Republican party in Georgia in the 1880's that its support of an Independent candidate was apt to be as the kiss of death. In writing of the Independent Movement in the South, a modern historian has said, "Once the color line was firmly drawn and the charge of the Independents' alliance with the Republicans fixed in the public mind, the third-party men had little chance."[39] In Georgia in 1882 the Democratic press hammered home with telling effect the constant refrain: "It is not independentism that is to be defeated at the polls . . . but the revival of republicanism which independentism has made possible."[40]

Dr. Felton had been pilloried by almost every newspaper in Georgia because, in his famous *Tribune* interview, he had dared to question the sacrosanct position of the Democratic party. Possibly he misjudged the times when he said for publication that the people of Georgia no longer regarded with horror the possibility of Republican supremacy. Or perhaps he misjudged the power of the Democratic press and what it could do with such a statement. A leaning toward the Republicans had been charged against Felton since his first campaign for Congress in 1874. Now he seemed convicted by his own words. He was referred to by the press as "the Republican Dr. Felton." It was rumored that if sent back to Congress he would vote with the Republicans in the election of speaker. Much was made of his readiness to join hands with "this disreputable element of Republicanism and of alleged pledges that he had made.[41] There is no way of knowing how Felton would have fared without the support of the Republicans in his district, but certainly he paid dearly for their votes.

Emory Speer also was having Republican troubles in the Ninth. In 1878, after his first election to Congress, Speer was termed by Henry Grady, his boyhood friend, as the finest campaign orator in the state and "the most promising youngster that Georgia has seen since Ben Hill first took his place on the hustings."[42] (Speer was only twenty-nine when first elected, the youngest man in Congress.) He was elected as an Independent in 1878 and in 1880. The usual charges of dickering with the Republicans were made against him in both races, and, in 1882, when the Independent Movement seemed likely to spread over the state, the accusations grew bitter. The issue of collaboration with the Radical and the Negro was in the forefront of the campaign.

The Athens *Banner-Watchman* threatened to print letters in its possession to prove Speer's "compromising correspondence" with Republicans. Speer succeeded in getting an injunction to prevent the paper from doing so, on the ground that the letters were personal ones. The paper insisted that they were political documents which proved that Speer was not only solely responsible for the recent appointment of the Negro, Madison Davis, as postmaster in Athens, but that he was gloating over "the degradation he had placed upon his white constituency."[43] Finally the Athens paper published one letter from Speer to Davis, evading the injunction by the claim that this letter had been picked up on the street and a copy forwarded to the paper by a friend. Addressed to "My dear Mat," the letter gave encouragement regarding the appointment and said, "You are in a position to do me great good with the mountain men and I rely on

• *Cooperation with the Independents* 75

you confidently to do so."⁴⁴ For the rest of the campaign, Speer was taunted with the "Dear Mat" letter and much was made of his Republican support.*

As a matter of fact, the Republicans in the district were never united in support of Speer, and the Negro voters in the Athens area were sharply divided, some preferring the regular Democratic candidate, Allen D. Candler. On October 2, when a Republican mass meeting held at the Athens town hall turned out to be a Speer rally headed by Davis, many Candler supporters left in disgust. During the course of the campaign, Davis was replaced by an anti-Speer man as chairman of the Clarke County Republican executive committee. Many Negroes objected to voting for Speer unless he declared himself as a Republican, but Davis denounced Negroes voting for the Democratic candidate as "republican renegades," and "traitors to race and party."⁴⁵

Emory Speer was not directly involved in the Markham House conferences or in the coalition movement headed by Felton and Longstreet (although he was in correspondence with both Felton and Farrow and entered the picture briefly in May as a spokesman for Stephens), but undoubtedly the effects of the move were felt in his own campaign. Any attack on the Democratic party was looked upon in some quarters as an attack on white supremacy, and, when Independent Democrats allied themselves with Republicans in a combination that threatened real danger to the party, the old cry of Radicalism and Negro domination was renewed in intensified form. It was clear that the Republican party in Georgia had not yet outlived the stigma of Reconstruction, nor was it likely to do so as long as it was so identified in the public mind with the Negro voter.

---

*Speer had become deeply involved in Republican patronage matters in Washington and was to become more entangled after his defeat for re-election to Congress. His relations with the Republican "syndicate" are recounted below, in Chapter VII.

VI

Lily-White versus Black-and-Tan

WHEN THE Radical Republicans in Congress gained control of the Reconstruction program in 1867 and gave the vote indiscriminately to all adult Negro males, some members of Congress were genuinely interested in equal rights for the freedmen. More of them were interested primarily in strengthening the Republican party. By providing a ready-made, easily-led electorate of colored voters, they hoped to extend the party into the Southern states and to make certain of continued control of Congress and of the presidency.[1] Through no fault of their own, the Negroes were made pawns in the white man's game of politics and were placed in a situation where they were much more likely to be exploited than advanced.

In Georgia, as in other Southern states, the organized nucleus of the Republican party was the Union League, and the bulk of its voting power from the beginning was that of the mass of newly freed Negroes. At first these were generally tractable and easily manipulated by the white leaders and they voted the Republican ticket with great unanimity. The strategy of Congress seemed successful as the Radicals won elections in one state after another in 1867 and 1868. But the victory was a pyrrhic one.

The political activity of the Negro perhaps more than any other factor caused the Conservative whites to band themselves together in the Democratic party to stamp out Radical rule. And inside the Republican party itself this political activity of the Negro was a primary cause of splits and factional fighting and of defections from the ranks. Thus it contributed to the weakening of the party both from without and within. In Georgia, the first crushing defeat suffered by the party at the hands of the Democrats came in November, 1868, and the deterioration from within reached critical proportions in 1872.

• *Lily-White versus Black-and-Tan* 77

It is true that the racial situation was not the only disruptive force within the Republican party in Georgia. The excesses of the Bullock administration had alienated many Moderate Republicans and there was a general exodus of white voters from the party in 1872. Among those that were left, the search for spoils was a constant source of friction. Underlying all this, however, and aggravating the other factors was the nagging fact that the great majority of party members were colored. To be an active working Republican in Georgia meant to work with Negroes, to meet with them, to be classed with them in the mind's eye of the public. This was unpalatable to most native whites and to many also who had come to Georgia from other sections of the country. Without a doubt it was a contributing factor in the withdrawal from the party of many of its representative white voters.

The Georgia press, overwhelmingly Democratic, was quick to center upon this vulnerable spot. The Atlanta *Constitution,* the Milledgeville *Federal Union,* and other powerful papers never lost an opportunity to point out the damaging fact that in Georgia most Republicans were Negroes. It seems apparent that this was done deliberately and with malice aforethought. Moreover, after the immediate danger of Radical rule had passed, some of the papers changed their tone from violent, slashing attacks on Republicanism to the more deadly weapon of ridicule. Republican conventions and mass meetings were reported in humorous vein, sometimes in Negro dialect, with invitations to the public to come out and see something "rich, racy and rare." This was hard for some of the whites to stomach. Jonathan Norcross protested hotly at this method of handling the news and blamed the *Constitution* for many of the disorders of the party in Fulton County.[2]

The Democratic newspapers also fostered distrust and resentment between the two races within the Republican organization. As early as 1870 the Athens *Southern Watchman* was warning that "These people [the Negroes] will find out, after awhile, that they are being badly cheated by the carpetbaggers and scalawags." The *Constitution* frequently expressed surprise that the Negroes would submit to the control of the few whites who dominated the party, and in 1876 pointed out that there were many colored men "of fine manners and more than ordinary education and . . . mental powers of no mean merit" who deserved to represent and be represented in party affairs.[3]

So long as the colored voters were willing to follow the white leaders and be content with the fragments of patronage thrown their way, there was no open clash between the two races within the party. In 1880, however, the Negroes took advantage of controversies between the whites to seize control of the party machinery, and that brought forth repercussions that were to shake the party for many years. Open splits in the party ranks and proposals for a separate white Republican party in Georgia were among the results.

There had always been some Negro leaders in the party—both good and bad—since its establishment. Aaron Alpeoria Bradley, Tunis Campbell, and H. M. Turner had made themselves heard very early, and Jeff Long had been elected to Congress in 1868. By 1880, however, a new type of colored leader had emerged. Young men, some of them college graduates, articulate and able, stood out in marked contrast to the illiterate black masses at party conventions. Before the state convention in April, 1880, it was reported that there was deep trouble in the ranks. The white leaders were fighting among themselves over the presidential candidate to be supported at the national convention, and the Negroes were reported as determined "to crawl from under the thumbs of the white republican officeholders."[4]

The convention met in the state Capitol on April 21, with the usual preponderance of colored delegates. J. E. Bryant, expecting to be re-elected state chairman, was profuse in his protestations of loyalty to his colored friends. Ordinarily Bryant was known as a shrewd and successful operator with the Negro element but on this occasion he made a blunder which was to cost him his leadership in the party. Trying to conciliate the colored delegates and to stave off discussion of the method of electing the chairman of the state central committee, he offered a resolution regarding the question of the distribution of patronage. His resolution would express the sense of the convention that the division of federal offices in Georgia should be half and half between the races. Others suggested that three-fourths for the Negroes would be more in keeping with the racial make-up of the party.

Ordinarily such utterances might have been meaningless platitudes, high-sounding resolutions to be filed away and forgotten in the archives of the party, but this time the Negro leaders were quick to take advantage of the opening. Edwin Belcher, a colored man from Augusta, characterized as the best speaker in the convention, offered a substitute proposal to test the sincerity of Bryant and the others. He moved that three-fourths of the delegates to the national convention in Chicago be colored men. Amid great enthusiasm and cheers from the colored delegates, the Belcher substitute was passed.

Bryant's friends made frantic efforts to have the motions tabled, but the damage was already done.

The meeting had gotten decidedly out of hand. To pass a resolution about patronage not controlled by the convention was one thing. To instruct the convention about its own choice of delegates to the national convention was an entirely different matter. When the committee on delegates submitted a report not in conformity with the three-fourths resolution, the list was revised to include fourteen colored and eight white members. Bryant's name was not included. There was only one white man among the four delegates-at-large, who were usually considered the leaders of the delegation.*

Having gained the lion's share of representation on the delegation, the Negroes continued to press their advantage. William A. Pledger was elected state chairman, the first Negro ever to serve in that capacity, and a new state central committee was named with a roster of twenty-four colored men and eight whites. Here again Bryant was omitted, as were most other white leaders of the party. The Negroes were definitely in the saddle; how long they could hold their seats was problematical.

William Anderson Pledger was an example of the new generation of Negroes in the party. Born in Fayette County in the early 1850's, he prided himself on being a self-made man. He had attended Atlanta University and had come to prominence in the party as editor of the Athens *Blade*. Later he practiced law in Atlanta and served as United States surveyor of customs in that city. Pledger never held elective office, although he ran for the state legislature from Clarke County in 1888. A party leader for many years, he remained continuously on the state central committee until his death and was a delegate to every Republican national convention from 1880 through 1900.

Pledger had become known first as a Republican leader in Clarke County, where he was recognized as "one of the shrewdest leaders of the Republican party" in that part of the state. "Pledger knows well how to speak and how to maintain his influence over the colored

---

*Contemporary accounts saw the Bryant resolution as a diversionary tactic which had backfired. The chief controversy on the first day and a half of the convention was between Grant forces and anti-Grant elements rather than between the races. There had been a tremendous fight over the election of the permanent chairman of the convention, a post won by W. H. Smyth, an anti-Grant man. Charges were made that Bryant had been party to a deal on the organization of the convention and the eventual selection of a mixed delegation in the interest of Sherman and Blaine. A Sherman agent was present at the convention, well equipped with funds, and was rumored to have been passing out "twelve dollar lunches" with great generosity. Atlanta *Constitution*, April 22, 23, 24, 1880.

people," said the Athens *Georgian* in 1876. When he became chairman of the state committee, the *Constitution* spoke highly of the Athens Negro, declaring him to be a good speaker, a ready debater, and a man of strong will and unusually quick intelligence. "If his head is not turned," commented the editor, "and he does not assume an offensive attitude, he can do a great work for his race in Georgia."[5]

As might be expected, the election of a Negro as state chairman and the resolution giving ascendancy to the colored members of the party were not well received by the white Republicans of the state. Almost immediately the repercussions started. The day after the close of the state convention there appeared in the Atlanta papers a call for white Republicans to assemble at the city hall on April 27 to make plans for a separate party organization. At this meeting Jonathan Norcross made a brief address, declaring that the movement was not a bolt but, rather, an attempt to strengthen the existing party. He stated that there were many thousands of white Republicans in Georgia who did not act with the party because such action would bring them in contact with colored men, against whom they were socially prejudiced. Resolutions were passed setting up a committee to correspond with men formerly prominent in the party to learn what practical steps could be taken to reawaken an interest in party matters and to enroll them again as active workers for the Republican cause. Norcross, W. L. Clark, and F. Reimann were appointed to the committee.[6]

On May 15, 1880, the committee issued a "Republican Address" which filled the greater part of a page in the Atlanta *Republican*. Recounting in some detail the situation in the party, the committee called for all white Republicans in the state to attend a meeting either in person or by proxy in Atlanta on June 22 for further consultation and action. An invitation was extended also to the Republican organization as then constituted (i.e., the Negro leadership) to hold a separate meeting at the same time and place and to cooperate through committees of conference. The committee emphasized the fact that the interests of both races were the same and that the movement was not intended to disturb or divide the existing Republican organization but to supplement it by bringing back some of the thousands of white men who had formerly worked with the party and who still believed in its principles.

While the address stressed the idea of cooperation, the committee chided the colored brethren for their rejection of their former leaders at the state convention and for their "anti-Republican" resolution demanding three-fourths of the offices. The Negroes were told em-

• *Lily-White versus Black-and-Tan* 81

phatically that if they should eliminate from the party all their white allies they would get no offices at all, and they were warned that the Democratic papers and partisans who encouraged them to turn out their white leaders were deceiving them for the purpose of destroying the Republican party in Georgia.

The meeting set for June 22 was held on July 6 in the state Capitol with only a small number of white Republicans in attendance. Norcross was made chairman and W. L. Clark, editor of the Atlanta *Republican,* secretary. A number of committees were named, including one to confer with the state central committee regarding the appointment of presidential electors, but little seems to have been accomplished. Although the address of May 15 had spoken hopefully of the organization of a new section of the party and of the nomination of a Republican electoral ticket "composed of such men as will canvass the State with effect, and such as no intelligent man is unwilling to vote for," apparently the movement died aborning insofar as any real effectiveness was concerned. The committee had engaged both legislative halls at the Capitol and had invited the colored Republicans to meet also and to form a separate organization; however, the Negroes spurned the proposal. Pledger, present on leave of the chair, spoke at length, arguing that the white movement was antagonistic to Republican interests in the state. He and Norcross exchanged sharp words.[7]

Judging from names appearing in contemporary accounts, Norcross's movement for a separate white Republican party did not have the support of the white officeholders, who composed the real power bloc in the party. His move seemed the bungling attempt of a well-meaning amateur. The professionals—the officeholders—held their fire for the moment, but when the time was ripe, in August, 1882, they made their move with a devastating force that unseated the Negro leaders and split the party in two. This time there was no talk of a separate white Republican party or of separate conventions of the two races. The 1882 move was simply a bid to gain control of the party organization and to wrest the leadership from the colored officers, with both factions vying for all possible support, whether white or colored.

Until 1880 the Republican leaders in Georgia had been men prominent in the party since the early days of Reconstruction. The state chairmen—Foster Blodgett, Henry Farrow, and J. E. Bryant—and the two Republican governors—Rufus Bullock and Benjamin Conley—had all been among the original members of the party in Georgia. All except Farrow had been members of the constitutional convention of 1867-68, and he had been president of the Union League in the state. Some of these leaders were still active in the party but there were new names and new faces in the forefront.

General James Longstreet, who had aspired to lead the party into a coalition with the Independents, was now United States marshal, located in Atlanta, and was still ready and willing to be tapped as head of the Georgia party. His was still a name to conjure with, although he never reached the expectations of his followers as a political leader. Of more force potentially was Alfred E. Buck, clerk of the United States district court, who had come to Atlanta from his native state of Maine by way of Alabama. Buck, who was to hold the office of state party chairman longer than any other man in the nineteenth century, came to Atlanta in 1873 and had been active in the party since his arrival. Both men were to play leading roles in the white man's resumption of control in 1882.

Ordinarily the party held quadrennial conventions and the chairman of the state central committee held office from one presidential year until the next. Under the 1868 constitution the term of the governor of Georgia coincided with that of the president, but when the new constitution was adopted in 1877 the term was reduced to two years. Thus Colquitt's second term was for two years instead of four and a new election was scheduled for 1882. White leaders of the Republican party saw in this development an opportunity to hold another state convention in 1882 and to get rid of Pledger and the predominantly Negro central committee elected in 1880. They spoke of failing to "re-elect" Pledger, although the chairman's term by custom had always been for four years.[8]

A state convention was set for August 2 and there were rumors in advance that fireworks could be expected. There was much talk of the "syndicate," the name given to a group of the white officeholders who reputedly were banded together to dispose of the federal offices in the state, keeping the best ones for themselves. It was reported that the syndicate members were determined to replace Pledger with one of their own number. The party executive committee, composed of the Negro leaders and a few of the white officeholders, met on July 31 to make plans for the convention and it was reported that feeling was running high within the group. Members of the party were said to be "red-hot" on the issue of control of the central committee, and the *Constitution* predicted that the convention by the first night would resemble Mount Vesuvius.[9]

Actually the eruption came on August 1, the night before the convention assembled, when each faction held a separate meeting to plan its strategy. One caucus was held in the printing office of the *Weekly Defiance,* engineered by Pledger and by J. H. Brown, colored editor of the *Defiance.* The other was held at the postoffice building under the leadership of Farrow and Longstreet. After the *Defiance* meeting broke up, Pledger, Brown, and a crowd of their supporters went to the federal building and tried to gain admittance to the other caucus. Barred by the doorkeeper, the Negroes forced their way in. Longstreet, as United States marshal, declared that he had charge of the courtroom, while Pledger, as surveyor of the Atlanta port, claimed to be custodian of the building. A general row ensued, followed by the arrest of Pledger and Brown, who made bond. Farrow declared that the two Negroes were drunk and termed the affair "one of the most disgraceful riots ever known in this city." Others insisted that there was no riot.[10]

In accordance with the call for the convention, issued on May 25 by Chairman Pledger, the meeting was scheduled to be held at the Capitol at ten o'clock on the morning of August 2, but the executive committee, controlled by the Farrow-Longstreet faction, held an early morning caucus and called for the convention to meet instead at noon in the United States courtroom. Dodgers were distributed which gave the impression that the new arrangement was the official one. In a statement issued later to justify this action, it was claimed that the executive committee, established by action of the state central committee on May 23 to handle party business until the assembling of the August convention, had the authority to set the time and place for the meeting and that Pledger had erred in issuing the convention call, although, admittedly, this was ordinarily the prerogative of the state chairman and secretary.[11]

The Pledger group, convening at ten, waited until eleven o'clock to open the meeting in the hope that delegates who had been confused by the second call would learn of the "true" situation and come back into the fold. Eventually both conventions got under way almost simultaneously and it was apparent that the party was completely split. Committees on conference, appointed by both groups, failed to make any headway at reconciliation. Most of the Negroes and a few of the whites were with Pledger, while the other faction was about equally divided between Negroes and whites. Among the white leaders who attended the Pledger meeting were J. E. Bryant, A. E. Buck, S. A. Darnell, and R. D. Locke. In addition to Farrow and Longstreet, the other group included the two Conleys, Walter H. Johnson, Tomlinson F. Johnson, and most of the other white delegates. In each case it was apparent that a studied effort was being made to recognize men of both races in committee appointments and in other procedures of the conventions. Each faction declared itself the true Republican party of Georgia and its convention the regular convention.*

A series of communications between the two groups showed that neither side was willing to yield in its claims to be the duly constituted convention of the party, although it was reported that Pledger was willing to retire as party chairman and would support either Buck or Locke for the place. The Farrow-Longstreet group, pushing former Governor Conley for the post of chairman, proposed that the party head be elected by a meeting of white delegates only, to be conducted jointly by Buck and Conley. To this suggestion Bryant took great offense, declaring that the communication from the Farrow committee was an insult to the Republican party and to the colored man.[12] The proposal that the chairman be elected by the white delegates only was defended on the ground that there were 40,000 more white than black voters in the state and that the white man seemed best able to lead the party and to attract accessions from the opposition. Not noted in the message was the fact that most of the white men present in the two convention groups were allied with the syndicate faction, which Farrow represented, and that a joint session composed *only* of the white delegates would swing the balance of control far over in that direction. This point, no doubt, entered into Bryant's indignant response to the proposal.

With all hope of conciliation cut off, each convention proceeded with its own business and drew up its own slate of candidates for state offices, both groups endorsing the candidacy of an Independent Democrat, General Lucius J. Gartrell, who was running for governor against Alexander H. Stephens, the regular Democratic nominee. The two factions scrupulously divided their other nominations between white and colored candidates. The slates were as follows:

Pledger Ticket
Congressman-at-large—R. D. Locke (w)
Secretary of state—R. R. Wright (col)

---

*This bifurcation of the Republican party in Georgia has been a frequent though not a continuous condition. As late as 1952, two separate conventions were held and separate delegations sent to the national convention, each claiming to represent the *real* Republican party in Georgia. The racial factor has entered into most of these divisions but has not always been the primary cause of dissension. At times the Negro question has been used as a screen to cover other conflicts, such as the fight for control of the state central committee, of patronage, or of the delegation to the national convention.

> Attorney general—George S. Thomas (w)
> Comptroller general—W. A. Pledger (col)
> Treasurer—F. F. Putney (w)
>
> *Farrow-Longstreet Ticket*
> Congressman-at-large—James Longstreet (w)
> Secretary of state—W. J. White (col)
> Attorney general—J. D. Cunningham (w)
> Comptroller general—Floyd Snelson (col)
> Treasurer—William F. Bowers (w)

Complete state central committees were named by both factions, with Benjamin Conley heading the Farrow group and A. E. Buck the Pledger party. Pledger himself had been nominated and had withdrawn in favor of Buck, probably in accordance with a prearranged plan.[13]

It is not clear from available accounts exactly how the differences between the two factions were reconciled. For weeks after the conventions there were references in the papers to the rival organizations and to the two Republican tickets in the field. From letters received and sent by Henry Farrow late in August and around the first of September it is evident that efforts were being made to compromise the situation and that various plans were being considered. Heads of the two factions met in Atlanta on August 30 and 31, and simultaneous meetings of the two state central committees took place on September 5 and 6. Committees representing the two groups conferred during the two days. The upshot of the negotiations was that Buck emerged as the chairman of a united front, with J. E. Bryant and Walter Johnson, from the two factions, as secretaries.[14]

A coalition slate of candidates was adopted and offered to the voters at the state election in October. Reports of the balloting show the following Republican candidates:

> Secretary of state—William A. Pledger
> Attorney general—Sion A. Darnell
> Comptroller general—Floyd Snelson
> Treasurer—William F. Bowers

The first two were of the Pledger faction, and Snelson and Bowers were candidates of the syndicate wing. The Republican candidates, like the Independent Democrat endorsed for governor, went down to overwhelming defeat.[15] C. D. Forsyth, the compromise candidate for congressman-at-large, was defeated in November, along with other Republican and Independent candidates for Congress.[16]

The new chairman of the state central committee, Colonel Alfred Eliab Buck, was one of the most interesting and one of the most capable figures to appear in the Republican party in Georgia during this period. Born in Maine in 1832, he was a graduate of Waterville College, was principal of the high school at Lewiston when the war broke out, and was an officer in the Union army throughout the war. After being mustered out of the service he went to Mobile, Alabama, and entered the iron business as a partner of his brother-in-law, Justice William B. Wood of the United States Supreme Court. He was a delegate to the Alabama constitutional convention in 1867, held various local offices, and was elected as a Republican to the Forty-first Congress. In 1873 Buck moved to Atlanta, where he was appointed clerk of the United States district and circuit courts. In 1889 he was to succeed Bryant as United States marshal and, after the election of William McKinley, to become minister to Japan.

From the time of his election to the chairmanship of the party in 1882 until his departure for Tokyo in 1897, Buck was the "boss" of the Republican organization in Georgia and held an unbroken tenure as its chairman. He was a member of the Georgia delegation to every national convention from 1880 through 1896. An interesting but little known facet of his army career contributed no doubt to Buck's success in Georgia politics. In the Union army he had served for about two years as the commanding officer of two regiments of colored troops. Since the Republican party in Georgia during his long tenure of office was composed so largely of Negro voters, his success in holding them in line may well have stemmed from his wartime experience with the colored soldiers.[17]

During the factional fighting of 1882, when the whites regained control of the party organization, the name of Jonathan Norcross does not appear. In 1884, however, he made another futile attempt this time working in conjunction with James Longstreet to establish a separate party for white Republicans. In these movements of Norcross there was never any bid for personal power. He was convinced that the only way to attract responsible, representative white men to the party was to make it possible for them to act as Republicans without mingling with the Negro members of the party. Yet he never advocated that the colored voters should be cast out or ignored. His theory, impractical and unworkable though it proved, was a matter of principle with him—a sort of premature "separate but equal" doctrine in the field of politics.

In sharp contrast was the motivation of most of the practical politicians who had wrested control from the colored majority in 1882.

With them it was primarily a question of personal power—of control of the party and of the *offices*. To this end they were willing and eager to use the Negroes and to work with them insofar as it was necessary—provided always that the black-and-tan masses should be kept subservient to the white leaders. In commenting on the situation in 1882, the *Constitution* had hit a vital point: "The negroes are afraid they can't get on without the white office-holders, and the white office-holders know they can't get on without the negroes."[18] The choicest political plums were apt to go to the men who could deliver the votes to a favored candidate at the national convention and this could be done only with a substantial following among the Negro members of the party.*

It is only fair to say that Farrow and some others who had labored long in the Republican party in Georgia saw clearly the party's dilemma in relation to the Negro. Admittedly it was to their advantage to keep the colored voter in tow—and they did this relentlessly—but it was not self-interest alone which led them to realize that the party could not be built up by eliminating the Negro. Writing to President Arthur early in 1883, Farrow complained of Longstreet and other "impracticables" who grumbled because they could not be furnished with *"a 'ready-made' respectable Republican Party."* "Unless they are willing to work among negroes, however disagreeable it may be," wrote he, "they will never find a point at which they will be willing to take hold and work earnestly for 'Republicanism in the South.' "

Farrow declared that Longstreet's idea of excluding the Negro from the Republican party in Georgia (or anywhere in the South) and of sending a "white-man's delegation" to the national convention stamped him "a political idiot." "[H]e has less political sense than any man I ever saw."[19]

By 1884 Longstreet had apparently given up hope of controlling the regular party organization in Georgia. In January he told a reporter for the Atlanta *Constitution* that, while he was a Republican, he had nothing to do with "the loud brethren" who were running the party in the state,[20] and shortly afterward he appeared in the forefront of the white Republican movement of 1884. This movement included a two-day conference in April, a state conven-

*In 1876, James Atkins's appointment as collector of customs in Savannah was attributed to the support he brought to Roscoe Conkling in the convention of that year, and J. E. Bryant's selection as United States marshal in 1884 was said to be a reward for his efforts in holding the Georgia delegation intact for President Arthur at Chicago. Atlanta *Constitution,* August 16, 1876, August 2, 1884; A. E. Buck to Henry P. Farrow, December 25, 1884, in the Farrow Collection.

tion in May, and a series of addresses directed to the white Republicans of the state.

The first meeting convened on April 8, the day before the state convention of the regular party organization. Again Jonathan Norcross was conciliatory to the colored members of the party, assuring them once more that the undertaking was not intended to trespass upon the rights and privileges of the Negro. (The gallery of the Senate chamber, where the meeting took place, was well filled with spectators, the majority of whom were Negroes.) Norcross still adhered to his idea of cooperation between the two races in separate conventions. His proposal to call the new party the "Whigs of 1884" was rejected but the conferees adopted the name "Whig Republican party." General Longstreet was named chairman of the executive committee and W. L. Clark, secretary. The call for the state convention went out over their names.[21]

The convention, held May 1-2, was called primarily to discuss the matter of sending delegates to the national convention in Chicago, but no delegation was named. The question of nominating candidates for state offices was also deferred. A motion was adopted that the state executive committee either call another convention to nominate or themselves nominate candidates and in the latter event that they declare for Longstreet for governor. All members of the convention voted "aye" except Longstreet himself.[22] The action recommending Longstreet for nomination was probably the basis for a statement in one secondary source that Longstreet was the Republican candidate for governor in 1884.[23] There seems to be no evidence that he was ever actually nominated even by this splinter group. Certainly he was not an official candidate of the Republican party organization and his name does not appear in the election returns.*

An unfortunate incident of the Whig-Republican convention occurred when Norcross took offense at criticism of some of his remarks about the Negroes. At the time he was with difficulty restrained from marching out of the meeting with his umbrella and his beaver hat, and he did not make an appearance on the second day

---

*This incident illustrates the difficulty in ascertaining the true facts about Republican party history from the fragmentary accounts in the Democratic press. Often a statement appears which seems to be a fact, only to be contradicted in a later issue or else never mentioned again. Allowance must be made, also, for the extreme bias with which much of the Republican news is presented. Longstreet's name appears in some secondary sources as the leader of the Republican party in Georgia at this time, but contemporary accounts do not indicate that he was ever accepted generally by the party membership as its leader.

of the convention. Feeling that he had been misunderstood, he wrote a letter to the *Constitution* explaining his reasons for leaving the convention and correcting a statement published the previous day. In justice to Norcross and in view of his reputation for race prejudice fostered by Avery and other historians, his sentiments should be judged by his own words:

[W]hat I did say ... was, that we have one white man's and negro hating party [the Democratic], and that was enough for Georgia, and that any party formed upon wrong cornerstones or in hostility to a portion of the voters would continue to be wrong in principles and practice, and that I could not and would not continue to act with any such a party.[24]

While Norcross, Longstreet, and a handful of associates were attempting to establish their separate lily-white party in 1884, the regular party organization was proceeding in accordance with a pattern which was to endure for many years. The brief interlude of Negro control under Pledger had proved abortive and the colored wing, although preponderant in numbers, had been set back firmly and decisively. The black-and-tan cohorts might furnish the votes and even receive some of the offices, but the white leaders would hold the reins. The balance might swing slightly from side to side as the years went by but the fundamental arrangement remained the same. The practical politicians of both races understood perfectly the necessity for this, and for the most part were able to hold in line the rank and file. Sometimes the truce was an uneasy one. Occasionally an insurgent upset a plan that had been carefully prearranged. But on the whole the two races were able to reconcile their differences and to maintain the *status quo*.

For the leaders it was a comfortable arrangement. What if it *did* discourage new accessions to the party? After all, there were not enough offices to go around as it was.

VII

The Syndicate

A PREOCCUPATION with the federal patronage had plagued the Republican party in Georgia almost from its beginning, and in the early 1880's the scramble for office reached a new peak of intensity and organization. The Republican "syndicate," a tight little combination of party leaders dedicated to the control of appointments in the state, was formed late in 1881. With slight alterations from time to time, because of expediency and the rise and fall of the personal fortunes of its members, the group was active for the next three years, through the administration of Chester A. Arthur.

The combination came into being just before the first Markham House conference. It included some of the Republican leaders who were most active in the coalition movement and was used for a time to promote the Independent cause, but there is no indication that the two moves were connected in the beginning. Since the syndicate was established originally on a confidential basis, with its members sworn to secrecy, it was not at first publicized or even recognized by the rank and file members of the party. Its history can be pieced together only from scattered correspondence from several different manuscript collections and from occasional references in the contemporary press.

Late in October, 1881, Henry Farrow received a confidential letter from his old friend, James S. Atkins, Savannah lawyer, who had been a leading Republican in Georgia since the days of Reconstruction. Atkins, who had lost his office as collector of customs in Savannah the previous year, proposed that a secret combination be formed to get all the offices they could and also to send a solid delegation to the next national convention. He suggested that Farrow make contact with a few of the "very truest, trusty, and congenially

• *The Syndicate* 91

harmonious Republicans" for this purpose. "Can this be done and the existence of such a thing never leak out?" he asked. Atkins outlined his idea in somewhat more detail, mentioning several possible members for the combination and several offices to be sought, but with no reference to the possibility of any cooperation with the Independents.[1]

In November and early December Farrow wrote to several friends *"in the most sacred confidence,"* inviting each one to join in a political combination to run through 1884. The question of patronage was suggested but not mentioned openly as the chief concern of the group. The stated objects of the combination (the term "syndicate" was not used in any of the early correspondence on the subject) were fourfold:

First, to secure recognition by the "powers that be" in Washington and also by the Independents in Georgia of the "right element" of Republicanism in the state;

Second, to secure proper recognition of Independents in Georgia not only by powers in Washington but also by Republicans in Georgia;

Third, to secure effective cooperation between Independents and Republicans in Georgia during the following year;

Fourth, to secure the Georgia delegation in 1884 for the combination represented by "Arthur, Grant, Conkling, *et al.*" as distinguished from the "James G. Blaine *et al.*" combination.

Farrow emphasized his belief that as scattered, isolated elements of Republicanism they could accomplish little, but by a fusion with the Independents they could carry the state in 1882. As for national politics, he was not proposing to drive the Blaine elements out of the party, said he, but he reminded his readers that the state party had been controlled for years by men from Maine—"understrikers" for Blaine—including J. E. Bryant, A. E. Buck, W. H. Smyth, C. H. Prince, and several others of the old carpetbagger faction who had held important federal offices and prominent positions in the party— "all *from Maine* and *for Blaine.*" All who entered the combination, said he, should agree upon a representative in Washington, and James Atkins had been selected for this post.[2]

Apparently the original membership of the syndicate, as crystallized at this time, consisted of six men: Atkins, Farrow, Charles W. Arnold, Walter H. Johnson, Alexander N. Wilson, and James Longstreet. The intermediate steps are not clear, but by the end of January all six men were in Washington, each thrusting a determined finger into the patronage pie.[3]

The inclusion of Longstreet in the group points up an interesting situation in the Republican party in Georgia. It seems evident that those who initiated the syndicate move did not want the General, did not really trust him, but were afraid to leave him out. Because of his long friendship with Ulysses S. Grant, Longstreet held a favored position with the "Stalwart" administration of Chester Arthur, and because of his wartime reputation, his potential influence in the state was not to be discounted. In Atkins's first letter to Farrow about the combination, he had said flatly, "I am against Longstreet for anything," but two months later he was urging Farrow and Wilson to "cultivate him assiduously," as he did not want the "C.B.'s" (carpetbaggers)* to capture him.[4]

It is not clear whether Longstreet was taken into the syndicate because of his part in promoting the coalition with the Independents or whether he was acting as an agent for the syndicate when he first approached Felton in the matter. The formation of the two movements was in progress at the same time and it is difficult to determine when they first converged. Longstreet's original letter to Felton regarding the possibility of the coalition was written on December 3.[5]

Even before the Markham House conference Farrow had protested to Felton that Longstreet was not versed in politics and would make costly blunders. He had recommended then that Atkins rather than Longstreet be chosen to represent the coalition in Washington.[6] Inasmuch as Atkins had already been chosen secretly to represent the *syndicate* in Washington, it seems evident that Farrow was trying to direct the two movements into the same channel, but there is no evidence that Dr. Felton was aware of this fact.

During January, 1882, both Longstreet and Atkins were in Washington. Both were in contact with the President and both were trying to influence him in dispensing the patronage.[7] That they were not always working in concert is shown clearly by letters from Atkins to Farrow. After a conference with the President, with Longstreet, Arnold, and Johnson also present, Atkins reported jubilantly that Arthur had deferred to his suggestions in several matters and had asked him alone for advice regarding a couple of appointments. He believed that Longstreet had been impressed.[8] A few weeks later,

---

*Antagonism between the native white Republicans and the carpetbag elements had existed to some extent from the beginning and it surged up periodically in some clash of personalities in the party. The particular target of members of the syndicate at this time was Andrew Clark, collector of internal revenue, who had been the open enemy of Farrow as district attorney and had tried to bring about his dismissal.

Atkins, Farrow, Johnson, Arnold, and Wilson (all in Washington) dispatched an urgent, confidential letter to Dr. Felton, asking that he see Longstreet immediately regarding certain matters of patronage.[9] Letters exchanged between Atkins, Farrow, and Wilson in subsequent months grew increasingly critical of the General.

President Arthur had already committed himself to a policy of cooperation with Independent elements in the South as a means of building up the Republican party in the Southern states. He was receptive to proposals from the Georgia Republicans that the federal patronage be used to further this purpose, and both Longstreet and Atkins were using this approach to gain their own ends. In the process of arranging for jobs for friends and supporters, it seems that each member of the syndicate had his own interest primarily in view. The flood of letters received by Farrow from Atkins and later from Wilson, who succeeded Atkins as the Washington representative, shows that dissensions and jealousies were frequent within the syndicate as well as among other party members.

Longstreet already held one of the top federal offices in the state, that of United States marshal, and seemed content with the post, but it was not long before other members of the syndicate were plotting for his replacement. Farrow was put forward first for collector of internal revenue to displace his old enemy, Andrew Clark, but, failing to get that position, was soon appointed collector of customs in Brunswick. Arnold, already postmaster in Albany, succeeded in having his brother, John W. Arnold, made postmaster at Columbus. Johnson, who had been postmaster at Columbus for a number of years, moved up to the internal revenue office. Wilson, after a few months in Washington early in 1883, was made collector of customs in Savannah. Atkins, coveting a fat plum for himself, was waiting for the creation of a proposed new judgeship for the northern district of Georgia. Early in April, 1882, he complained to Farrow that he was "mighty sick" waiting for an office to be created for him. After months of obtaining appointments for others, "I begin to feel like an office-broker," he wrote.[10] The bill setting up the new district court was already in Congress, however, and with its passage Atkins set to work in earnest to secure for himself the appointment as judge, pressing all his friends to his support.

During these months of preoccupation with the patronage there was almost no mention of the Independent movement in the correspondence between members of the syndicate. All thought and pretense of using the appointments to foster the cause of the coalition had seemingly been put aside. Although the members of the syndicate had been the chief Republican supporters of cooperation with the Independents, little had been done to implement the agreement. Farrow, distressed at the inactivity, wrote long letters to Longstreet and to Felton during the month of May, complaining of lack of cooperation among Republican leaders and making suggestions that were never carried out regarding the organization of the pending campaign. Even before Stephens's rejection of the Independent nomination for governor, it was clear that the coalition had failed.

Embittered by the turn of affairs and piqued by an appointment given to one of his political enemies, Dr. Felton wrote to Farrow in June that he had withdrawn all his recommendations to the President for office. "I am satisfied," he wrote, "the cause of Independentism has been irreparably damaged by the unseemly fight in Washington among Georgia Republicans over the federal offices." The great mass of the people who did not seek office, said he, were disgusted. He deplored the fact that a good cause had been ruined by personal factions among Republicans.[11]

While Chester Arthur seemed genuinely interested in the attempted cooperation with the Independents in Georgia, he was more directly concerned about his own chances for renomination in 1884. His willingness to cooperate with the Georgia syndicate was undoubtedly influenced by the fact that its members were pledged to his support and hoped to take a solid Arthur delegation to the national convention.

During the spring of 1882 it became apparent that a battle royal was shaping up for the control of the party in Georgia. White leaders were determined to take the power from the Negroes who had headed the party since 1880, and it seemed certain that William Pledger would be replaced as chairman. Actually, Pledger's power had already been undermined, and the main question was *which* group of white men would take over. It was obvious that the change would be made at the state convention scheduled for August, and the faction that gained control at this time would be in position to appoint the delegation to Chicago in 1884.

Most of the members of the syndicate were too practical in their approach to politics to think that they could obtain or retain control of the party without the support of a sizable bloc of colored voters, but, as a group, they felt little attachment for the Negroes. Longstreet was never popular with the colored men and was eventually to go off into the white Republican movement. Atkins, in first writing to Farrow about the syndicate, had declared that he never intended to strike another blow in politics unless he could see a tendency toward the upbuilding of a white Republican party in the state. No colored man had been taken into the original membership of the syndicate and none had been invited to participate in the coalition with the Independents. On the other hand, A. E. Buck and J. E. Bryant, leaders in the other faction of the party, were outstanding in their success with the colored voters and were working hand in glove with the Negroes.

Anxious to placate Pledger and hoping, no doubt, to gain his support in the coming shift of power, the syndicate arranged for his appointment as surveyor of the port of Atlanta, with the aid of Congressman Emory Speer and in spite of the opposition of Longstreet. Pledger was delighted with the office, and in thanking Farrow for his part in the matter, added the postscript, "The hatchet is and ought to be buried."[12] At about the same time, L. M. Pleasant, another influential colored Republican, was made collector of internal revenue for the third district of Georgia.[13]

As the months passed, however, and it seemed less and less certain that the syndicate faction would prevail, the little center core of the combination—Atkins, Farrow, and Wilson—evidently decided on a drastic action. Five additional members, three of them Negroes, were admitted to the syndicate. It is not clear whether the new combination replaced the old or whether the new members were simply added, possibly in a secondary capacity; but on July 12, 1882, an agreement was drawn up, headed "Terms of Combination" and signed by Atkins, Farrow, Wilson, R. D. Locke, S.A. Darnell, L. M. Pleasant, Edwin Belcher, and James M. Simms.* That they were actually taken into the group is indicated by the fact that Atkins referred later to the document as "the syndicate paper."[14]

Members of the syndicate were not alone in their concern over the control of the convention and of the new state central committee. Chester Arthur was also keeping an anxious eye on the situation in Georgia and was disturbed by the possibility of losing the state's twenty-four convention delegates.** Late in July Atkins reported to

---

*The "Terms of Combination" document, in the Farrow Collection, is partially destroyed and it is impossible to determine its full significance. Attached to it is a fragment dated August 22, 1882, referring to unanimous resolutions regarding the signatures and membership of Darnell and Locke. The implication is that they were expelled from the combination after going over to the Buck-Pledger faction in the split convention of August 2-3. Darnell and Locke are referred to as traitors in a letter from Atkins to Farrow, August 11, 1882, in the Farrow Collection.

**At the time, Buck, Bryant, Pledger, and other leaders of that faction of the party were thought to be for James G. Blaine and against the nomination of Arthur, but by the time of the 1884 convention all had swung to Arthur's standard.

Farrow that the President was not pleased with the prospect of not carrying the state convention. Atkins urged Farrow to spare no effort to control the meeting. "You must control it if you have to kill some fellows," he wrote.[15]

The syndicate's desperate effort to control the convention, which led to two separate meetings, two separate state central committees, and two separate slates of candidates for state offices, has been recounted above, in Chapter VI. The eventual compromise, with Buck as chairman, seemed a setback for the syndicate faction, but a merger was going on behind the scenes which brought forth a revised combination and resulted, after all, in a solid Arthur delegation at the national convention in 1884.

After the state convention in August, 1882, the center of power shifted perceptibly. First to fall was James Atkins, who had been riding the crest for seven months as the syndicate's contact man in Washington. During these months Atkins had dispatched a veritable flood of letters to Farrow, the group's anchor man in Georgia. Filled with grandiose schemes, pontifical advice, and an abounding self-assurance, his letters gave no hint that he himself would be the first major casualty in the struggle for patronage. Atkins had set his heart on the new judgeship and apparently believed that he was going to get it. He actually did get the nomination from President Arthur but there was probably never a chance that he would be confirmed. With the exception of Emory Speer, the Georgia congressional delegation was solidly and vigorously against him and the judiciary committee of the Senate refused to send his name to that body for consideration. Atkins's past record in federal office and in the state legislature would hardly commend him to the bench. When it became clear that he could not be confirmed, he withdrew his name, just before the August convention.*

A week later, Atkins wrote Farrow that he had left Washington and was returning to his home in Savannah, where he expected to settle permanently into his profession of law. "I am crushed and shelved, so need not be considered," wrote he. "I have ended my days of political usefulness and it may be of all other sorts."[16] At various times during the next year or so, friends of Atkins reported to Farrow that he had become sour and embittered and was still brooding over his loss of the judgeship, which he blamed on every-

---

*Appointed to the judgeship was Henry Kent McCay, former member of the Supreme Court of Georgia. McCay was a Republican but was never active in organization politics.

body except himself. He remained in the inner circle of the syndicate and occasionally emerged from his depression for a brief spurt of political activity but he was never again an influential figure in the party. Three years before his death, in a letter to John Sherman, Atkins complained bitterly that to be a Republican in active politics in the South was to be "a foolish martyr."[17]

Another casualty from the top ranks was James Longstreet, who had been on the way out for longer probably than he himself realized. It is not clear exactly when and under what circumstances Longstreet was dropped from the syndicate. His name does not appear on the "Terms of Combination" paper of July 12, 1882, but he was still spoken of by the press as a leader of the syndicate wing in reports of the August convention and he certainly worked together with Farrow at that time. After the convention his name appeared less frequently in connection with the party organization and not at all in the connection with the syndicate except in reference to plans for getting him out of the marshal's office.

Around the first of the year (1883), Alexander N. Wilson replaced Atkins as the syndicate's representative in Washington. For several months his reports to Farrow came thick and fast. Even after he returned to Savannah as collector of customs about the middle of the year, he continued to correspond regularly with Farrow about party matters. Wilson was a school teacher by profession, a Unionist and Republican by conviction, and a politician of some standing. He had grown up in East Tennessee with Andrew Johnson and reportedly had been offered the post of provisional governor of Georgia in 1865 but had declined. He had attended the first Markham House Conference in December, 1881.*

In July, 1882, Walter Johnson had taken over as collector of internal revenue, a move that brought him to Atlanta and put him in a position of increasing prominence in the party organization. After the compromise between the two factions, Johnson became secretary of the state central committee, sharing the office with J. E. Bryant, member of the other faction. Farrow, confirmed in March, 1882, as collector of customs in Brunswick, continued to spend long periods in Atlanta and Washington, intent on party business. Presumably C. W. Arnold remained a member of the combination, although

---

*After filling several federal offices, Wilson went back to teaching and eventually became assistant superintendent of schools in Atlanta. On his death, he was described as a teacher to three generations, respected and loved. Atlanta *Constitution*, June 23, 1893.

never a very powerful one. Still postmaster at Albany and chairman of the Second District Republican executive committee, Arnold wrote frequently to Farrow, quarreled mildly with him on occasion, and was rumored at times to be after his job and also that of Wilson.

The big news in the syndicate by early 1883 was the addition of at least two and possibly three new members, powerful members. A. E. Buck and Emory Speer were definitely *in*, and there are indications that J. E. Bryant was either admitted with Buck or came later into the combination. It seems clear that Buck's entry came as a result of (or possibly as a *part* of) the compromise that united the two factions of the party in the fall of 1882. Did the price of admission include pledges on the part of Buck and Bryant to support the renomination of Chester Arthur? It seems not unlikely. Buck led the unanimous Arthur delegation to Chicago in 1884 and Bryant was one of its members.

Emory Speer had worked with the syndicate behind the scenes from its beginning. Georgia's only Independent member of Congress in 1881-1882, Speer owed his election partly to the Republicans and was in close touch with party leaders. Moreover, he was well-liked by President Arthur and was consulted by him in matters of patronage, a circumstance of great importance to the syndicate. Apparently Farrow had written to Speer when the combination was first projected, as Speer had responded early in December, 1881, that both Atkins and Farrow were his friends and that he would do all he could to help either of them. "I believe that Atkins is the best man you could get for your purpose," he added, referring, apparently, to the plan for Atkins to represent the group in Washington.[18]

During 1882 Speer's name appears often in the correspondence of members of the syndicate and he was himself the author of numerous letters to Farrow. The tone of some of these leaves no doubt as to his deep involvement with the Independent Movement of 1882 and with Republicans, especially those Republicans of the syndicate faction.[19] When Speer was unexpectedly defeated for re-election to Congress in November, 1882, an awkward situation developed. A vacancy in the office of United States attorney for the northern district of Georgia had been allotted to C. D. Forsyth, Rome Republican, but Speer wanted the place and members of the syndicate felt that he should have it.

In January, Farrow wrote to Buck regarding the situation. "There is but one course for us to pursue," said he, "and that is to come speedily, speedily, to Speer's support—that is, take Speer into our

• *The Syndicate* 99

combination without a moment's delay."* Farrow expressed the opinion that the group would be much stronger with Speer and that, moreover, he would probably go to some other combination if not taken into the syndicate.[20]

A few weeks later Buck was in Washington taking a hand in matters of patronage and he and Speer went together to see President Arthur to show that they were in harmony. The joint visit was Speer's suggestion. "The President was highly pleased and so expressed himself," reported Wilson to Farrow.[21] Speer was assured of the appointment as district attorney, but it could not be given to him until after the expiration of his term as congressman.

On Buck's return to Atlanta a few days later he wrote Farrow a long, confidential letter regarding several appointments either made or projected. Of one arrangement (involving two Negro Republicans), Buck reported that he had consented because it was Speer's wish and because he wanted "to tie him [Speer] to us." Besides, as Buck admitted to Farrow, he wanted Speer to take immediate steps to get Longstreet out of the marshal's office in order that Bryant might be appointed to the place.[22]

For months, Farrow, Wilson, and Atkins had become more and more exasperated with Longstreet. Speer showed a disposition to agree but did not want to rush the matter. Almost a year before, Speer had expressed the *"sub rosa"* opinion that Longstreet's conduct was such that it would be impossible to avoid an issue with him, but he wished to do so if possible.[23] Wilson reported early in 1883 that Speer was not willing to ask Longstreet's removal until he reached Atlanta and saw for himself the operation of the marshal's office. Speer acknowledged that Longstreet was of no use as a politician. In fact, said Wilson, there was no one who had an idea that Longstreet was of any practical value in politics, but he had a national reputation, was old, and General Grant was his friend.[24]

Longstreet's friendship with Grant was still a matter of importance in the minds of many. Farrow himself had felt constrained to write the former President a long letter of explanation when a rumor was published that he was trying to put Longstreet out of office. Farrow denied that he had ever "sought directly to throw him out of office," though he had been forced to the conclusion "that God never intended him for a political leader."[25]

---

*That Speer actually became a member of the syndicate is indicated in later correspondence. "If *our crowd* will hold steady and hang together now, with Speer in the lead, we will come through all right. . . . Speer is our *strong tower*." Alexander N. Wilson to Henry P. Farrow, June 1, 1883, in the Farrow Collection.

Colonel Buck put his case to Speer frankly on the basis of political expediency. Since Speer himself was about to be named district attorney and Wilson was to be appointed to the customs office, said Buck, taking two from the syndicate side with no counterbalancing appointments would make it hard for him to hold his forces together if Longstreet remained. If Bryant, who had opposed the syndicate, was appointed marshal, all would be well. If the President could provide for Longstreet elsewhere, he would be glad to see it done, said Buck, but if not, "why he ought to go, for political reasons if for no others."[26]

Eventually Longstreet *was* replaced by Bryant but not until the summer of 1884. An investigation ordered by the President showed the Marshal's accounts badly out of line and his office poorly administered.* Even so, the President did not act at once, choosing to wait until after the Republican national convention. Arthur was defeated by James G. Blaine for the nomination, but the Georgia delegation held firm and gave its twenty-four votes to Arthur all the way. His appointment of Bryant as marshal, soon after the convention, brought charges that a deal had been made. There seems no reason to doubt that this was true. Buck himself substantiated the fact in a letter to Farrow several months later.[27]

According to the story, the "deal" was twofold. Even before Bryant's appointment, the New York *Times* and other papers over the country had published rumors that the price of Georgia's twenty-four votes would be the marshal's office for J. E. Bryant and a judgeship for Henry Farrow. Buck admitted that the President had told him that he would have no occasion to be disappointed over the two appointments.

For many months—perhaps years—Farrow had aspired to the judgeship held by John Erskine.** He had served for eight years as district attorney with Judge Erskine, when his was the only United States district court in Georgia. After the separation of the northern and southern district in 1882 and the appointment of an additional judge, the original court became the southern district court with

---

*Even his enemies did not usually question Longstreet's personal honesty. Ill health and general unfitness for the responsibilities of the office had made him easy prey for corrupt and incompetent associates.

**Judge Erskine had come to Atlanta originally in 1855 but had gone North during the war. In 1865 he had returned to Georgia when appointed to the judgeship by Andrew Johnson. Erskine described himself as "a republican in principle," but he was never active in the party organization. He retired, it was said, "without a single enemy." Atlanta *Constitution,* December 20, 1883, a reprint in the Farrow Collection.

headquarters in Savannah. It was known that Erskine would be seventy years old in September, 1883, and that he planned to retire soon after that, and it was known too that Farrow had already staked out a claim to the office. There was no secret about his ambition. As early as March, 1883, he wrote President Arthur that he had "long been 'in train' for that office" and would be supported for it in all Republican circles.[28]

Erskine's resignation was not announced formally until late in December but Farrow had been busy with preparations all year—marshaling his supporters, collecting letters of endorsement, arranging for resolutions to be passed by various groups of Republicans, and preparing a long and elaborate brief for submission to the President.[29] The retiring judge was in poor health and asked to be relieved from his duties, and it was generally assumed that the President would nominate his successor during the session of Congress that convened in December, 1883.

In January, rumors were abundant of others who were trying for the judgeship, both Republicans and Democrats. It was not thought that Arthur would name a Democrat, however, and Farrow had the endorsement of most of the leading Republicans of the state. All but six of the eighty members of the state central committee had come out for him, most of the district chairmen, and hundreds of the rank and file members of the party. The Republican executive committee of Glynn County, where Farrow was then residing, had placed him in nomination in November. The Fulton County committee had passed similar resolutions in October. The state central committee sent a petition to the President asking his appointment. His ten-page printed brief carried the names of more than fifty Democrats, along with his Republican endorsers. These included some of the most prominent men in the state, most of them lawyers.[*] It would seem that his position was impregnable. But the President did not act.

Farrow himself had taken a leave of absence from his collectorship in Brunswick and was in Washington pushing his plea. He was in constant communication with Buck, Wilson, and Walter Johnson, back in Georgia. James Atkins had shown a strange reluctance to join the cause. Wilson and others said he had a dog-in-the-manger

---

[*]Among the Democrats who endorsed Farrow (if a Republican was to be appointed) were James Jackson, chief justice of the Georgia Supreme Court, J. H. Lumpkin, reporter of the Supreme Court, Henry Jackson, chairman of the Democratic state executive committee, and former Senator John B. Gordon. Independent Democrats William H. Felton, Lucius J. Gartrell, and Emory Speer were included in the list.

attitude. Having lost his own try for a judgeship, he seemed to begrudge Farrow the chance for appointment. He finally agreed, conditionally, to help, but he blew hot and cold, alternately friendly and aloof, and could not be counted on. Finally it became apparent that Arthur would make no nomination before Congress adjourned. Farrow and the others concluded that he was waiting deliberately until after the national convention; so it became all the more important to take a solid slate for Arthur to Chicago.

When Congress convened again in December, 1884, it was obvious that the appointment would have to be made soon. The November elections were over and the Democrats had won the presidency. Arthur would go out of office on March 4, and he could not wait much longer and be sure of time for the Senate's confirmation. Besides, Judge Erskine had left the bench and a substitute was holding court for him. A replacement was long overdue and badly needed.

On December 1, Buck, Bryant, and Johnson, officers of the state central committee, wrote the President a formal letter asking that the appointment be made. A little later, Buck sent Arthur a personal telegram urging action.[30] By the middle of December, Atkins and Bryant were in Washington, and telegrams were flying back and forth. On December 16, Atkins reported to Farrow that a basketful of dispatches had been received, supplementing previous endorsements. But still the President did not act. Atkins and Bryant talked frequently with Arthur but got no satisfaction. Both men, astute politicians, diagnosed the situation after a conversation with the President. Bryant wrote that Arthur had delayed sending any name to the Senate because he hesitated to nominate Farrow and yet wanted to please the group. He appeared to have some doubt whether Farrow could be confirmed. (Farrow had frequently been under fire as district attorney and in his present job. After Atkins had been rejected for the other judgeship in 1882, Farrow's name had come up but had quickly been discarded.) Atkins said flatly that Arthur was simply not in favor of Farrow and would not talk about the case with any satisfaction.[31]

The barrage of telegrams continued. Christmas came and went. But still the President did not act.

When Atkins went home to Savannah at Christmastime, he ran into a bit of news that confirmed a suspicion that had been growing in his mind for some time. On January 5 he wrote to Farrow that lawyers in Savannah were telling him that Emory Speer was acting as though he was to be connected with that bar. (Speer was then attorney for the northern district court, centered in Atlanta.) An old college chum of Speer's had told Atkins that Speer had some axe to grind in connection with the Savannah bar. Atkins had asked him innocently whether Emory expected to be judge. The answer was emphatic: "That's it; that must be it; that accounts for it." "The question was to the mind of the college chum a *revelation*," wrote Atkins. "He . . . settled on his conclusion at once." Atkins protested to Farrow that he was not really suspicious of Speer but he knew the President was "an Emory man," warm toward Speer generally and cold toward Farrow's candidacy, and he might settle the difficulty in the appointment by naming "one whom he really desired all the time."[32]

There is no indication that Farrow distrusted Speer or had considered him a rival for the judgeship. In December, in a letter to the President, Speer had renewed his endorsement of his old friend, Henry Farrow, but a careful observer might have noticed that his description of the type of jurist needed would fit himself quite as well as Farrow.[33]

In the middle of January the suspense was ended. Word came from Washington that the President had made up his mind not to appoint Farrow, and that Emory Speer had applied for the office and was confident that he would be appointed. Farrow, stung to the quick, got off an angry telegram to the department of justice charging Speer with dereliction of duty as district attorney. He attacked Speer bitterly and signified his intention of following up the charges. Speer expressed surprise at Farrow's attitude. He protested that he had made no move to seek the appointment until Farrow was out of the picture. Moreover, he said that it had been understood with Farrow, Buck, Bryant, and Johnson that his name was to be presented if it should become apparent that Farrow could not be appointed.[34]

On January 19 the President signed Speer's nomination and sent it to the Senate. Confirmation was expected at once. Farrow dropped his active opposition after Bryant assured him that the President had, indeed, definitely discarded his name before Speer made his application. Buck and Bryant came out for Speer, and it was thought at first that both Georgia senators would support him. A complication developed almost immediately, however, when Senator Alfred H. Colquitt objected to the nomination. The judgeship had been vacant for fourteen months, said he; another six weeks would make no difference. Colquitt declared frankly that the appointment should be deferred until Grover Cleveland should take office, in order that a Democrat more acceptable to the people of the state could be named. The Georgia delegation in the House of Representatives, one hundred per cent Democratic, endorsed this stand. Senator Joseph E. Brown came out in support of Speer.[35]

There followed one of the most unusual proceedings ever seen in the Senate. The two Georgia senators met in head-on collision over the issue. The nomination was tied up for several weeks in the judiciary committee of the Senate and was then debated long and furiously on the Senate floor. On February 18, after a four-hour executive session, largely taken up by Brown and Colquitt, Emory Speer was finally confirmed. Brown was the only Democrat in the Senate who voted for the nomination.* Only four Republicans opposed it.[36] So an Independent Democrat was named to the federal bench in Georgia, as one of the last official acts of a Republican President and a Republican Senate, while the man endorsed almost unanimously by the Republican party of the state was rejected.

Perhaps it was just as well that the Democrats had won the presidency. The syndicate, like Humpty-Dumpty, could never be put back together again. But, with Grover Cleveland in the White House, there would be mighty few jobs for Republicans anyway. There would be a respite for at least four years from the feverish striving for office, the virus of *federalitis*, which had crippled and almost paralyzed the party in Georgia.

Henry Farrow did not retire from politics because of his defeat, but he spent more and more of his time at his country place at Porter Springs, where he owned a resort hotel and other property. He retained his post as collector of customs in Brunswick until his resignation in October, 1885, and subsequently served as postmaster both at Porter Springs and at Gainesville. In 1896 he ran for Congress and the following year waged a campaign (unsuccessfully) for appointment as auditor for the navy department. But things were never again the same. He was never again the center of power in the party. The show now belonged to Alfred Eliab Buck, and Buck made the most of it for the remainder of the century.

---

*Republicans in Georgia often complained that the state's senators, though Democrats, had too much influence over the appointments made by Republican presidents. Brown, charged by his enemies in both parties with being the "boss" of the state, was generally friendly with the syndicate. When Farrow had written to him in March, 1882, about his own confirmation as collector of customs, the Senator had responded, "Leave the matter in the hands of your old friend & have faith." Five days later he wired Farrow that he had been confirmed. Joseph E. Brown to Henry P. Farrow, March 24, 29, 1882, in the Farrow Collection.

VIII

Fusion with the Populists

DURING THE decade of the 1880's Republicanism in Georgia continued to decline. The party usually elected a few scattered members of the General Assembly, but even the most optimistic Republican in Georgia could hardly hope for success on a statewide basis. It was clear that the only possibility of breaking the political stranglehold of the Democratic party was to combine with other forces. For a while, in the late seventies and early eighties, cooperation with the Independents had seemed the answer, but that had proved disappointing. Now, as a new decade got under way, a new possibility of combination appeared. This time the magic word was *fusion*—fusion with the Populists.

Cooperation with the Populists—the People's party—seemed to offer more chance of success than did the old tie with the Independents. The trend toward Independent candidates was never an organized one. It depended primarily upon a few strong individuals, such as William H. Felton and Emory Speer. The attempt to organize a separate coalition party, sparked by the Markham House conference in December, 1881, never materialized. The Populist party, on the other hand, was a going concern. Growing out of the Farmers' Alliances in the South and the Northwest, it had a large and enthusiastic membership and by 1892 was sufficiently well organized nationally to nominate a candidate for president. There were more Populist candidates, more Populist voters, and infinitely more room for political maneuvering and bargaining than had been present in the earlier attempts at cooperation with individual Independents.

The Farmers' Alliances were originally non-partisan, non-political organizations. They grew out of the agricultural distress that gripped both the West and the South during the eighties and were dedicated to the interests of the farmer as contrasted with the monopolistic practices of big business. At the beginning, both the Northern Alliance and the Southern Alliance tried economic methods to bring prosperity to the farmer. Various ventures into cooperative buying and selling were made and a wide variety of educational and social activities was sponsored. Some of the cooperatives succeeded; others failed miserably. At best they brought only a small measure of relief to agriculture. The conviction grew that the remedy for the farmer's ills lay in political action.[1]

In the Northwest, in every state where the Alliance was strong, third-party tickets were in the field by 1890. In Georgia, however, as in other Southern states, Alliance members were slow to accept the idea of a new party. They preferred to work through the framework of the Democratic party rather than to run the risk of dividing the white vote of the state. In 1888 there were many Alliance men among Democratic candidates in Georgia and they were successful in a large number of cases.[2]

By 1890 there were more than one hundred thousand members of the Alliance in Georgia and the farm group had become so powerful politically that it had virtually captured the Democratic party of the state. The two principal candidates for governor were both Alliance men and all ten of the congressmen elected from Georgia gave lip service at least to the Alliance program. In the General Assembly the Alliance elected three-fourths of the senators and four-fifths of the representatives.[3] In terms of action, however, the results were disappointing. Alliance members elected as Democrats tended to think and act like other Democrats instead of pushing the movement for reform. In the Congress, Thomas E. Watson of the Tenth District was the only Georgia Representative who refused to be bound by the Democratic caucus. In the General Assembly some reform legislation was passed but the accomplishments of the Alliance were not extensive.

The same situation was general in other states where Alliance members were working through the old, established parties. In May, 1891, the People's party as a national organization was launched at a convention of Alliance men in Cincinnati. On October 1, 1891, Tom Watson published in Atlanta the first issue of his *People's Party Paper*, which was to appear weekly for the next eight years. In 1892 the Populist party entered Georgia politics by naming "dirt farmer," W. L. Peek, as its candidate for governor.[4]

Republican leaders in Georgia had watched with interest these developments leading to a third party in the state. In 1890 there had been Republican candidates for Congress in every district except the Sixth and Eighth but none had polled an impressive vote. Only three Republicans were elected to the Georgia House of Representatives. No opposition vote was listed against W. J. Northen for governor or against other statehouse officers. The exciting event in Georgia politics in 1890 was the upward surge of the Alliance within the Democratic party. Republican voting power was a negligible factor.[5]

In 1892, with the advent of the third party, the political situation in the state was both complicated and confused. Members of the Farmers' Alliance, overwhelmingly Democratic, were torn between their loyalty to the old party and their desire to endorse the reform principles of Populism. There were rumors that some of the incumbent congressmen would go over to the new party but all except Watson remained in the Democratic ranks. Those Alliance men who did espouse the People's party were largely from the less privileged class of farmers, the "wool hat boys" of Georgia politics. They were fiercely opposed to the old Bourbon leadership of the Democratic party but many of them were equally opposed to the idea of seeking or accepting help from the Republican party. The Republicans, also, were divided on the question of cooperation. The issue of fusion with the Populists was an explosive one which was to plague the Republican party in Georgia for almost a decade. While it was a well-established policy of the party to support individual candidates who opposed Democratic nominees and who were pledged to carry out measures in the interests of the people,[6] official endorsement of the candidates of another party was something new and was a hotly fought issue among party leaders and rank and file members.

On the national level the two parties—Republican and Populist—had little in common. In most respects their platforms were diametrically opposed. On the local level, however, there were factors that tended to draw them together. First, of course, was their common hostility to the Democratic party. United action was a matter of expediency, with the alluring possibility of electing some candidates of both parties who could not otherwise hope for success. But there was more to bring them together than common opposition to the Democrats. In the Republican party the bulk of the white membership (except for the controlling clique of officeholders) was composed of small farmers—former Unionists or their sons—mainly in the mountainous sections of north Georgia. Scratching out a living on the rocky upland slopes, these sturdy yeomen had little kinship with the prosperous lowland planters who had been the slaveholders before the war. Many of them became Republicans soon after the war and stayed in that party in spite of its vicissitudes.[7]

These small farmers had their counterparts in other sections of the state, but most of the latter had remained in the Democratic organization until the formation of the Populist party. Those who joined the People's party in 1892 had much in common with the white rank and file of the Republican party in Georgia. Moreover, many of these habitual Republicans themselves had good reason to embrace Populist doctrines, which were designed to aid poor, distressed farms. The Republican party in its early days had championed the poor and the oppressed, and "the heady Populist doctrines were good Republicanism," writes a modern authority on politics. "The Republican fusion with the Populists in the 1890's was not solely a marriage of political convenience."[8]

If the white Republicans only had been involved, fusion between the two parties might well have been a success, but the white members of the Republican party in Georgia made up a very small percentage of its total. Effective fusion, from a numerical standpoint, must necessarily include the mass of Negro voters. And the racial angle brought serious complications, as it always had within the Republican party itself.

During the summer of 1892, rumors were prevalent that Georgia Republicans would combine forces with the Populists for the state and national elections. Leaders of both parties denied this. United States Marshal A. E. Buck, chairman of the Republican state central committee, stated that he was not apprised of any such movement and was satisfied that there was none upon either side. Sion A. Darnell, United States district attorney, who had been defeated in his campaign for Congress in the Ninth District in 1890, declared that he was opposed to any alliance with any other party and felt sure that there would be no fusion in his district. The Independents had wanted Republican votes in the past, said he with some bitterness, but had always shown "a most singular unwillingness to have any relations with the republicans," except when their votes were wanted.[9]

The Republicans had held a convention in April to choose delegates to the national convention but had deferred other matters until August, when the adjourned meeting was to re-convene. On August 10, the day before the convention, the state executive committee held a secret meeting where the question of fusion was heatedly discussed. It was reported that the majority, led by W. A. Pledger, opposed the idea. At the convention on the following day the same situation prevailed. Pledger made a long and forceful speech urging the convention to nominate a Republican slate of candidates for state offices. Since the white voters were divided, said he, the Republicans would have their best opportunity in many years of putting across their own candidates. Apparently he had little support for his plea, and Buck's motion against putting out a state ticket was passed almost unanimously. No action was taken in the matter of supporting Populist candidates but the failure to nominate a state ticket was seen as opening the way for a deal with the third party.[10]

It was reported that Peek had been approached by Republican leaders regarding the possibility of endorsing him officially but that he had been somewhat cool to the proposition. He would welcome their votes, said he, but would make no compromise of Populist principles.[11]

After the August convention had refused to nominate its own candidates or to endorse those of the third party, individual Republicans felt free to support any candidates in the field. Governor Northen during his first term had won the approval of the colored people by providing more money for Negro education and by coming out vigorously against lynching and lynch law, and many Republican Negroes, including Pledger, determined to support him for a second term.

It had become evident early in the campaign that the Negroes could hold the balance of power, and both parties were bidding for their vote. The Populists tried to enlist their support through the Colored Alliance. In 1890 the president of the colored farm group in Georgia, Ed S. Richardson, a conservative Negro, had declared that his organization had persistently refused to meddle with politics and did not propose to be led into the same trap as had the white Alliance. The pressures were strong, however, for the Negroes to go Populist. After all, most colored men in Georgia were farmers and they belonged very definitely to the lower economic and social levels that were most attracted by Populist doctrine.[12] The national supervisor of the Colored Alliance, R. M. Humphrey, a white Southerner, had declared himself in favor of the third party movement as early as 1890.[13]

In their platforms Southern Populists denounced lynch law and the convict lease system and spoke out for the political rights of the Negro. Negroes were made welcome at Populist rallies, and picnics, barbecues, and camp meetings were arranged for them. Tom Watson, writing on the Negro question, contended that the "accident of color" could make no difference in the interest of farmers, croppers, and laborers. He believed that when the Negro once realized this self-interest would compel him to vote with the Populists.[14] (Watson's feeling about the colored voter at this point was very different from his later attitude.)

It would seem that any rational appraisal of the situation would have drawn the Negroes to Populism and that the colored Republicans would have been strong supporters of the idea of fusion. There were factors, however, pulling in the other direction. The Democrats had long since learned the value of the Negro vote, even though they did not welcome the colored man into their party councils. Many inducements were held out to persuade him to cast the Democratic ballot. In state elections especially, where there were few Republican nominations, many Negroes who considered themselves good Republicans chose to vote for the regular Democratic candidates when they were opposed by Independents or by third-party men. The size of the colored vote for a particular candidate might depend primarily upon the personal popularity of that man with the Negroes and upon his record in matters relating to the colored people, regardless of his political label. Alfred Colquitt always had effective Negro support, and Northen was widely approved on the basis of his first term in office. Even before the Republican convention in August, "Northen Clubs" were being formed among the colored men, and after the Republicans declined to nominate a ticket Pledger and others were openly campaigning for the Democratic Governor.

Later in September Colonel Buck dropped a bombshell on his followers by sending out circulars advising all Republicans to vote with the People's party. When questioned, the Colonel denied that any general fusion was involved but he expressed the opinion that the majority of Republicans would vote for Populist candidates.[15] Party members all over the state were in a turmoil. In Macon the county executive committee held a secret meeting and resolved that the Republicans of Bibb County should support the People's party —state ticket, congressional ticket, and legislative ticket. In Rome Buck met with party members (principally the white element) in the office of Postmaster Zack Hargrove and heard them pass a resolution to the effect that it was the *duty* of Republicans in the approaching election to support the candidates of the People's party. Others fell into line, but all was not peace and harmony on the Republican front. Negroes in Thomasville (and the same was true in other locations) were described as "highly wrought up" over Buck's "order" that they should vote the third party ticket.[16]

• *Fusion with the Populists* 111

Perhaps the most articulate opposition to fusion at this point came in an open letter issued by a group of Negro Republicans who were delegates to the state convention in August and most of whom were members of the state central committee. This letter reminded Republicans through the state that it was under the advice of Buck himself that the convention had decided not to put out a state ticket and had refused to endorse candidates of any party, thus leaving every member free to vote for whom he pleased. "No republican ought to be controlled by Mr. Buck where there is no republican ticket in the field. We . . . prefer in the campaign to follow the plan mapped out by Hon. W. A. Pledger and vote for Governor W. J. Northen."[17]

The Democratic press, quick to seize upon any sign of dissension in the Republican party and to give a few well-aimed blows to the dividing wedge, made much of the situation. The *Constitution* declared that the Buck circular wes "rebounding like a destructive boomerang into the bosom of republicanism." Democrats are "laughing in their coat-sleeves." Colored voters are "not as thick-skulled as Colonel Buck fancies them in the full realization of the purpose of that circular."[18]

The Atlanta *Journal,* with implied approval, printed a letter from a "prominent Negro" of Athens to another Negro, whom he commended for supporting Governor Northen.[19] T. W. Reed, editor of the Athens *Banner,* commenting on the dissension caused by Buck's circular, predicted that the Negro vote would divide very evenly between the Democracy and the third party.[20]

That Buck's action met with the approval of national Republican leaders seems evident. Shortly after the circular was issued Pledger was called to New York, ostensibly to confer with party heads about the national election and to receive speaking assignments for the Harrison campaign. Many speculated that the real reason was to get him out of Georgia until the state election was safely over. Interviewed in Washington, Pledger predicted Northen's re-election by a majority of forty thousand. He expressed the opinion that colored men in Georgia had fared better under the Northen administration than under any other government since they were freed.[21]

The real victim of the Buck manifesto, according to his own testimony, was W. L. Peek, the Populist candidate for governor, the man who presumably should have been most benefited. After his crushing defeat (by a majority of more than seventy thousand votes) Peek declared that Buck's attempt at support had injured the Populist cause "more than a little." The support of the ticket by

Republicans, said he, led many to suppose that there was something in the party that savored of Republicanism, "and their votes scared away at least two for one."[22]

During the flurry of excitement preceding the election, there were rumors that Buck's advice to Republicans to vote Populist was part of a deal leading to a coalition slate of presidential electors. It was said that both parties would withdraw their electoral tickets and substitute a fusion ticket made up of five third-party men and five Republicans. After the tremendous defeat suffered in the state election, however, it was evident that even a combination electoral ticket would have no chance of beating the Democrats. Moreover, the Republican candidates for elector refused to withdraw; so each party put forward its own ticket. The third-party men were said to be relieved. The idea of fusion was thought by many to belong to Buck, without Populist consent.[23]

Outspoken against any proposal to combine forces with the Republicans was Tom Watson, running for re-election to Congress from the Tenth District. Whenever the matter came up he expressed himself unequivocally, rejecting and denouncing fusion with either Republicans or Democrats. "My policy is for a straightout fight. I whip the other fellow or he whips me. . . . [N]o republican must vote for me under the impression that I am heading for the republican camp."[24] In the national election in November, as in the state election, the Democratic victory was complete. Watson went down in defeat along with other Populist and Republican candidates.

In 1894 there was a great deal more fusion between the two parties than in 1892. The Populist candidate for governor, Judge James K. Hines, was a more capable man and apparently more willing to negotiate with the Republicans than Peek had been. Moreover, the Democratic candidate, W. Y. Atkinson, was less popular than his predecessor and in his first race for governor he did not have the confidence of the Negroes that Northen had possessed. The election was bitterly fought and the margin of victory for the Democrats dropped from over seventy thousand to around twenty-five thousand votes. The elections of 1894 have been characterized as "the most exciting as well as the most degrading since the overthrow of the 'carpet-bag' government."[25] Each party strove openly and shamelessly for the Negro vote, while at the same time denouncing the other for catering to the colored citizens.

The Republican state convention was held in Atlanta on August 29 and was preceded by the usual rumors of consolidation with the Populists. That this was the leading issue of the convention was evi-

• *Fusion with the Populists* 113

dent even before the delegates convened. District caucuses held the night before were marked by hot debate over endorsement of Populist candidates. In the Fifth District meeting, fusion won by a bare majority, and a fusionist, C. C. Wimbish, Atlanta Negro, was endorsed as temporary chairman of the state convention. On the following day, however, he was defeated for the chairmanship by another Negro, Henry Lincoln Johnson, who opposed fusion. So the anti-fusionists chalked up the first victory of the day. Johnson, who was to be a power in the party through the first quarter of the twentieth century, was a young Negro from Butts County, then practising law in Atlanta as a partner of W. A. Pledger. His victory over Wimbish at the state convention was a triumph for Pledger, foe of fusion.[26]

Alfred E. Buck, displaced as marshal by the Democratic administration of Grover Cleveland, was still chairman of the state central committee but was not present at the convention. He was reported sick at his old home in Hallowell, Maine. One of his chief lieutenants, Walter H. Johnson of Columbus, was elected permanent chairman of the convention and seemed to be in charge in Buck's absence. Walter Johnson was the son of James Johnson, provisional governor of Georgia immediately after the war. He had served as postmaster in Columbus from 1873 to 1882, then as collector of internal revenue in Atlanta for a number of years except for brief intervals during the administrations of Cleveland. He was to succeed Buck as state Republican chairman in 1898 and also to serve as United States marshal for many years.[27]

At the state convention in 1894, Walter Johnson did not take an open stand on fusion but "talked on the edges of the question of endorsing the populist ticket." Not so cautious were some other members of the convention. The best speech of the day was said to have been made by a colored preacher, A. P. Grant, "who talked right out in meeting on the subject of a trade with the populists." Grant, like many others present, was willing to support Hines and Watson if the Populists would endorse Republican candidates for the legislature where there was a chance of electing them.[28]

The vital issue at the convention was whether to endorse Hines and Watson, but the question never came to a vote. The nearest approach came in the fight that developed over the report of the resolutions committee. The Populist supporters on the committee made a great effort to get a direct endorsement but failed. The resolutions as originally presented, however, denounced any Republican who should "canvass, vote for or in any other way aid the democratic nominees in the October election," but without a similar ban on Populist candidates. This omission was hotly protested and the resolution was amended to disown Republicans who should go into caucuses and primaries with "other parties." The resolution as adopted made no specific mention of *voting* for such candidates. Indeed, in most cases, there were no other candidates available.[29]

Accounts of the October election indicate that Republicans *did* vote for Populist candidates in great numbers, and it was said that the state central committee had admonished them to do so in spite of the convention's refusal to endorse the third party. Reports from many counties emphasized the large Negro vote for the Populists. In fact, in Carroll County the Democrats claimed that more than four hundred Negroes voted *illegally* for Populists. In Gwinnett County between six and seven hundred Negroes who usually voted with the Democrats when there were no Republicans in the race were said to have been thoroughly organized against the Democrats and to have voted solidly with the Populists. Many in Ware County were surprised at the solid support of Populists by the local Negroes, although it was known before the election that they had been "besieged for their votes" by the Populists. In Putnam County it was reported that perhaps three-fourths of the third-party votes were cast by colored men. "The Negroes had evidently been well drilled," said a dispatch from Terrell County, "and they voted almost solidly for the third party ticket. Not since the days of radical rule have they stood so firmly together."[30]

Actually the Negro vote was not so solid on a statewide basis as such reports would imply. It was conceded that both the Democrats and the Populists had made a determined bid for the colored vote and that Negro votes were bought by both sides and voted many times. Intimidation, bribery, and other forms of corruption were reported, including the falsification of election returns. In the congressional election in November, the fraud was especially notorious in the Tenth District, where Thomas E. Watson was again running for Congress. Because of obvious irregularities in this district, the Democratic winner resigned and a new election was held, but Watson was again defeated.[31] The atmosphere was reminiscent of Reconstruction days. The play for Negro votes startled and disgusted many observers and set in motion a reaction which, a few years later, would practically disfranchise the Negro in Georgia.[32]

In spite of the slump in the Democratic majority for governor, the Republican party gained little if anything in the elections of 1894. It returned a typical quota of members to the Georgia legislature—three in the House and one in the Senate. It aided in the election of some Populist legislators but made little impression in the balloting in its own name. Forty-nine Populists won seats in the General Assembly, a decided gain over 1892.[33]

In 1896 the chief political interest in Georgia lay in the presidential campaign. (The part played by Georgia Republicans in McKinley's election is described below, in Chapter IX.) In the presidential race, the term "fusion" was used primarily in connection with the combination between the Populists and the Democrats.* In the state election, however, and the congressional races, "fusion" still meant cooperation between the Populists and the Republicans and it was still sought and fought. During the summer the usual crop of rumors flourished, and, as usual, Colonel Buck denied categorically that there was any danger of fusion with the Populists—or the Prohibitionists. (Buck described himself as "a prohibitionist, one of the dyed-in-the-wool variety" and said that he personally would not hesitate to vote for a Prohibitionist candidate for governor if no Republican ticket was put out.) He denied that Populist leaders had agreed to support Republican candidates for Congress in return for Republican support of the Populist state ticket.[34]

A controversial, all-white ticket of presidential electors had already been selected at a session of the Republican state executive committee in Macon, and Buck was said to be reluctant to call the usual convention of the party in August for fear of stirring up more dissension. Some members of the party were eager to run a state ticket, and Tomlinson Johnson of Savannah, collector of customs under Harrison, was talked of as a candidate for governor. Buck, however, was rumored not to want a ticket. A meeting of the state central committee was held in Atlanta on August 17 but no convention was called. No state ticket was named but the Populist candidates were not endorsed. An address to the Republicans of the state was drawn up, explaining the decisions of the committee. Members of the party were urged to concentrate their energies upon the election of Republican congressmen and presidential electors but were specifically left free to vote "as individual judgment may dictate" in the state election.[35]

The day before the meeting of the state central committee, the

---

*The Populist electoral ticket for William J. Bryan and Thomas E. Watson was eventually withdrawn in Georgia when Democrats, supporting Bryan and Arthur Sewall, refused to collaborate. In this connection, a pithy quip is attributed to Watson, that the Democratic idea of fusion was "that we play Jonah while they play whale." Quoted in Arnett, *Populist Movement*, 204.

Atlanta *Constitution* had stirred up a hornet's nest by printing the details of an alleged "secret deal" between Populist and Republican leaders. As the story was told, the Populists had agreed to give the Republicans two places on the statehouse ticket in return for Republican support, but the Populist convention had failed to make good on the promise. On Saturday, August 15, said the paper, a conference was held between Judge Hines and Buck and Walter Johnson to work out a new agreement to be considered by the Republican committee at its meeting on Monday. It was understood that the Populist leader had expressed regret over the breakdown of the plan and had offered the Republicans two places on the electoral ticket. After consulting with other Populist leaders Hines was said to have dictated a statement and sent it over to Buck's office. The contents were not disclosed.[36]

The publication of the story brought dissension into both camps (as it was no doubt intended to do). Hines, criticized by the Populists for dealing with Buck, issued a card branding as "pure fiction" the statement that he had made a proposition for a combined electoral ticket. He admitted that he had urged Buck and Johnson to give the Populists their support in 1896 as they did in 1894. Declaring that there was an impassable gulf between the two parties in national affairs, the Populist leader pointed out that in state affairs both parties were interested in honest elections and other reforms. "If, on these high grounds, the republicans can vote our state ticket, I want their help and vote," said he.[37]

Walter Johnson, interviewed by a *Constitution* reporter, stoutly maintained that the Populists still owed the Republicans two places on the state ticket. Buck, with characteristic adroitness, could not be pinned down by the reporter.[38]

Some of the Negro leaders, already smarting at their exclusion from the Republican electoral ticket, boiled over with indignation at the disclosure of the attempted deal. Pledger, Henry Lincoln Johnson, and others were said to be bitterly opposed to the plan. The *Constitution* reported that the Negroes of the party were said to be almost solid in their support of Governor Atkinson. "Ninety-nine per cent of the negroes much prefer Atkinson to Seab Wright." (Seaborn Wright was the Populist candidate for governor in 1896.)[39]

The paper's figures might be open to question but there seems little doubt that, among the Negroes, the pendulum had swung somewhat away from the Populists since 1894. In the first place, Atkinson, like Northen, had during his first term conciliated the

Negroes by his proclamations condemning lynch law and by other public acts directed toward their welfare. Democratic party leaders had capitalized upon this to the fullest and many colored Republicans were now Atkinson's supporters. In the second place, the colored voters had already discovered that the Populists wanted their votes but not their company. In fact, Henry Lincoln Johnson, showing keen insight into the matter, stated, "The intelligent negroes of Georgia know that there is far more hate and spleen against the negroes in the populist camp than in the democratic."[40]

The typical white Populist in Georgia was found in the less privileged brackets of society. His prejudice against the Negro was apt to be tinged with his own feeling of insecurity and with the fear of economic competition. He was far more liable to feel a personal sense of resentment and hatred against the "nigger" than were the more prosperous members of the planter class and the business community who, for the most part, composed the leadership of the Democratic party. The latter had no intention of according to the Negro any recognition of equality—socially, politically, or economically—but, so long as the colored man "kept his place," relations between the two races were apt to be cordial and cooperative. The old ante-bellum attitude of paternalism and genuine affection for the plantation "people" was still prevalent to a great extent with whites of the higher levels of society. Except when their fear of Negro domination was uppermost (as during Reconstruction), they were accustomed to dealing with the black man in a kindly and conciliatory manner.

The state election was set for October 7, the first Wednesday in October. As the time approached, pressures were brought to bear upon Republican leaders to lend more active support to the Populist candidates. Visits were paid to Buck by H. W. Reed, national financial head of the Populist party, and John Cunningham, chairman of the state executive committee, and it was rumored that the Populist leaders had even telegraphed Mark Hanna, chairman of the Republican national committee, to enlist his aid. Whatever may have been his original intentions, Buck responded on October 1 by issuing his "usual ante-election circular," urging Republicans to vote for the Populist candidates. Recognizing that his action was not consistent with the address sent out six weeks previously, which expressly left party members free to vote either ticket, the Republican chairman conceded that his party had nothing in common with either the Populist or Democratic party as to national issues. On state issues, however, he pointed out, the Populist platform pledged honest elections, destruction of the convict lease system, and other reforms which could be obtained only by the overthrow of the Democratic party in Georgia.[41]

Dismissed by the Democrats as "just Boss Buck's biennial play," the open letter of the chairman was resented by the Negroes as an attempt at coercion and was promptly answered by Pledger in vehement terms. The Negro leader declared that he expressed the feelings of the great majority of colored Republicans in Georgia in opposing Buck's effort to force them to break alliances specifically authorized by the address of August 17. He reminded his readers that he had for years urged the nomination of a Republican ticket for statehouse and county officers and also for congressmen. "As often as I have asked it, so often have I been informed that it was not politic to do so." Pointing out that there were 90,000 registered Negro Republicans in the state and "let us say" 40,000 white Republicans, Pledger asked, "What is the matter with electing something ourselves?"[42]

If Buck's circular was simply his usual pre-election maneuver, it was followed by the usual post-election result. The Democrats swept the field. Atkinson was declared the winner by nearly thirty-five thousand votes. Only three Republicans went to the General Assembly, and the number of Populist legislators was sharply cut.[43]

No sooner was the state election over than rumors were published regarding a deal in the Fifth District whereby W. L. Peek, the Populist candidate for Congress, would withdraw in favor of Republican J. C. Hendrix. The Democratic candidate, Leonidas Livingston, incumbent congressman, insisted that such an agreement was part of a trade which had led to the issuance of the Buck circular. Peek denied this vigorously but ten days later he announced his withdrawal from the congressional race. He was described as unwilling and bitter. The Republicans had candidates in seven of the eleven congressional districts but carried hardly a dozen counties in the entire state. As usual, eleven Democrats were elected to Congress.[44]

After the Populist fiasco in the presidential campaign of 1896, when it virtually merged with the Democrats in its nomination of Bryan, the party was never again a serious factor in national politics, although it nominated a candidate for president as late as 1908. At the state level, also, it declined rapidly. In Georgia, in 1898, events followed the pattern established in the past few elections. The old question—to fuse or not to fuse—was argued by the Republicans but this time apparently it inspired little feeling and less

• *Fusion with the Populists* 119

hope. Fusion was an old story by now and had lost its ability to excite. Besides, with the departure of Colonel Buck for Tokyo in 1897, a certain something had gone out of the Republican party in Georgia. Walter Johnson, a far less colorful and controversial figure, was serving as chairman *pro tem* and the party had subsided into comparative peace and harmony—and apathy.

In 1898 no state Republican ticket was nominated; only in the Eleventh District was any appreciable effort made to elect a fusion candidate for Congress; and nobody was surprised when the Democrats captured all the major offices and most of the minor ones. The Populist candidate for governor, J. R. Hogan, lost to Allen D. Candler by 66,614 votes, with little mention of Republican support. In 1900 Candler was re-elected by a somewhat greater margin over Populist J. H. Traylor. Since the 1896 state election the Populist vote had dropped from 85,832 to 23,235.[45] And the Republicans had almost dropped out of the public eye as well as out of the running.

It is questionable whether the Populist party in Georgia derived any real benefit from attempts at fusion with the Republicans. If a general fusion had been effected the gain in voting strength might have outweighed the disadvantages, but with the halfhearted, spasmodic sort of cooperation that existed on both sides, little was accomplished even on a short-term basis. The Populist party never elected a governor of Georgia, never elected a congressman, and its triumphs in the legislative races were short-lived. On the debit side was the stigma attached to Republicanism and to the Negro vote in the eyes of most of the white people of Georgia. Many believers in Populist doctrine left the Populist party when it became evident that the white voters in Georgia were being divided and that the Negroes would hold the balance of power in state elections.

As for the effects of fusion on the Republican party in Georgia—it would be hard to discover any genuine short-term benefits, and the long-term results were disastrous. Nothing else could have so alerted and solidified the white voters of the state as the threat of "Negro supremacy." The Democratic party in Georgia came out of the Populist ordeal more united than ever before and more determined than ever to destroy the political power of the Negro.

As early as 1892 the danger was seen. Former Governor Joseph E. Brown emerged from his retirement to warn the white people of Georgia. Success of the People's party, said he, would almost inevitably involve a union with the Republicans and a sharing of state offices with Negroes. The only way to maintain the Solid South and white supremacy, he declared, was for the whole white race to vote the Democratic ticket together.[46]

Events of the next few years in Georgia, especially the disreputable elections of 1894, had a sobering effect upon many, but it was the political situation in North Carolina which brought the matter to a head. In North Carolina, fusion between the two parties was so successful that by the end of 1896 the coalition had captured the state. The governor and other statehouse officers, the two United States senators and all but one member of the congressional delegation, a majority of both houses of the state legislature, and hundreds of local and county officers were either Populists or Republicans after the elections of 1896. In some of the counties where the bulk of Republican voters were Negroes, this meant Negro officeholders in large numbers. Whole counties were said to be "negroized." A Raleigh correspondent wrote to the Atlanta *Constitution* that there were "no less than a thousand" Negroes holding office in North Carolina and that the Negroes were preparing to make the state a place of refuge for their race from all over the South. Democrats were said to be determined to overthrow Negro rule, peaceably if possible but by force if necessary. Conflict between the races was freely predicted.[47]

The intense excitement felt in North Carolina was communicated to neighboring states, and white Southerners who remembered the evils of Reconstruction were greatly aroused. In Georgia the Democratic press played up avidly the reports of "Negro domination" and the threats of violence. For weeks before the Georgia state elections of 1898 the Atlanta *Constitution* carried feature stories on the situation in North Carolina with the warning that the same thing could happen in certain counties of Georgia if the Democrats should become overconfident.[48]

Populists in Georgia and other Southern states were urged to return to the Democratic party in order to avoid splitting the white vote. Many were ready to abandon the third party in order to prevent the Negroes from regaining political power. The race question aroused more feeling than any reforms that Populism could offer.[49] Without a doubt, the object lesson presented in North Carolina was a factor in the rapid decline of the Populist party in the South after 1896. It was a factor, too, in the move to suppress or nullify the Negro vote in Georgia as in other Southern states, and an inevitable result was the further decline of the Republican party in the South.

Fusion with the Populists was an incongruous sort of situation

• *Fusion with the Populists* 121

from the beginning. In the West, where the Republican party was the dominant one, the Populists fused with the Democrats. In the South they fused with the Republicans. In some Southern states in 1896 they fused with Republicans in the state elections and with Democrats on the national ticket. The absurdity of the situation was well expressed by Tom Watson when he remarked: "Suppose I were to go into North Carolina to speak. What could I say? I could only repeat the Ten Commandments, say the Lord's Prayer and dismiss the Congregation."[50]

In the eyes of many Republicans in Georgia, the "congregation" was indeed dismissed after the failure of the attempts at fusion with the Populists.

IX

Triumph with McKinley

FOR REPUBLICANS in Georgia, one of the few bright spots in the disappointing decade of the 1890's was the election of William McKinley in 1896. While there was no chance of the Georgia electoral vote going Republican, the return of a Republican to the White House, even without the Georgia vote, meant a great deal in the way of patronage to party leaders in the state. This was especially true since the Georgia delegation to the national convention had been almost solid for the winning candidate. The election of McKinley, after four years of a Democratic administration, was like manna from heaven to the party faithful.

The campaign was an exciting one and it had seemed, for a brief moment, to offer new hope to the Republican cause in Georgia. The impetus did not come from within the state party itself. It stemmed partly from the political genius of Mark Hanna and the peculiar personal charm of McKinley and from the fresh new approach instituted by those two individuals, but that was not the full story. By 1896 many prominent men in the state had come to believe in the Republican doctrines of sound money and a high protective tariff. Many Democrats were dissatisfied with the administration of Grover Cleveland and were ready to be wooed by the Republican party on the new issues—if only the old traditional lines of division could be forgotten or glossed over in some way. The Democrats who were attracted by Republican principles at this time were at the opposite pole from those who were acting with the Populists. They were usually men of substance—businessmen, industrialists, or large-scale planters—men who would be benefited by Republican policies and who would have brought to the Republican party in Georgia that aura of "respectability" so sorely needed.

The fact that the Republican party, as then constituted in Georgia, was totally unable to adapt itself to the situation and to seize the opportunity presented was one of the last and greatest misfortunes that it encountered during the nineteenth century. There was a momentary triumph with McKinley, replete with benefits for the fortunate few, but the chance to revolutionize and regenerate the party slipped from the grasp of those who recognized and tried to take advantage of the opportunity.

On the state and local levels, Republicans in Georgia might work with the Populists or with Independent candidates or might even cast their votes for the Democrats, but, when it came to presidential elections, most of them remained loyal to the Republican ticket. The time had long since passed when the party constituted a threat in the election itself but it still carried a great deal of weight at the national convention. The Republican party allowed two delegates for each member of Congress regardless of Republican voting power in the state. The Georgia delegation—twenty-six strong in 1896—would have more weight in the convention balloting than many states whose electoral votes were found consistently in the Republican column.

It was not strange that delegates from Georgia—and the other states of the Solid South—were in great demand at the national conventions. Candidates for the nomination vied with each other for months ahead of time in lining up delegates, and the peculiar composition of the Southern parties made them vulnerable to the crudest sorts of appeals. In Georgia the white leaders and the colored masses alike became imbued with this convention fever, and every fourth year the party was in a ferment. In this quadrennial scramble for convention delegates there was nothing novel about rumors of "boodle," but with the McKinley campaign came a more subtle approach, with far greater potentialities than the methods usually employed.

Perhaps there was no member of the Republican party more highly respected in Georgia than William McKinley, and none more closely identified with the ideas of sound money and the protective tariff. In 1888 he had been invited to Atlanta to speak at the Piedmont Chautauqua on "The Taxing Power of the Government" and had been given a royal welcome on his visit to the city. The Atlanta *Constitution,* never enthusiastic about the financial policies of Grover Cleveland, then nearing the end of his first term, had greeted McKinley with extreme cordiality, describing him editorially as "the ablest republican in America, and a statesman of the very highest character." The paper emphasized the fact that McKinley's visit was not a political one and that his welcome to Georgia would come not from "the colored people alone" (i.e., the Republican party of Georgia) but from the whole people, irrespective of party and race. He would be greeted by the "best people" and given a fair hearing. The visit was a great success, and some of the "best people" became McKinley's close friends and enthusiastic admirers. He used the private car of former Governor Joseph E. Brown en route to Atlanta and was met up the line by an escort of prominent citizens, including the mayor and the president of the Chautauqua. Colonel Alfred E. Buck and former Governor Rufus Bullock were on the special car, and Buck made the introductions. McKinley's address at the Chautauqua was well received and Georgians in general were favorably impressed with the man and with his message.[1]

Long before the 1896 convention, McKinley, now the governor of Ohio, was recognized as one of the leading candidates for the nomination for president, although by no means the only one. Following the Republican victory in the congressional elections of 1894, it became evident that the Democratic administration was in serious trouble and that chances for a Republican triumph in the presidential election of 1896 were bright. Almost immediately there began one of the most remarkable pre-convention campaigns in the history of the American presidency, and in a large degree this campaign was centered in Thomasville, Georgia.

McKinley's campaign manager, Marcus Alonzo Hanna, was a controversial figure in his own day, and historians do not yet agree as to the extent to which he dominated McKinley or as to the methods he used in securing the nomination. Certainly none would question his political sagacity and his devotion to the Ohio Governor. Hanna was a Cleveland industrialist, a wealthy man, who, in his middle years, developed a taste for politics. Whether it was a case of disinterested public service or an overweening personal ambition might be (and has been) debated, but it is a matter of record that Hanna became the political "boss" of Ohio and that, in January, 1895, he retired from business and became a full-time politician. As McKinley's campaign manager he made his one great object in life the securing of the presidential nomination for his friend.[2]

As a businessman, Hanna applied business methods to politics. He had been a delegate to the national conventions in 1884 and 1888, and he knew how the Southern delegates had been exploited and all too often purchased outright. Not waiting until convention time to dicker with individual delegates, he went to the heart of the matter. He knew that state and district conventions were usually dominated by small groups and he concentrated his efforts on those leaders, arranging far in advance to control every possible unit down to the lowest levels at which delegates were chosen. His agents laid down the strategy by which the various conventions could be controlled for McKinley.[3] The large bloc of Southern delegates was Hanna's particular goal. With this in mind, in January, 1895, he rented a large house in Thomasville, Georgia, and prepared for guests—important guests. All winter a steady stream of Southern politicians flowed through the house on Dawson Avenue, and in March Governor and Mrs. McKinley paid him a visit of two weeks' duration. This visit assured the Governor of a large majority of delegates from the deep South.[4]

En route to Thomasville, on March 12 the McKinleys stopped off in Atlanta with Colonel and Mrs. Buck. Mark Hanna joined them there, and the Buck home on Peachtree Street was the scene of a number of conferences. That evening the gentlemen of the party went to the Aragon Hotel, where McKinley greeted those who called to pay their respects. The crowd included many of those "best people" who remembered the Ohio Governor so favorably from 1888.[5] In accepting the Bucks' hospitality, the Governor had stressed the fact that he was going to Thomasville "for a little rest and outing" and had no idea of making any speeches while in Georgia.[6] This was part of the Hanna strategy. McKinley was at his best in an informal conference. From all accounts, he was a sociable man with a great deal of charm, who made friends easily and seemed genuinely interested in those he met. For the entire Thomasville venture, *sociability* was the keynote. Mark Hanna knew the strong points of his friend and he sensed, too, that personal attention and the social approach would win converts among the Southerners.

On the surface the Thomasville trip was simply a friendly house party—with Governor and Mrs. McKinley visiting their old friends, the Hannas, in search of recreation and a little Georgia sunshine. (Mrs. McKinley was a chronic invalid, subject to distressing spells of "nerves," and found the severe Ohio winters hard on her health.) If there were political implications to the trip—and few doubted that there were—they were kept nicely subordinated to the social. There had grown up in Thomasville through the years an aggregation of rich Northerners, including Hanna's brother, Mel, who already owned an estate there. Most, if not all, were Republicans with protectionist views, and the McKinleys and the Mark Hannas fitted right into the group. It was only natural, moreover, that the well-to-do citizens of Thomasville should mingle with the visitors on a friendly social basis and vie with each other in welcoming the newcomers.

The McKinleys were honored at a round of social events, the two most important being a large public reception held at the Mitchell House and a brilliant affair at the home of the Mark Hannas attended by a hundred invited guests. The Mitchell House reception assembled about five hundred residents and visitors, with the scores of ladies in party attire emphasizing the social nature of the gathering. A prominent Thomasville attorney, a Democrat, W. M. Hammond, delivered an address of welcome, several times interrupted by spontaneous applause. McKinley's response was a gracious one, paying tribute to the re-united country and to the hospitality of the people of Thomasville. The affair was a veritable love feast, and the Governor apparently made a happy impression on all.[7]

The two elaborate receptions at Thomasville were no doubt valuable in establishing a favorable image of McKinley (and unquestionably there was a certain amount of "snob appeal" involved), but the real object of the visit was being accomplished quietly day by day in a series of informal conferences between the candidate and political and business leaders from all over Georgia and from other Southern states. It was rumored that Republicans came from as far away as Arkansas to consult with the prospective nominee. With all of them, both white and colored, McKinley was affable and cordial, and they were impressed by his tact and his engaging candor. In spite of an encounter by the honor guest with the grippe which disrupted plans for a few days, the house party was a great success.[8]

On March 27 the McKinleys left Thomasville for a quick swing into Florida and then concluded their Southern tour with an overnight stop at Savannah. In Savannah, as in Thomasville, the Ohio Governor was given a hearty welcome by Democrats as well as Republicans. Highlights of his visit included an elaborate tour of the city and an informal reception at the Commercial Club. Sandwiched between the two was a meeting with a group of colored Republicans at one of the local Negro churches—apparently the only formal meeting during the Georgia tour. Professor Richard R. Wright, president of the Georgia State Industrial College, and a leader among Georgia Republicans since 1880, presided, and the main address was made by the Reverend E. K. Love. In attendance were about fifty colored preachers, teachers, lawyers, and politicians. Called upon for a few remarks, McKinley spoke pleasantly of the reception given him and made reference to the advancement of the colored race, both in education and in a material way.[9]

There was much speculation around the state as to the real purpose of McKinley's visit and his plans for the campaign. Even before he left Thomasville the rumor was being circulated that he intended to lay aside the Negro and to build up a white Republican party in the South. It was said that the tariff question would be the main issue, and force bills and election laws were to be eschewed entirely.[10] No doubt McKinley would have liked to lay aside the entire Negro *problem* (if not the Negro himself), but the matter was not that simple. In Georgia, as in most of the other Southern states, the great majority of Republican voters were Negroes. Mark Hanna was a practical politician and he undoubtedly knew that to antagonize the Negro seriously, at least before the conventions, would nullify his plans for the Southern delegate vote.

It was reported from Jacksonville that the committee on arrangements had kept the movements of the Governor secret all of one day for the purpose of shutting out the Negroes. There were none present at the hotel and few at the depot. Their invitation to McKinley to attend a formal reception of colored people was courteously declined. A Florida observer concluded that, while the color line seemed to have been drawn, it had been done so diplomatically that the Negroes themselves did not realize its real significance. McKinley and his campaign managers were said to have conducted all their communications with the Negroes quietly and in such a way as not to offend the Southern whites, even though they were surreptitiously bidding for Negro support at the same time.[11] Such reports, published in a Savannah paper just before the party's arrival, may have influenced McKinley to accept the invitation of the Savannah Negroes for the meeting in that city.

From the beginning of McKinley's Georgia tour there were reports that he would make protection his chief and almost his only plank, on the assumption that the South was about ready to accept the protection policy as an overture to the manufacturers of the East.[12] The businessmen and industrialists of the "New South" had turned their eyes toward the East, and the old agrarian tie with the Midwest no longer attracted them. The fact that the Populist move was in full swing just at this time seems paradoxical, but the willingness of the small farmer in Georgia to ally himself with his Western counterpart was, to some extent, a protest against these very "New South" tendencies of the Bourbon Democrats.

The rise of sentiment for the protective tariff had been in process for several years. During the Harrison campaign in 1888, Buck had declared that there was a "host of protectionists" among the Democrats of Georgia. He was astonished at the great number of Democrats who were delighted at the idea of McKinley's coming to Atlanta and who were outspoken against the free trade element controlling their party. Buck related the incident of one prominent rice planter of south Georgia who had made the statement that rice planters in Georgia would either have to abandon their plantations or quit the Democratic party and he thought he would do the latter.[13]

A year later, Buck reported directly to President Harrison that both Henry W. Grady and Evan P. Howell, editors of the Atlanta *Constitution,* were in favor of protection, and that Howell, the chief editor, had pledged himself in December, 1888, to come gradually to the support of the Harrison administration, to fight the free traders with his paper so vigorously as to make a permanent breach between the protectionists and the organized Democracy, and to join with the Republicans in 1890 in support of candidates for Congress. The Republican chairman commented bitterly on the fact that Grady and Howell had shortly afterward thrown aside the cause of protection and were running the paper on the race issue in order to make it solid once more with the Bourbon Democrats.[14]

The views of Colonel Buck might be discounted on the ground of political bias but his statements are corroborated by a non-political observer writing to John Sherman from Atlanta early in 1888. He suggested to Sherman that a special Southern wing of the Republican party he established under the name of "High Tariff" or "Protection Party." "It is a fact," he wrote, "that there are thousands upon thousands in the Southern states who would willingly vote the Republican principles under another name . . . and the Republicans if sharp ought to break the *New South* on Protection. The *Constitution* now is advocating Republican principles but dare not call them by that name."[15]

By March, 1895, the editor of the Savannah *Morning News* saw indications that the Republican party was about to gain a strong foothold in the South. Dissatisfaction with the financial policies of the Democratic Congress could make the Republican party "a very respectable party in the South," said he. It was not uncommon to hear influential Democrats say that they would not object to the return of the Republican party to power (nationally). In South Carolina a number of prominent young men were talking seriously of joining the Republicans, and some of the most influential sugar planters in Louisiana had already allied themselves with the party.[16]

This feeling of dissatisfaction with the Democratic party among elements that would never turn Populist was present in Georgia as in other Southern states and Mark Hanna was clearly conscious of the fact. It was probably no coincidence that the same papers that announced McKinley's impending arrival in Atlanta reported also the formation there of a Republican club headed by James D. Collins, erstwhile Democrat, and a preliminary conference looking toward the establishment of a protection league.[17]

James D. Collins was a former officeholder in Fulton County and was, also, a businessman of some prominence. Interviewed by a local reporter, he spoke freely about his conversion to Republicanism and his belief in the protective tariff. He stated that the club, to be called the "Southern Republican Club," had several hundred members, most of whom had not before been affiliated with the Republican party. He declined to give their names but told the reporter that some of the strongest men in town were in the movement. They were all protectionists, said he, and now proposed to cast their votes on that line. They disagreed with the course of the national Democratic party and Collins believed that most people in Georgia felt the same way. "It has been mainly prejudice that has kept people from joining the republican party in this state, anyhow," he declared.[18]

In commenting on the organization of the club, the editor of the *Constitution* warned that it would not do for the Democrats of Georgia and of the South to ignore the tendency toward Republicanism found in business circles. With discontented farmers turning to the Populists and many of the "town boys" now on the verge of going into the Republican camp, it would be well for Democratic leaders to open their eyes. Another straw in the wind noted by the editor was the meeting held in Atlanta on March 11 to discuss plans for the formation of protection leagues in the state. It was decided to perfect local organizations first, with the eventual goal of putting Georgia into the American Protective League. Among those who attended were R. D. Locke and James F. Hanson, both of Macon. Locke was a Republican of long standing and Hanson a recent convert.[19]

Hanson was one of the leading industrialists in Georgia, the founder of the Bibb Manufacturing Company, a man with many business interests, and outstanding in civic and social affairs. As early as 1881 he had been recommended to Dr. William H. Felton as "entirely trustworthy," and as one who might be weaned away from the Democracy on the issue of the tariff.[20] Probably Hanson and McKinley had been friends long before the latter came to Georgia for the first time, as the Macon man had attended a tariff convention in New York in 1881 and had been an active advocate of protection for many years. Learning of McKinley's impending visit to Thomasville, Hanson was eager to have him stop and deliver a speech in Macon and he wrote the Ohio Governor to this effect. McKinley replied that he would be glad to see Hanson on the Georgia trip but that he doubted the propriety of doing otherwise than going directly to Thomasville. "I cannot get the consent of my mind," he wrote, "to do anything that places me in the position of seeming to seek an office and anything I might say or do would be at once interpreted as an effort in that direction." The Governor suggested instead that Hanson join the party in Macon "and run over to Thomasville" with him.[21]

Hanson was in Atlanta on the night before McKinley's arrival and was no doubt among those who conferred with him and with Mark Hanna on that occasion. Apparently he was ready now to take an open stand as a Republican and to work for the party on the state as well as the national level. Soon his name began to be noised abroad as a new leader in the Republican party in Georgia. It was rumored that he would be one of the delegates-at-large to the national convention and would be the Republican candidate for governor in 1896.[22] It seems evident that the McKinley wing of the Georgia party planned to push the new recruit as fast and as far as possible and to make political capital of his prestige and prominence in order to attract to the party other men of the same type. As might have been expected, the effort to promote a newcomer to such a position of leadership met with bitter opposition.

Nor was McKinley to get the Georgia convention delegation by default. There were several other hats in the ring and it was not long before the other candidates for the nomination recognized the Hanna-McKinley strategy in the South and sent their own agents posthaste to enter the competition. In Georgia, by the end of 1895, it was clearly a matter of McKinley against the field—and the field included such formidable adversaries as Thomas B. "Czar" Reed, Speaker of the House of Representatives, Levi P. Morton, New York governor and former vice president under Benjamin Harrison, Senator Matthew Quay, Republican "boss" of Pennsylvania, Senator W. B. Allison of Iowa, and Senator Shelby M. Cullom of Illinois.

T. Thomas Fortune, Negro editor of the New York *Sun,* spent some time in Georgia in the interest of Governor Morton and was one of the featured speakers at a meeting of the Republican state central committee in Atlanta on December 28. James S. Clarkson, chairman of the Republican National Committee, was also in town at the time of the meeting, ostensibly to see the Cotton States and

International Exposition but incidentally "to feel the republican pulse for Allison for president."[23] The usual rumors of "boodle tactics" went the rounds. A Savannah editor berated Republican statesmen of the North who criticized the South for not raising the Negro to a higher plane and then sent money to buy his vote.[24] McKinley money was said not to be lacking, but McKinley himself indignantly denied any intention of using "financial or any other ulterior considerations" to influence the selection of Southern delegates.[25] In reply to a letter from E. K. Love, colored preacher of Savannah, reporting the use of money by some candidates, the Ohio Governor wrote that he "would be loathe to believe" that the Republicans of the state could be improperly influenced.[26]

McKinley found it necessary, also, to deny the "base charge" that he was not in sympathy with the colored Republicans in their struggle for equal rights and recognition. The candidate cited his record in Congress to disprove the rumor that he was not interested in civil rights. Insinuations that he favored the organization in the South of a new Republican party composed largely of white men and controlled by white leaders, he declared to be utterly without foundation.[27]

The state convention had been set for April 29 and a hot fight was predicted. There had been turbulence in almost every district, with contesting delegations, fist fights, and charges of political deals.[28] The division was not primarily along racial lines, although McKinley's alleged preference for a white party had been used against him. Many Negroes were enthusiastic followers of McKinley, while others opposed him. The whites were also divided. The obvious alignment was that brought about by support of different candidates, but underlying this was a struggle for control of the party. There were factions and bitter controversies even among supporters of the same candidates. Buck was managing the campaign for McKinley, and Pledger the forces of the "combine," representing Reed, Morton, Allison, Cullom, and Quay.[29]

District delegates to the national convention had already been chosen, and the great fight of the state convention was over the selection of the four delegates-at-large. The McKinley forces, confident of success and expecting to elect all four delegates, were playing a lone hand and making overtures to no other candidates. The supporters of all the others had united to try to stop McKinley and to send a delegation to St. Louis that could be "handled" to suit conditions as they arose. It was rumored that the slate to be presented by Buck would be made up of two white men and two Negroes—Buck himself, J. F. Hanson, John Deveaux, secretary of the state central committee, and H. A. Rucker, long active in the party and a son-in-law of Jeff Long. Many McKinley supporters, however, felt confident that R. R. Wright would be one of the delegates.[30]

The most vulnerable spot on the Buck ticket was that occupied by Hanson. Although it was conceded that he was an outstanding man, he had not been received cordially by one wing of the party. Many were more interested in preserving the *status quo* than in any attempt to regenerate the party. Pledger, several months earlier, had announced his intention of defeating the Macon man. The Negro leader had a personal candidate for the delegation, his law partner, Henry Lincoln Johnson, and he was determined that Johnson should be included among the delegates-at-large. There was some talk that Deveaux might be sacrificed for Johnson but it seemed apparent that Pledger had centered his fight on Hanson. Leaders of the combination appealed to the Negroes with the argument that they should have more than half of the delegates-at-large since there were so many more colored Republicans than white in the state. The district delegates, already chosen, showed a heavy majority of colored men.[31]

Never in the history of political conventions in Georgia had delegates been so openly and so lavishly courted by prospective candidates for the nomination. On the day before the convention, according to the newspapers, Atlanta's Decatur Street looked like the midway at the fair! The principal headquarters for the McKinley forces were on the second floor of the Young Men's Library building on Decatur Street and the "combine" had its meeting place across the street at the Imperial Opera House. Both were decked with bunting, pictures of the candidates, slogans, and mottoes. A special feature of the McKinley headquarters was a large room where only delegates were admitted, "fitted up with tables fairly groaning with eatables and drinkables, sandwiches and cakes, and a hogshead of lemonade." Cigars were passed out with a free hand, a bootblack dispensed free shines, and everyone apparently was happy. The headquarters of the "combine" presented a lively appearance also, with the Atlanta Dixie Band as the star attraction. Thomas Reed and Matthew Quay were the candidates most featured, and hundreds of campaign buttons were thrown to the crowds in the streets. Trains were met, delegates were pounced upon and taken to reception rooms, and the carnival spirit prevailed in spite of the fierce competition.[32]

The convention itself was one of the most riotous ever held by the Republican party in Georgia. The leaders of both factions had met privately the night before the convention and, as it developed later, Buck and Pledger had reached a compromise which they believed would insure a peaceful session. Instead, the "harmony" move completely disrupted the convention. Because of numerous contests, a fight had been expected on the report of the credentials committee, but Buck had bypassed the committee and had the roll of delegates prepared in advance in his office by Secretary John Deveaux. When Pledger moved the acceptance of the Buck roster as presented, the motion appeared to be a sure if somewhat surprising forerunner of harmony. Even more surprising to his followers was Pledger's endorsement of the nomination of Buck as chairman of the convention and his reference to his own act as "a prelude to peace." When he continued, "Will you stand by me, friends, in our arrangement for peace?" he was met with a chorus of unbelieving cries. "Yes!" "Yes!" "What is your arrangement?" "No!" "No!" "Not on your life!" Someone near the speaker's stand shouted, "He's drunk! Take him out!"

An attempt had been made to admit delegates by card only, but the crowd had rushed the doors, and the convention hall was filled with a large and unruly mass representing both factions. Both sides had been primed for a close fight over the delegation and both had hoped for success. It was evident that most of those present were caught completely by surprise at the idea of a deal between Buck and Pledger. Pandemonium began to break loose. Colonel Buck, feeling a bit unwell, turned the gavel over to Walter Johnson, who rapped in vain to gain order.

Then came the critical moment. R. D. Locke, with a large United States flag sticking from his coat pocket, placed in nomination the "harmony" slate of delegates: Buck, Rucker, Deveaux, and Henry Lincoln Johnson. The nomination caused a stampede. Not only had Hanson been sacrificed for the Pledger partner, thus giving a vote to the "combine" (needlessly, in the eyes of most McKinley supporters), but R. R. Wright had also been passed over. Wright had been a McKinley man from the beginning, had established a cordial relationship with the Governor on his Georgia trip, and had apparently felt sure of a place on the delegation.[33] There were yells, catcalls, and hisses, intermingled with loud and continuous cries of "Wright!" "Wright!"

A mass of shouting Negroes crowded around the speaker's desk and nobody could get a hearing. Walter Johnson claimed that he put a motion to elect the four delegates and that it was carried by acclamation. He claimed, too, that he put a motion to elect as alternates Wright, Locke, B. J. Davis, and L. M. Pleasant. Others denied that such a motion was ever made. The Buck faction declared that Buck and Deveaux were re-elected officers of the state central committee and authorized to appoint the other members of the committee. The meeting was then hastily adjourned and the Buck contingent and Pledger left the hall.

Amidst the confusion, few of the delegates realized what was happening until it was all over. Wright and his supporters, protesting the alleged irregularities, especially the failure to take a proper vote, remained in the hall and proceeded to hold another convention. Committees were named and reports heard; a platform endorsing McKinley was adopted; a new state central committee headed by the Reverend E. K. Love was elected; and a slate of delegates-at-large to the national convention was chosen. This delegation was composed of Wright himself, Buck, Henry Lincoln Johnson, and J. H. Hetherington. Disinterested observers saw little likelihood that the Wright-Love party would displace the old order of things, but there was a great deal of sympathy for Wright in his resistance to the steamroller tactics of Buck and Pledger. McKinley, commenting on the split between Buck and Wright, expressed regret at the "falling out" but assured Buck of his full confidence.[34]

Newspapers all over the state termed the convention a disgraceful spectacle. The Macon *Telegraph* went so far as to call it "nauseating."[35] If the disorder had been deliberately planned to discourage the acquisition of those new "better elements" so earnestly sought by some, it could hardly have done it more effectively. Businessmen attracted by Republican principles might vote for a Republican president but few of them would ally themselves openly with the party on the state and local levels.

An exception was J. F. Hanson. Although rejected by the party at the state convention and, to all appearances, "sold out" even by the men who had been most diligent in seeking his acceptance, the Macon man evidently understood the political facts of life in Georgia and was willing to continue in the effort to build up the party in the state. No more was said about his possible candidacy for governor but he became one of Buck's chief lieutenants. He and W. H. Smyth represented the state chairman before the Republican national committee on the eve of the St. Louis convention and were successful in winning every case where there was a contest for seats in the Georgia delegation. The net result was twenty-two Georgia votes for McKinley and two each for Reed and Quay.[36]

After the national convention was over and McKinley was safely nominated with the help of the Negro delegates, Republican leaders in Georgia made a bold move to make the party more palatable to the white businessmen of the state whom they had hoped to attract on the issue of protection. On July 25 the state central committee held a secret meeting in Macon and chose an all-white slate of presidential electors, with Hanson and General James Longstreet heading the list as electors-at-large.[37] It is not clear whether the colored members of the committee were out-voted or simply persuaded to go along with this strategy. William A. Pledger said later that he had agreed to the all-white ticket and had induced most of the Negro committeemen to support the move because he was informed that Northern Republicans believed that it would secure accretions from the Democratic party.[38]

Ordinarily the electors were chosen at a second state convention held late in the summer, and the matter of a state ticket was discussed at the same time. Having named the electors themselves, the central committee did not set a date for a convention but empowered the chairman to do so if it should seem desirable. This, Buck declined to do. It was charged that he was *afraid* to do so, for fear that a convention would reverse the action of the committee in setting up the white slate of electors.[39]

During the summer and early fall, the party was in a turmoil over the question of fusion with the Populists in the state election and in the congressional districts, but the campaign for McKinley went on apace. Colonel Buck, approached by a reporter for news regarding fusion, found the Chairman stamping a pile of letters in red with this message: "The republican party stands for honest money and the chance to earn it. William McKinley." "I like the way it reads," said Buck.[40]

After the state election in October, the Republican headquarters in Atlanta became even busier. McKinley literature and gold circulars and pamphlets were mailed throughout the state. Meetings at strategic points were addressed by Buck, Hanson, Longstreet, and others. It was rumored by the Democrats that Mark Hanna had sent "a big lump" of McKinley money "for the purpose of buying up every possible floating vote in Georgia." A cartoon in the *Constitution* showed Hanna with his money bags, pouring out Georgia's share.[41]

On election day, the results in Georgia were gratifying and the results nationwide were exhilarating. A Republican was headed once more for the White House! Moreover, McKinley had polled a larger percentage of votes in Georgia and a larger numerical total than any

Republican candidate since 1872.⁴² The unfortunate fact that a large number of those who voted for McKinley were strictly "presidential Republicans" and could not be counted on to swell the party ranks at the grass roots was largely lost sight of in the Atlanta celebration that followed the victory.

Far into the night the celebration continued. The colored Republicans assembled first on Decatur Street and paraded through the city, their enthusiasm fanned into wild excitement by the strains of a brass band. A Democratic mob formed at the corner of Peachtree and Marietta streets, furious at the exultation of the Negroes. Hoodlums in both mobs were armed with pistols, rocks, and clubs, and police were powerless to restore order. However, the spirit of the whole affair seemed more rowdy than vicious and there were no serious casualties. An observer commented philosophically that it was like the aftermath of the great Auburn-Athens football game on Thanksgiving two years before, "when the Athens boys went perfectly wild over their victory."⁴³

The National Party and the South

THROUGH ALL the vicissitudes of the Republican party in Georgia and the other Southern states in the last quarter of the nineteenth century, the national party leadership never gave up the hope of strengthening the party in the South and bringing it back to a position of power. Contrary to popular belief, Republicans in the South were not abandoned after the removal of the troops in 1877.[1] The "Southern Question," the most important political issue during Reconstruction, was still a serious problem for subsequent presidents. Every Republican who occupied the White House for the remainder of the century tried in his own way to handle the problem and to build up the party in the South. The fact that the top strategists of the party did not always agree on the proper course and that the policy was so often shifted accounts partly for the failure to re-establish the Republican party as a serious contender in Southern politics.

Grant's policy was one of force, the Military Reconstruction which he had inherited from the preceding administration. One of the primary purposes of the program adopted by the Radical Congress in 1867 was the creation of a ready-made Republican party in the South by the enfranchisement of the Negro. Subsequent legislation tried to force the South to give the colored man full political and civil rights. This policy succeeded only so long as the Conservative whites could be kept under foot. The carpetbag-scalawag-Negro governments could be maintained only by the use of federal troops and by political maneuvers backed by the Radicals in Congress. In Georgia the failure of the policy of force could be seen as early as November, 1868, in the tremendous victory of the Democratic candidate for president. Before Grant ever took office, the Republican party in Georgia had passed its peak, and by the end of Grant's first term the Radical government of the state had toppled and the Conservatives were back in power.[2]

Unquestionably the decline of Republican voting power in Georgia was accelerated by devious methods on the part of the Conservative whites.[3] This, however, was an almost inevitable result of the congressional policy. Force gave rise to force, intimidation to intimidation. The activities of the Ku Klux Klan and other agencies in discouraging Negroes from voting were desperate measures of desperate men, who saw no other way to defend themselves and to restore order in the state. The policy of imposing military rule and Negro suffrage upon the South had a paradoxical effect in Georgia, as in other Southern states. The Radicals had hoped to divide the whites, to force the recognition of Negro equality, and to promote the cause of Republicanism. Instead they united the whites and brought about a racial solidarity and a consciousness of race prejudice which slowed the advancement of the Negro and resulted, politically, in a Solid South that resisted all subsequent efforts to strengthen the Republican party.

While the Republican kept the presidency for twenty years after the war, the margin of victory was rarely a safe one. After the election of 1872 there was a long period of equilibrium between the parties. The Republicans depended for victory on very small margins in a few key states. The idea that the Republican party did not need Southern votes to secure its position is a mistaken one, but the policies of the Grant administration seemed designed to alienate the native white element in the South. Preference given to carpetbaggers and Negroes in the matter of patronage and the support by force of the most Radical elements in the state governments offended many white men who might otherwise have worked with the local Republican parties.

By 1876 it was clear that the policy of force and intervention had not resulted in Republican strength in the South. By this time, also, the climate of public opinion in the North had changed. The bloody shirt, while still used as a campaign issue, was becoming somewhat frayed. Most people in the North had tired of lurid tales of outrages upon the Negroes. In fact their enthusiasm for the Negro had cooled perceptibly. The South was receiving more favorable reporting in Northern journals, and businessmen in the North and East were more than ready to forget the past and to take advantage of the rising economy of the South. Thoughtful Republicans began to reassess their policy toward the Southern states and to realize what a dismal failure it had been.

• *The National Party and the South* 139

Rutherford B. Hayes came to office pledged to a new policy. Much has been written about the "Compromise of 1877," and Hayes's removal of the troops and his more conciliatory attitude toward the South have been considered as part of the agreement which brought him to office. Even in his letter accepting the nomination, however, written long before there was any thought of a disputed election or a compromise, Hayes had held out the hope of self-government for the South. He insisted that Southern people must obey the new amendments and give colored people all their rights but he made it clear that he was not in sympathy with the "ultra measures" relating to the South. Letters written by Hayes early in 1877 show that the Southern problem was very much on his mind and that he had a great desire to unite the sections and to promote the prosperity of the South. His inaugural address reiterated the sentiments of the letter of acceptance, and it was endorsed by many leading Republicans.[4]

Hayes had a great ambition to build a strong Republican party in the Southern states. He was convinced that the only way to attract Southern whites to the party was to lessen its dependence on the Negro and the carpetbagger. He hoped to rebuild the Southern wing of the party along economic rather than racial lines. He himself had been a Whig, a staunch believer in the economic principles of that party, and he hoped to realign Southern politics along the old Democratic-Whig division and to convert conservative whites to Republicanism. This he proposed to do primarily through a judicious use of the federal patronage.[5]

Hayes was the first Republican president to try the experiment of appointing regular Democrats to important positions in Georgia and the other Southern states in the hope of prying them loose from the Democratic party. He hoped, too, to present a more favorable image of the Republican party by filling federal offices with people acceptable to their respective communities. His purpose was to rehabilitate the party by the acquisition of Southern whites with Whiggish tendencies. The experiment was an important one because of its sharp departure from Radical policies during Reconstruction. The strategy was never approved wholly by a majority of Republicans in Congress. It was received with suspicion by Democrats in the South and with hostility by most Southern Republicans. Hayes seldom received credit for honest motives in the matter, as the public generally regarded the move as part of the bargain that made him president.[6]

Convinced that the policy of force under Grant had served only to thwart Republican chances in the South, Hayes swung far to the other side in his attempt to conciliate Southern Conservatives. Wishing to include a Southerner in his cabinet and not finding an appropriate Republican, he appointed a Democrat, a former Confederate officer, David M. Key of Tennessee, as postmaster general. This was, perhaps, the most important patronage-dispensing position in the government. Key's appointment met with opposition from both sides. Republicans objected to having a Democrat in such a sensitive position in the cabinet, while Democrats felt that the new postmaster general was, after all, not a very representative member of their party. He had been defeated for Congress and had been sent to the Senate by the governor to succeed Andrew Johnson. Just a few weeks before his appointment as postmaster general, he had been defeated for re-election to the Senate, receiving his chief support from the Republican minority in the Tennessee legislature.[7]

It was understood that Key had been invited to the seat in the cabinet to represent the South and to give personal attention to patronage in that section.* He stated this frankly in an interview with the New York *Times* a week after his appointment. The *Times* reporter wrote that Key would appoint men without regard to politics who had the capacity and disposition to help the administration bring about a reconciliation between the sections.[8]

In making appointments in the Southern states the policy was laid down and frequently reiterated that preference would be given to Republicans where suitable Republicans were available. On many occasions, however, in Georgia and in other states, Democrats were appointed to office. Even where Republicans were named, the nominations were often subject to approval by the state's Democratic members of Congress. Senator John B. Gordon was said to be a powerful figure in controlling patronage during the Hayes administration, and Georgia Democratic congressmen were consulted about appointments in their districts as though they were members of the President's own party.[9] In this way, Hayes hoped to make appointments that were acceptable to the conservative whites and to reduce the influence of the carpetbagger and the Negro. His conciliatory attitude toward the South no doubt made some friends among the Democrats in Georgia, but there is no evidence that it won converts for the Republican party or votes for Republican candidates. On the other hand, his policy alienated and offended most Georgia Republicans, especially the Negroes.

*The objection of Republican congressmen to having a Southern Democrat in charge of patronage matters led Hayes to retain former Postmaster General James N. Tyner of Indiana as the first assistant in the department, to handle patronage in the Northern states. This was made plain in the contemporary press.

Early in his term of office, in September, 1877, the President made a Southern tour, including a visit to Atlanta. According to contemporary accounts, he and Mrs. Hayes received an enthusiastic reception all along the way, and they made an extremely favorable impression in Atlanta. Correspondents for Northern newspapers expressed amazement at the cordiality of the people of Atlanta. "It taxed credulity," wrote one, who mingled with the crowds and was astonished that "the undertone on the streets, among all sorts of people, was so unreservedly hearty."[10] Said another: "It was plain to one on the platform, looking into the eyes of the multitude, that the people liked his face and manner to begin with; and before he had spoken a dozen sentences there could be no doubt that they liked his speech, for their applause was unmistakably spontaneous and earnest."[11]

The speech in question, which brought spontaneous applause from the crowd, chilled the hearts of many Republicans who heard it. Hayes spoke plainly about the withdrawal of the troops and told the colored people that he was satisfied that they were better off at the hands of the Southern whites and that their rights had been better respected during the previous six months than at any other time since the war. He made it plain that the Negro could expect no more federal intervention in his behalf. He made it plain, also, that he had no sympathy for carpetbaggers, when he expressed himself as favoring government of the people by the people's own representative men. A few days later, a meeting of Negroes in Atlanta, called to ratify Hayes's Southern policy, was characterized as "about the slimmest ratification meeting of a presidential policy ever held in the Union." Negroes had been advised by their preachers not to attend the meeting nor to endorse the policy of Hayes, "who had basely turned his back upon his party and upon the loyal men . . . of the South."[12]

Hayes was never popular with Republicans in Georgia. The Georgia delegation to the national convention in Cincinnati, which nominated him, had been almost evenly divided for James G. Blaine, Oliver P. Morton, and Roscoe Conkling, with a few votes for Benjamin Bristow. Not until the seventh and last ballot did Hayes receive any Georgia votes at all and then only seven out of a total of twenty-two.[13] Georgia Republicans had little enthusiasm for the candidate, and the candidate was obligated in no way to them.

In addition to this, the leadership of the party in Georgia represented the very elements that Hayes found most objectionable. During most of Hayes's administration the chairman of the state central committee was John E. Bryant, one of the most notorious carpetbaggers ever to operate in Georgia. In April, 1880, Bryant was replaced as chairman by a Negro, William A. Pledger, and for the last year of Hayes's term the Negroes filled three-fourths of the places on the state committee and controlled the state organization. Carpetbaggers and Negro politicians were not necessarily vicious or corrupt, but their presence as party leaders and officeholders was apt to be resented by native white members of the organization. Hayes felt that their influence must be reduced or, if possible, eliminated in order to attract Southern whites. It was not strange that there was little sympathy or cooperation between the President and Republican officials in Georgia.

A link between the administration and the Republicans of Georgia was John Sherman. As secretary of the treasury under Hayes, Sherman had many jobs at his disposal, and he himself had presidential aspirations. Over a long period of time, he carried on a voluminous correspondence with Southern Republicans, and they wrote him frequently of their grievances. Typical, perhaps, of the frustration felt by Negro members ambitious for recognition was the experience of Edwin Belcher, who corresponded with Sherman for almost a year regarding an appointment for himself. Belcher, who had been active in the Georgia party since its inception, was serving as a mail agent but was eager for an appointment as deputy collector at Savannah. He felt that the job had been promised to him but he never received the appointment. He complained to Sherman that President Hayes had not been very liberal in the distribution of his favors to colored men. Belcher pointed out that no Negro in Georgia had been appointed to a position above that of mail agent under the administration. "General Grant was more liberal to the Colored people and not quite so generous to democrats," he wrote.[14]

Convinced finally that he had been passed over in consideration for the job, Belcher noted rather bitterly that Hayes had expressed great solicitude for the "poor colored people" when his own election was in doubt but, once in office, had ignored them in matters of patronage. When General Gordon was made the dispenser of federal patronage in Georgia, said he, it was "tantamount to the declaration that no Negro need apply."[15]

The Negroes were not alone in their grievances regarding patronage. One of the appointments most resented by Georgia Republicans was that of a Democrat, O. P. Fitzsimmons, to the much sought after post of United States marshal.

W. L. Clark, editor of the Atlanta *Republican,* reported to Sherman that he admired Hayes's courage in breaking with many in the party in order to get it on higher ground, but that most of the officeholders in Georgia were "very hostile" to his administration. His own business had suffered, said he, because of his support of Hayes. Colonel Buck, clerk of the federal courts, had told Clark in 1878 that if he ran an administration paper he would not give him the "slightest support," a pledge that Buck had "faithfully kept."[16] In full sympathy with Buck's attitude was J. E. Bryant, state party chairman from 1876 to 1880, who referred later to "the infernal administration of that man Hayes." "Our party was humiliated by his conduct," said he. "It was worse than a democratic administration." Bryant's remarks, made on the floor of a state convention in 1882, were greeted with a chorus of approval.[17]

The true measure of the success of Hayes's policy was not his own popularity with either Republicans or Democrats, but the extent to which it broke into the Solid South and strengthened Republican organization in the Southern states. The results were discouraging. In the congressional and state elections of 1878, Southerners turned their backs upon the President's conciliatory gestures. Every Republican candidate for governor in the South was defeated and Republican members of Congress were cut from ten to three. A comparison of Republican votes in 1878 with those of 1876 in the predominantly white counties and the predominantly black counties of the South showed a marked decline in both categories. The new strategy had not only failed to gain a substantial number of white votes, but had cut drastically into the usual Republican majorities in counties with a high percentage of Negroes.[18]

Hayes was greatly disappointed in the election returns of 1878 and admitted publicly to the press that the experiment was a failure. Privately, however, he still continued to hope for success and he held to his course. The election of 1880 proved conclusively that his strategy had not worked. After almost four years of the new policy the party failed to carry a single Southern state in the presidential race. In eight of the eleven Confederate states James A. Garfield polled a smaller percentage of the total vote than had Hayes in 1876. It was plain that Hayes had failed to convert Southern whites to Republicanism.*

---

*Georgia was one of the three states which showed an increased ratio of Republican votes in 1880. This was probably due mainly to a lack of enthusiasm for the Democratic candidate, as the Democratic vote dropped from 130,088 to 102,470, while the Republican total increased by less than four thousand votes, from 50,446 in 1876 to 54,086 in 1880. Stanwood, *History of the Presidency*, 383, 417.

During Hayes's administration the trend toward Independent candidates was becoming pronounced, and in many individual instances Republicans supported such candidates, as in the cases of William H. Felton and Emory Speer in Georgia. The President, however, turned down all offers of coalition with the Independent Democrats of the South. He rejected also proposals to establish a compromise party in the South under some such name as National Union Party. Nor was he interested in a suggested revival of the old Whig party. He hoped to attract former Whigs and other conservative elements in the South into a union with the conservative Republicans of the North, but he insisted that this be done under the regular Republican name and based on Republican principles.

The most promising Independent movement in the South at this time was the Readjuster movement in Virginia, which developed in 1878 under the leadership of William Mahone, a former Confederate general. Contending with the regular Democratic element in Virginia on the issue of the settlement of the public debt in the state, the Readjusters had the support of many Republicans, both colored and white, in winning the state election in 1879. Some national Republican leaders, as well as those in Virginia, favored a coalition with Mahone as a means of breaking the power of the Democratic party in the state. This proposal Hayes rejected, as he felt that the Readjuster movement smacked of repudiation and was in direct conflict with Republican principles and the conservative union that he was determined to promote.[19]

With the election of James Garfield in 1880, it was evident that there would be a change in the national party's policy toward the South. Garfield had at first concurred with Hayes's plan but had become very critical of the new departure, as had other influential Republican leaders. During the next administration, Garfield and Chester Arthur completely abandoned the Hayes strategy, but they did not abandon attempts to win Republican votes in the South. Garfield had time only to discuss and put into partial operation his own plans, but Arthur followed and expanded the program with a policy of full and wholehearted cooperation with the Independent movements in the South, including that in Georgia.[20]

Garfield himself was committed only to partial cooperation with the Independents. It happened that Mahone, now a member of the Senate, held the balance of power between the two parties when the new Congress met in special session in the spring of 1881. It was generally acknowledged that his price for aiding the Republicans in organizing the Senate would involve a deal whereby he would control the federal patronage in Virginia and support would be given by the administration to a coalition of Republicans and Readjusters on the state level. Increasing pressure was brought to bear upon Garfield to come to terms with Mahone. Apparently the President agreed to some sort of limited alliance with the Readjusters but he was unwilling to sacrifice the identity of the Republican party in Virginia. Many of its members opposed a coalition. The details of the alliance had not been completed when Garfield was assassinated.[21]

When Chester Arthur became president in the fall of 1881, he was convinced that the best hope for Republicanism in the South was a policy of complete cooperation with the Independent movements. He was willing to go much further than Garfield. Not only did he go all the way in his cooperation with Mahone, turning over to him a tremendous amount of federal patronage to aid in the state elections of 1881, but he courted economic radicals wherever they might be found. In general, Arthur proposed to unite Republicans, Readjusters, Greenbackers, Independents, and so-called "Liberals" under his banner in the attempt to break the hold of the Democratic party in the South.[22]

In Georgia the administration endorsed the efforts of Georgia Republicans to form a coalition with Independents led by W. H. Felton. The backing of the President and other national Republican leaders was never openly acknowledged, but their support is clear from correspondence of the period and from the handling of certain federal appointments in support of the movement. Even before the Markham House conference in December, 1881, General Longstreet wrote to Felton suggesting that the President be approached about appointments favorable to the Independent cause.[23] Shortly after the conference he went to Washington to confer with Arthur, and he wrote to Felton suggesting that the latter come to Washington to talk with the President about the policy to be followed in Georgia.[24]

After James Atkins went to Washington to represent the coalition (and the syndicate) in January, 1882, he reported to Felton that President Arthur was convinced that the move for a coalition differed from former sporadic cases of Independentism in Georgia and that he was ready to take steps to show his support.[25] Atkins had already written to Farrow a long enthusiastic account of a meeting at the White House when he, Longstreet, C. W. Arnold, and Walter Johnson had been granted an audience with the President. The group asked Arthur to make one or two changes immediately to furnish a signal to the Independents that he was with them. The President, wrote Atkins, grasped the whole subject at once and said that the plans were feasible and well laid.[26]

While the evidence would suggest that Atkins and some of the others were more interested in controlling the patronage than in forwarding the cause of the Independents, there seems little doubt that President Arthur, in working with the syndicate faction, was attempting to aid the coalition with the Independents. Indicative of the understanding that existed between the President and the syndicate was a letter from Longstreet to Arthur recommending the replacement of two minor officials in the state. "The incumbents seem to be attentive officers," wrote the General, "but do not seem to appreciate the importance of their positions in extending that aid which we so much need." It is significant that one of the replacements proposed by Longstreet was described as a special friend of Alexander H. Stephens, who would be extremely useful in the district to which he would be assigned.[27] (At this time, the Independents were still hopeful that Stephens could be persuaded to be their candidate for governor.)

One of the appointments made by Arthur during the spring of 1882 was that of Henry Farrow as collector of customs at Brunswick. From this vantage point Farrow would have opportunity for much political maneuvering in behalf of the expected Independent campaign. In May, he received a letter from Emory Speer, Independent congressman from the Ninth District, relaying a message from the secretary of the treasury that any leave of absence that he might take for the purpose of his work in Atlanta the department "would entirely overlook." (Speer's reference to the projected Independent mass meeting and to plans for the nomination of Stephens left no doubt as to the nature of Farrow's "work" in Atlanta.)[28]

Democratic leaders in Georgia and the Democratic press were always quick to seize upon and magnify any evidences of cooperation between Independent candidates and Republicans. They were quick to realize that the coalition movement of 1881-1882 represented something more than casual cooperation. Senator Benjamin H. Hill warned Felton that the Stalwart Republicans under Arthur had entered upon a new attempt to get Republican party control of the South. "This second attempt is far *more adroit* and in many respects more infamous than that of 1867," he wrote. Hill predicted that the move would not only fail but would bring political odium upon all in the South who lent themselves to it.[29] Alexander H.

Stephens, while deploring Hill's attack upon Felton, cautioned his friend about the policies and objects of the Radical party and expressed regret that Felton had seen fit to endorse the Arthur administration in an interview with a correspondent for the Chicago *Tribune*.[30] The Atlanta *Constitution* recognized the fact that the administration was behind the coalition and working with the syndicate and declared bluntly that the move was a scheme not only to disrupt the Solid South but to obtain a second term for Chester Arthur.[31]

While Arthur's approach to the problem of building Republican strength in the South was quite different from that of Hayes, he, like Hayes, subordinated the Negro to the white Southerner. In order to exploit Democratic divisions in the South, Arthur felt that he must relegate the colored man to a minor position in the party. In Georgia, the President continually ignored the recommendations of Pledger, the colored chairman of the party, and, implicitly at least, concurred in his replacement in 1882. The national committeeman from Georgia, James B. Deveaux, another Negro, was also ignored. Arthur, like Hayes, tried to placate the Negroes by rewarding a few of their leaders with offices, but this failed to satisfy the mass of colored Republicans, who felt that they had been abandoned a second time. Hayes had tried to attract Southern conservatives, while Arthur leaned toward economic radicals, but in both cases Republican appeals in the South were directed primarily toward whites instead of Negroes.[32]

As in the case of Hayes, the acid test of Arthur's policy came at the ballot box. Here again, in 1884 in the presidential election, Republican strategy proved a complete failure in breaking the Democratic South. Not an electoral vote in the South was won by James G. Blaine. His aggregate popular vote in the Southern states surpassed that of Garfield and Hayes, but his over-all proportional vote in the section fell slightly below the figures of 1876 and 1880. In the congressional elections of 1882, eight Southern Republicans had been sent to Congress and eight Independents. For the moment, the policy of cooperation seemed to have gained results, but in 1884 all the Independents were defeated. There were still eight Republicans, substantially more than in 1878 but fewer than in 1876 or 1880. Certainly the new policy showed little promise for the future. What small gains had been made were only through a Republican-Readjuster-Independent coalition, at the expense of orthodox Republicanism, and these gains had not been permanent.[33]

By the mid-eighties, Republicans were discouraged about their chances to win the South. The failure of two major attempts to crack the Solid South and the dissatisfied, divided condition of Republican parties in the old Confederate states were disheartening. The loss of the presidency to the Democrats in 1884 was a serious blow. The White House had always taken the lead in determining and directing the party strategy regarding the Southern states, and there was no further organized effort to build up the party in the South until the Harrison administration. In the meanwhile, party leaders seemed more interested in building up their own chances for the presidential nomination in 1888 than in a real regeneration of the party. In the election of 1888, Harrison polled a smaller percentage of Southern votes than had any Republican candidate since the war, and in Georgia his numerical total was much lower than that of any previous Republican candidate for president.[34] It was plain that a new policy was badly needed. Floods of suggestions as to the "Southern Question" poured in upon Harrison between his election and inauguration. He moved slowly and was cautious about expressing himself, but he frequently repeated his insistence upon the old Republican demand for a free ballot and a fair count.

Harrison, like many other Republicans in the North, was convinced that the failure of Republicans to win victories in the South was due primarily to the fact that their votes had either been suppressed or not counted. Concluding from Hayes's and Arthur's experiences that it was almost impossible to convert Southern Democrats to Republicanism, he determined to concentrate on protecting the voting privileges of existing Southern Republicans, especially the Negroes. His major effort to win back the South, therefore, centered around the Federal Elections Bill of 1890—the "Force Bill," as it was promptly termed. This bill, introduced in Congress in March, 1890, provided for federal supervision of elections and empowered the President to use the Army and Navy if necessary for its enforcement. It passed the House of Representatives but met strong opposition in the Senate, where it was first postponed after a filibuster and finally, in January, 1891, removed from the legislative calendar.

Even in the North, public opinion was not wholly in favor of the Force Bill, but many people felt that the defeat of the measure represented still another abandonment of the Negro by the Republican party. The party platform as usual had pledged the enforcement of the Fourteenth and Fifteenth amendments, and Harrison himself, long before his nomination, was personally committed to a free ballot and full political rights for Negroes. He learned, however, as had his predecessors, that the problem was not a simple one. People in the North as well as the South were weary of attempts to revive sectional strife and violence. The defeat of the elections bill reflected the growing desire of Republican leaders to focus their attention upon the tariff and monetary policies and to forget the old issues of Reconstruction.[35]

While the Force Bill never became law, the attempt to push it through Congress had brought to the surface waves of sectional animosity which, for a short time, had threatened to bring back the old bitterness of Reconstruction. Advocates of the bill collected and publicized evidence to show the alleged suppression of voting rights in the South, and all sorts of outrages were recounted. Those opposing the bill responded in kind. To most white people in the South the measure was grimly reminiscent of the days of Grant, and the Democratic press brought out once again the old threats of Negro supremacy and bayonet rule. The Atlanta *Constitution* saw the bill as "infamous," " a monstrous scheme to upset all local authority," utterly without excuse except as a partisan measure intended to place Southern congressional districts in control of the Republicans. "All that can come of it," protested the editor, "is confusion, bitterness, race conflicts, and the destruction of our industrial progress."[36] The bill ostensibly applied to all sections of the country but it was generally recognized as an attempt by the administration to increase the Republican vote in the South. Its defeat brought great relief to most people in Georgia, but the Negroes understandably were disappointed.

Thwarted in his first attempt to strengthen the party in the South, Harrison was soon presented with another opportunity. By 1892 the farmers of the South and West had joined forces in the People's party and were ready for a full scale political effort on the national as well as the state and local levels. Many Republicans felt that the party should take advantage of the Democratic split in the South by forming a coalition with the Populists in Georgia and other Southern states. Harrison was never very hopeful of success in this venture. He had seen the meager fruits of Arthur's attempt to cooperate with the Independents a decade before. Nevertheless he agreed to support the policy, and in July, 1892, the Republican national committee announced that it would make a vigorous effort to break the Solid South in the elections of that year. Chris Magee, a Pennsylvania Republican, was placed in charge of the campaign to unite the Republican and Populist groups for the 1892 campaign.[37]

In September, 1892, just before Colonel Buck issued his first circular advising Georgia Republicans to vote for Populist candidates, Magee was in Atlanta and conferred with the state chairman. The visitor was quoted as saying that he did not believe that the third party would amount to anything but that Democrats who went off into the People's party would eventually land in the Republican party.[38] In Georgia the results of the state election in October proved conclusively that few Democrats had as yet landed in the Republican party and not many had found their way into the Populist ranks. W. L. Peek, the Populist candidate, was defeated by a majority of more than seventy thousand.[39]

Although Harrison had been lukewarm over the idea of fusion, he had apparently been persuaded by party leaders that the strategy had a good chance for success. When the results of the Georgia election came in, the President was reported to be in a "furious rage," complaining bitterly that he had been duped by Southern Republicans as to the condition of political affairs in the South. "I have washed my hands of the south," Harrison reportedly said. "It is a land of rebels and traitors who care nothing for the sanctity of the ballot, and I will never be in favor of making an active campaign down there until we can place bayonets at the polls. I am now more than ever in favor of ramming a force bill down their throats."[40]

As the story was told in a special dispatch from Washington, the President sent word to the "managers" in New York to dump the Southern program overboard and in the future to confine operations and money to the pivotal states in the North.[41] A month later Harrison himself was defeated in his bid for re-election. The program of fusion with the Populists continued in a halfhearted way in most Southern states. It had the blessing of the Republican national committee but, except in North Carolina, it never came up to the expectations of its sponsors.

With William McKinley and the election of 1896 came a new era in American politics. McKinley and Mark Hanna made another attempt to convert the Southern white to Republicanism, but this time it was on the basis of valid issues. The tariff and the monetary question took the place of the old sectional appeals, and the "Southern Question," as such, was not agitated. In Georgia in 1896 the McKinley vote was larger proportionally than the Republican vote in any other presidential election since 1872. In every other Southern state except Texas, however, McKinley polled an even smaller percentage of the total state vote than did Harrison in 1888. For the South as a whole, Republican strength was at its lowest point to date, McKinley receiving less than thirty per cent of the popular vote in the eleven Southern states.[42]

Twenty years of planning and scheming had not secured one Republican electoral vote in the South. Instead, Republican strength in the section had declined steadily since 1876. As the century neared an end, it seemed improbable that the situation would improve.

XI

Conclusion: Eclipse on the Georgia Scene

THE REPUBLICAN party never disappeared completely from the Georgia scene. Its eclipse was not a total one, but by the end of the nineteenth century the party had so declined in power and prestige that it was scarcely visible on the political horizon. Every four years, when a president was to be nominated and elected, there was a flurry of activity, but in the intervening years the organization was almost obscured by the all-powerful Democratic party.

Many of the ills of the Republican party in Georgia were self-inflicted and self-perpetuated, but just at the close of the century the party suffered a blow which was not of its own making and which pushed it still further into obscurity. This blow was not aimed at Republicans alone but it had the effect of stifling *all* opposition to the Democratic party. It was the establishment of the Democratic white primary in Georgia. When the Democratic state executive committee adopted the statewide primary in 1898 and made it mandatory for all counties, the emphasis in Georgia politics shifted from the general election to the Democratic "election." And when the primary was made the *"white* primary" in 1900, this action seemed finally to set the seal on the old claim of the Democracy that it was the white man's party in Georgia. Opposition to Democratic candidates in the general election virtually ceased after 1900.

The nomination of Democratic candidates had long been more meaningful than the contests in the general election, but so long as the nominating was done by conventions it did not take the place of the election in the eyes of the mass of voters. After the change in the method of choosing candidates, most voters who exercised their

• *Conclusion: Eclipse on the Georgia Scene* 153

franchise in the Democratic primary felt that the election had been held and that the results were final. The general election, established by law, became anticlimactic and had little meaning or interest. At best there had been few Republican candidates on the state and local levels since the 1870's. After 1900 white Republicans tended more and more to vote in the Democratic primaries for state and local officials and to save their Republicanism for the presidential elections. For colored voters, whether Republican or Democratic, there was little incentive even to register to vote.

While the system of primaries was not aimed originally at the Republican party in Georgia, the move to make it mandatory and statewide was influenced by the fusion threat in the last decade of the century. Nominating candidates in the direct primary was considered more democratic and less subject to corruption and machine rule than the convention and caucus methods formerly employed. It had the added attraction of enabling the Democrats to fight out their factional battles within the party itself with less danger of disaffected elements entering the general election.

By 1898 almost two-thirds of the states had laws, relating to primaries, beginning with California in 1866. In Georgia primaries had been used for the nomination of county and municipal officers in scattered instances since 1874. Fulton County and the City of Atlanta both held primaries in that year.[1] By 1880 a few counties had begun to hold primaries to elect delegates to the Democratic state convention, where nominations for statehouse officers were made. By 1898 a majority of the counties were using this method of choosing delegates, but the rules formulated by the state executive committee in that year provided for a statewide primary not to choose delegates but to nominate *directly* the governor and other statehouse officers, justices of the supreme court, and judges of the superior courts. In 1900 the rules were amended in several respects, including the proviso that limited the primary to white voters.[2]

The General Assembly had been slow to pass laws regulating primaries, since they were established and financed by the Democratic party, not the state. In 1887 the legislature for the first time defined primaries and included them in a measure regulating the use of liquor in elections. In 1891 it passed a law to protect primaries from certain corrupt practices, but expressly left the formulating of rules to the political party holding the primary.[3] This made possible the exclusion of Negroes by party action rather than by state law, a circumvention of the Fifteenth Amendment which was upheld by the United States Supreme Court for many years.[4]

Long before 1900 some Georgia counties had recognized the value of the white primary as a means of excluding Negroes from any meaningful participation in the electoral process. As early as 1876 a white primary was held in Augusta. This evidently caught the colored voters by surprise, as numbers of Negroes applied at the polls and were refused, even though they avowed their loyalty to the Democratic party. The Augusta *Constitutionalist* termed the move a "blind stroke of policy on the part of the Democratic managers" and expressed anxiety that it might cause dissension in the Democratic ranks.[5] The institution of a white primary in Clarke County in 1888 met with general approval on the part of white voters, who rejoiced that the Negro would no longer be a principal factor in county elections.[6] In Atlanta in 1892 the Democratic city executive committee decided to hold a white primary. The rival candidates were said to be satisfied, but a group of Negroes presented a petition asking for a primary for all qualified voters without regard to color.[7] By 1898 a number of counties had party rules barring Negroes from their primaries, and in practice the colored voters were quite generally excluded, but it was not until 1900 that the restriction was written into the formal rules of the Democratic state executive committee.[8]

While the Negro did not always vote Republican, he had always been identified primarily with that party. The Democrats needed him only when the white vote was divided. At such times they had welcomed and even courted his vote, but he was never made an integral part of the party. In the Republican organization he held most of the offices and supplied an overwhelming majority of the party vote. Any development which discouraged large numbers of colored men from registering and voting would inevitably cut down on the number of potential Republican ballots. At the state and local levels where there were few Republican candidates, these ballots might be cast for Independents or even for Democrats, but most of them could be counted on for the Republican ticket in the presidential election and in other cases where there were Republican candidates.

The white primary was hailed as the solution to the problem of Negro suffrage in the South, "an escape from negro domination on the one side, and from warfare upon the suffrage on the other." On the day of the first statewide white primary in Georgia, the Atlanta *Constitution* in a featured two-column editorial explained the meaning of the new system. It would permit the conservative people of the state to control affairs without depriving any person of the vote.

• *Conclusion: Eclipse on the Georgia Scene* 155

If the colored voters could present a better ticket or make a more successful appeal at the general election, they had the right to do so.[9] It was significant that no mention was made of the Republican party. To most people in the state the Republican party and the colored voter were synonymous. In a state with a normal two-party system of politics, the institution of the direct primary should have stimulated and invigorated both parties. In those Southern states which had one invincible party, the coming of the primary simply pointed up the impotence of the Republicans and left the field to the Democrats. "In Georgia the primary is the election," declared the *Constitution,* and few would have argued the point.[10]

The ineffectiveness of the Republican party in Georgia was clear to all. To explain the reasons for the ineffectiveness and for the decline and virtual dissolution of the party would necessarily involve a repetition of much that has been written in previous chapters. The identification of the Republican party with the abuses of Reconstruction and the consequent image of the Democracy as the party of Redemption, the party of white supremacy, had imposed a handicap that was almost insuperable. "No greater insult could be offered to a decent white man than to call him a Radical," one Georgia editor had written in 1872, just after the Conservatives had regained control of the state.[11] This had expressed the sentiment of a large portion of the people of Georgia. In the face of such hostility and contempt it was asking a great deal of any "decent white man" to expect him to adhere to the party. Some did, and made honest efforts to redeem it, but public opinion and the forces of social discipline eventually drove most of them out of its ranks.

After the unexpected exit of Governor Bullock and the virtual collapse of the Republican organization, frustration and defeatism had taken their toll. With the passing of the years the party had settled down into a rut of inaction and disrepute. The continued predominance of the Negro, the factional fights and the conflicts among party leaders, the greed for office and corruption in office, the questionable character of many of the leaders, the unsavory reputation of Southern delegates to national conventions, the failure to put up candidates for office, and the apparent lack of a real desire among the leadership to expand the party and to win elections—all these were factors which contributed to the deterioration of Republicanism in Georgia. In justice to the party and to its leadership, however, it should be remembered that powerful forces from the outside were also involved in its fall from power. The Ku Klux methods of the early days, the more refined suppression of votes which came later, and the relentless campaign of vituperation and ridicule on the part of the Democratic press all aided in breaking it down.

Certainly its failure did not mean that there was no need or desire for a strong second party in the state. A reporter for the *Atlantic Monthly* touring the South in 1882 was impressed with the number of so-called Democrats who did not care for that party and would have welcomed another. He reported that large numbers of men prominent in the Democratic party had said to him, "I wish to God we might have an administration party, a republican party, in our State, that a gentleman could belong to without the sacrifice of all honesty and self-respect." Many such speakers identified themselves as former Whigs who hated the name of Democrat.[12]

The failure of the national Republican party to make use of the old Whigs, the Douglas Democrats, and other Unionist elements, in their attempts to form a second party in Georgia immediately after the war was a major tactical error. Benjamin H. Hill, himself a former Whig who had become a leader in the Democratic party, complained bitterly that Republicans in Congress had failed to perceive the distinction between the original secessionists and the Union men in Georgia and had treated them all alike. The old Whigs and Unionists had expected to take control of affairs in the state after the war, said he, and might well have formed the nucleus of a Republican party if they had been treated with more magnanimity. The Reconstruction Acts of Congress, which indiscriminately disfranchised the whites and gave the Negro the ballot, had driven most of them into the Democratic party.[13]

Many of the difficulties of the Republican party in Georgia grew out of the Radical program of Reconstruction. The determination to build the party around the Negro voter and the preference given to carpetbaggers and to others who were willing to work with the Negroes discouraged most of the native whites who might otherwise have acted with the Republicans. Some of those who aligned themselves with the party in 1868 helped to defeat it in 1870, after the split between the Radicals and the Moderate Republicans during the Bullock administration. Many others left the sinking ship in 1872. Since that time there had been few new recruits and little to attract the "respectable" white voters of the state to Republicanism. Even when they agreed with the party on issues they were deterred from joining it by the unpalatable nature of the organization in Georgia.

Theodore Roosevelt expressed the opinion that the disruption and destruction of the Republican party in the South had been brought

• *Conclusion: Eclipse on the Georgia Scene* 157

about by the refusal to face the truth, that "under existing conditions there is not and cannot be in the Southern States a party based primarily upon the Negro vote and under Negro leadership or the leadership of white men who derive their power solely from Negroes."[14] The continued attempts to maintain and bolster such a party resulted only in its further decline. Rutherford Hayes saw this clearly, but his new-departure Southern policy was a case of "too little and too late." The mold was already set and he was powerless to change the course of affairs.

The Republicans never found a formula by which they could join large numbers of Negroes and whites in the same party. Trying to hold on to the Negro vote with one hand while beckoning the white Southerner with the other proved fruitless. This they learned to their sorrow in the attempted coalitions with Independents and with Populists. In commenting upon this situation, one of the best known modern students of government declares that "the stigma of blackness in the end deprived the Republicans of any chance for the white support they needed to become a political force."[15]

In addition to discouraging new acquisitions to the party in Georgia, the predominance of the Negro caused frequent upheavals within the organization, as has been recounted above.[16] The conflicts between the lily-white and the black-and-tan factions arose partly from prejudice and partly from the conviction that the party could never hope to become a significant factor in state politics so long as the Negro was predominant. Divisions were brought about also by jealousy over federal appointments and by the almost constant struggle among the white leaders for control of the party and of the patronage. The cleavages were never entirely along racial lines. White men were to be found on both sides, but the white leaders who were most successful in the Georgia party were those who cast their lots with the Negroes and were able to maintain themselves in power with the backing of the bulk of the colored membership. The white leaders may have manipulated the Negro masses but they were completely dependent upon them for their position in the party.

In spite of the various attempts to form a white (or more nearly white) party in the 1880's, and in spite of the all-white electoral ticket in 1896 and a repetition of that strategy in 1900, the end of the century found the Republican party in Georgia more completely in the hands of the Negroes than at any previous time. At the state convention in March, 1900, the delegates-at-large chosen to attend the national convention included three Negroes and one white man.

The four officers of the newly elected state central committee also included three Negroes and one white man.[17] The white man in both cases was the same, Walter H. Johnson, who had succeeded Colonel Buck as head of the party after the latter's departure for Tokyo as minister to Japan.* This prevalence of the Negro was to become even more pronounced during the early years of the twentieth century.

Periodic protests regarding conditions in the party had not been lacking. Often they came from former leaders of the party who had either retired voluntarily or had been shunted aside by their successors. An interesting example of this occurred in 1890 when a former Bullock aid, A. L. Harris, turned away from the party in disgust and made public his opinions of Republicanism in Georgia. Harris had been a carpetbagger during Reconstruction and was considered at that time to be a prime mover in the Radical wing of the party. He had retired from active politics when the party passed out of power in the state but had remained a Republican. His discontent at the condition of the party boiled over when he went to Colonel Buck in behalf of a friend seeking a federal appointment and was told that he would have to have the endorsement of C. C. Wimbish, Negro chairman of the Fifth District Republican committee and surveyor of the port of Atlanta. In a card which appeared in the Atlanta press, Harris paid his respects to the party in no uncertain terms, and his sentiments were echoed by other men who were Republicans in principle but not in participation. Their comments are significant because they help to explain the disrepute in which the party was commonly held.

In the first place, said Harris, there *was* no Republican party in Georgia. There was only a "small close corporation" of a few Negroes and white men who kept up just enough organization to send themselves as delegates to Republican national conventions and to keep themselves in office. They wanted no accession to their number, he charged, nor did they really desire success at the polls for the party. "[A]ll under heaven they want are the offices in the gift of the national republican administration, and they get them." Harris

---

*Johnson, the first native white to serve as party chairman since 1876, was later forced to step aside because of an order of the department of justice barring federal officials from positions on party committees. (He was currently serving as United States marshal.) William A. Pledger, vice-chairman, became chairman nominally but with the understanding that Johnson would retain the active control. It was thought expedient to have a white man at the head although all the other officers were Negroes. When Buck died in Japan in 1902 he was referred to still as the leader of the party in Georgia, but it was said that his death would mean no change in party organization in the state. Atlanta *Constitution*, December 6, 1902.

• *Conclusion: Eclipse on the Georgia Scene* 159

pointed out the fact that the party was dominated by Negroes, and not the most learned, broad-minded colored men at that. There were thousands of men in Georgia who were strong protectionists, said he, who would vote with the protectionists if the Negro was eliminated from politics or from domination of the Republican party in Georgia.[18]

The Atlanta *Constitution,* quick as usual to exploit dissension in the ranks of the enemy, sent a reporter around with the Harris letter to other Republicans of long standing who were no longer active in the state organization. In a follow-up story several of these were quoted, all affirming and some elaborating on the criticisms made by Harris.[19]

A frequent critic of Buck's control of the party was Rufus Bullock, now a respected and successful businessman in Atlanta. Bullock had been acquitted in 1878 of charges of fraud growing out of his actions as governor, but had taken little part in state politics since his return to Atlanta in 1876. Ignoring the fact that the downfall of Republicanism in Georgia stemmed largely from events of his own Radical administration, he occasionally delivered a blast at the party for its current misdeeds and deficiences. Late in 1895 he and Buck had exchanged sharp words over a letter from the former Governor which had appeared in the New York *Herald.* Among the remarks made by Bullock in the published letter was the comment that no self-respecting white man could subject himself to the control of the party as then constituted.[20] A few months later, after the "disgraceful exhibition" (the state convention of 1896) at which J. F. Hanson and R. R. Wright had been rejected as delegates to St. Louis, Bullock amended his remarks by adding that "no self-respecting *colored man"* should subject himself to the control of the Buck organization. Friends of Buck rushed to his defense in the matter, stating that he had worked tirelessly for four months to secure the endorsement of Hanson and had tried to persuade Rucker or Deveaux to yield place to Wright.

"Governor Bullock knows too much and has grown to be too good for practical republican purposes," declared William Pledger, who criticized Bullock for being a *national* Republican only, while others remained both state and national Republicans.[21] Buck had already commented rather bitterly upon this same point and upon the fact that it did not accord with the "social environment" of Bullock and some others to stem the tide of public opinion and work actively in the party. "It is very easy to criticise and sneer," said he.[22]

Bullock at this period, along with hundreds of other prominent and well-to-do men of the state, illustrated the phenomenon of "presidential Republicans" so characteristic of the party in Georgia and in other Southern states. This situation was especially marked in Georgia in 1896, when many prominent men were attracted to McKinley and the principles of the national Republican party. Then and in subsequent elections they voted for Republican candidates for president but refused to be identified with the state organization. With "presidential Republicans" on the one hand and "postoffice Republicans" on the other, it was small wonder that the party could make no progress in Georgia. The former group preferred to have a Republican in the White House but were not willing to work for the party on the state and local level. In fact, they would have shuddered at the very thought of turning over the government of the state to the party as it existed.* The latter group were interested chiefly in the spoils of office for themselves and their friends. The last thing they wanted to see was an expansion of the party which would have resulted in more hands stretched out for the federal patronage.

One of the most frequent charges made against the leadership of the Republican party in Georgia grew out of its failure to put up candidates for office and its apparent lack of interest in winning elections. Most party officials seemed to think almost wholly in terms of controlling the state party machinery rather than of building up a party worthy of the name. The high point in party politics lay in the selection of delegates to the national nominating conventions. To nominate candidates for the state and local officers and to conduct an all-out campaign for the party were less attractive to most of the leaders. Their reluctance to do so was understandable, in view of the failure through the years to elect Republican candidates on those occasions when nominations had been made. It was clear, however, in the controversies over the question which arose in almost every state convention, that most of the party leaders simply did not want Republican candidates in the field. It is a recognized fact that the easiest way to keep a political party small is to fail to put up candidates. By 1900 the failure in Georgia had become chronic and the smallness was acute. And the strangest thing about the situation was

---

*A visitor from the North attended a dinner at the home of Henry Grady and found there among the guests Rufus Bullock and I. H. Kimball. He was surprised at the general agreement as to state policy. He reported later in his autobiography that he did not find in Atlanta any prominent business Republicans who desired Republican control in the state. *Colonel Alexander McClure's Recollections of Half a Century* (Salem, Mass., 1902), 401-402, quoted in Woodward, *Origins of the New South*, 16.

• *Conclusion: Eclipse on the Georgia Scene*

that most of the people in the state—Republicans as well as Democrats—seemed content to have it so.*

One critic of the party leadership in 1890 had expressed the opinion that the party in Georgia was just where it wanted to be. Certainly there was more than a grain of truth in his comment.[23]

---

*Such statements, while apparently true, should not be taken as a blanket indictment of all leaders or members of the Republican party in Georgia. No doubt there were sincere and dedicated workers in the organization, as in most organizations. The conditions in Georgia, however, as described above, were general throughout the South and have been so recognized by disinterested students of government. Heard, *A Two-Party South*, 97-102, describes the same situation for the South as a whole.

Appendices

APPENDIX A
REPUBLICAN MEMBERS OF CONGRESS FROM GEORGIA*

40TH CONGRESS
(1867-1869)

Biographical Directory of the American Congress, 1774-1961. (Washington, 1961), 187, 192, 197, 202. Unless otherwise noted, members took their seats at the opening of their respective Congresses.

Senate—Both seats vacant
House—District 1—Joseph W. Clift, Savannah
　　　　　　　　(Seated July 25, 1868)
　　　District 3—William P. Edwards, Butler
　　　　　　　　(Seated July 25, 1868)
　　　District 4—Samuel F. Gove, Griswoldville
　　　　　　　　(Seated July 25, 1868)
　　　District 5—Charles H. Prince, Augusta
　　　　　　　　(Seated July 25, 1868)
　　　District 6—Contest between John A. Wimpy (Republican) and John H. Christy (Democrat); neither seated.

41ST CONGRESS
(1869-1871)

Senate—Joshua Hill, Madison (Seated February 1, 1871)

Appendices

House—District 2—Richard H. Whiteley, Bainbridge
        (Seated February 9, 1871)
    District 3—Marion Bethune, Talbotton
        (Seated January 16, 1871)
    District 4—Jefferson F. Long, Macon
        (Seated January 16, 1871)

42ND CONGRESS
(1871-1873)

Senate—Joshua Hill, Madison
House—District 2—Richard H. Whiteley, Bainbridge
    District 3—John S. Bigby, Newnan
    District 4—Thomas J. Speer, Barnesville
        (Died August 18, 1872)

43RD CONGRESS
(1873-1875)

Senate—Both seats held by Democrats
House—District 1—Andrew Sloan, Savannah
        (Seated March 24, 1874, after contest)
    District 2—Richard H. Whiteley, Bainbridge
    District 5—James C. Freeman, Griffin

APPENDIX B

REPUBLICAN PRESIDENTIAL ELECTORS
FOR GEORGIA,* 1868-1900

*1868—Certified List in Farrow Collection, Correspondence folder, January-June, 1870.
1872—Printed circular, "Regular Republican Ticket," in Farrow Collection.
1876—Atlanta *Constitution*, August 17, 1876.
1880—*Ibid.*, September 8, 1880.
1884—*Ibid.*, August 10, 1884.
1888—*Ibid.*, September 5, 1888.
1892—*Ibid.*, October 20, 1892.
1896—*Ibid.*, July 26, 1896.
1900—*Ibid.*, July 6, 1900.
As most of these lists were published at the time of appointment it is possible that some changes occurred before the elections in November. Names are given as listed in the sources cited.

1868
At large—H. P. Farrow,
    A. T. Akerman

1872
At large—A. T. Akerman,
    Benjamin Conley

District 1—F. M. Smith
District 2—John Murphy
District 3—E. J. Higbee
District 4—W. H. Whitehead
District 5—J. E. Bryant
District 6—S. C. Johnson
District 7—J. L. Dunning

District 1—Amherst W. Stone
District 2—Joel Johnson
District 3—W. B. Jones
District 4—W. W. Merrill
District 5—Joel R. Griffin
District 6—John F. Shine
District 7—C. D. Forsyth
Distirct 8—George S. Fisher
District 9—C. A. Ellington

1876
At large—Dawson A. Walker,
    E. C. Wade
District 1—John T. Collins
District 2—C. W. Arnold
District 3—B. F. Bell
District 4—R. D. Locke
District 5—J. A. Holtzclaw
District 6—J. F. Long
District 7—Z. B. Hargrove
District 8—V. M. Barnes
District 9—R. M. Archer

1880
At large—James Atkins,
    George S. Thomas
District 1—A. N. Wilson
District 2—
District 3—W. P. Pierce
District 4—J. N. Wimbush
District 5—E. Pinckney
District 6—Peter O'Niel
District 7—C. B. Forsyth
District 8—W. J. White
District 9—W. T. Crain

1884
At large—Jonathan Norcross,
    James Atkins
District 1—Henry Blunn
District 2—Charles Wesolowsky
District 3—Beverly C. Mitchell
District 4—Harrison J. Sargent
District 5—George S. Thomas
District 6—Owen W. Sherman
District 7—C. D. Forsyth
District 8—W. F. Bowers

1888
At large—James Atkins,
    C. C. Wimbish
District 1—Tomlinson F. Johnson
District 2—Benjamin F. Brimberry
District 3—J. A. Dudley
District 4—R. J. O'Kelley
District 5—Richard T. Dow
District 6—Benjamin J. Jones
District 7—J. Spillman
District 8—William F. Bowers

• *Appendices*

District 9—John M. Allred
District 10—J. T. Denning

District 9—John W. Garren
District 10—$\begin{cases}\text{James T. Denning}\\ \text{R. R. Wright}\end{cases}$
(2 factions)

1892
At large—Chas. W. Arnold,
           Judson W. Lyons
District 1—Richard W. Collins
District 2—Benjamin F. Brimberry
District 3—Mitchell G. Hall
District 4—James R. Thomason
District 5—George S. Thomas
District 6—
District 7—Aaron Collins
District 8—Monroe B. Morton
District 9—John W. Parks
District 10—John M. Barnes
District 11—Floyd Snelson

1896
At large—J. F. Hanson,
           James Longstreet
District 1—W. R. Leaken
District 2—C. W. Arnold
District 3—J. H. Gano
District 4—M. L. Covington
District 5—W. H. Smyth
District 6—Marion Erwin
District 7—J. A. Crawford
District 8—William Powers
District 9—S. A. Darnell
District 10—W. H. Stallings
District 11—C. Downing

1900
At large—J. F. Hanson, John Oliver
District 1—Henry Blunn
District 2—J. E. Peterson
District 3—W. B. Seymour
District 4—E. N. Clemence
District 5—H. L. McKee
District 6—T. W. Thurman
District 7—Charles Adamson
District 8—D. F. DeWolf
District 9—A. S. J. Hall
District 10—S. P. Vaughn
District 11—W. Blook

APPENDIX C

DELEGATES TO REPUBLICAN NATIONAL CONVENTIONS*
1868-1900

*Proceedings of the Republican National Convention, 1868-1900 (published contemporaneously). Some discrepancies appear in names and addresses; errors have been corrected where the proper form was obvious.

1868

At Large

Foster Blodgett
Joseph E. Brown
J. R. Parrott
Henry K. McCay

Districts

1. T. P. Robb
   Isaac Seeley
2. F. O. Welch
   D. B. Harrell
3. I. G. Maull
   W. C. Smith
4. G. G. Wilbur
   J. B. Etze
5. D. G. Cotting
   William Gibson
6. Madison Bell
   E. Hulbert
7. L. P. Gudger
   W. H. Watson

(Neither alternates nor addressses are given in the convention list of the Georgia delegation for 1868.)

National Committeeman—John H. Caldwell, LaGrange

1872

Delegates	Alternates

At Large

Benjamin Conley, Augusta	Amos T. Akerman, Cartersville
Dawson A. Walker, Dalton	
John S. Bigby, Newnan	Thomas J. Speer, Milner
Moses H. Hale, Savannah	William J. White, Augusta
Richard H. Whiteley, Bainbridge	Philip Joiner, Albany
John F. Quarles, Augusta	
W. B. Higginbotham, Rome	
James M. Simms, Savannah	

Districts

A. W. Stone, Savannah	1	J. T. Shufton, Brunswick
L. M. Pleasant, Lawton		

• *Appendices*

A. C. Bell, Preston Elbert Head, Americus	2	P. M. Sheibley, Rome
T. M. Hogan, Columbus I. H. Anderson, Fort Valley	3	D. C. Gresham, Greenville
George Fisher, Augusta Jefferson F. Long, Macon	4	John L. Conley, Atlanta
C. H. Prince, Augusta Edwin Belcher, Augusta	5	Isham S. Fannin, Madison
A. T. W. Lytle, Gainesville Madison Davis, Athens	6	Roderick D. Badger, Atlanta
George P. Burnett, Rome William Finch, Atlanta	7	D. D. Snyder, Atlanta

National Committeeman—Isham S. Fannin, Madison

1876

Delegates *Alternates*

At Large

Delegates		Alternates
Henry P. Farrow, Atlanta		William H. Smyth, Atlanta
James Atkins, Savannah		Eugene R. Belcher, Augusta
Henry M. Turner, Savannah		Benjamin Conley, Atlanta
George Wallace, Macon		W. J. White, Augusta

Districts

John H. Deveaux, Savannah J. T. Collins, Brunswick	1	W. M. Craft, Savannah Stephen T. Moore, Savannah
Edward C. Wade, Quitman Francis F. Putney, Albany	2	Charles L. Bradwell, Thomasville William L. Noble, Albany
S. Wise Parker, Americus Elbert Head, Americus	3	Peter Griffin, Americus
Randolph L. Mott, Columbus Walter H. Johnson, West Point	4	Curtis Bell, Columbus John M. Ward, West Point
George B. Chamberlin, Atlanta Jones O. Winbish, Atlanta	5	L. W. Wimby, Atlanta George W. Ware, Atlanta
Jefferson F. Long, Macon James B. Deveaux, Macon	6	George Wallace, Macon W. W. Brown, Macon

William L. Goodwin, Cartersville
J. N. Van Meter, Kingston

7 W. H. Higginbotham, Rome
Jesse A. Glenn, Dalton

Edwin Belcher, Augusta
C. H. Prince, Augusta

8 J. W. Lyons, Augusta
John Heard, Greensboro

Isham S. Fannin, Augusta
Madison Davis, Athens

9 Jefferson J. Findley, Gainesville
Richard S. Taylor, Athens

National Committeeman—James B. Deveaux, Macon

1880

Delegates   *Alternates*

At Large

E. C. Wade, Savannah
W. A. Pledger, Athens
Edwin Belcher, Augusta
J. F. Long, Macon

R. R. Wright, Cuthbert
Harrison Harris, Madison
W. H. Smyth, Atlanta
C. O. Fisher, Griffin

Districts

Louis B. Toomer, Savannah
Floyd Snelson, A. & G.R.R.

1 Thomas Butler, St. Mary's
S. H. Morse, Savannah

B. F. Brimberry, Cuthbert
John Few, Thomasville

2 S. M. Griffin, Quitman
H. R. Stewart, Bainbridge

Jack Brown, Washington
Elbert Head, Americus

3 W. D. King, Hawkinsville
S. S. Smalls, McVille

R. D. Locke, Columbus
J. C. Beall, Hamilton

4 A. W. Port, Newnan
H. M. Dougherty, Hamilton

A. E. Buck, Atlanta
H. A. Rucker, Atlanta

5 E. M. Brown, Griffin
George E. Holmes, Decatur

W. W. Brown, Macon
James B. Deveaux, Macon

6 P. O. Holt, Macon
Peter O'Neil, Milledgeville

A. M. Middlebrooks, Cartersville
W. B. Higginbotham, Rome

7 H. S. Ober, Rome
J. C. Upshaw, Rome

C. H. Prince, Augusta
Judson W. Lyons, Augusta

8 W. F. Holden, Crawfordville
John Heard, Greensboro

• *Appendices* 169

S. A. Darnell, Atlanta   9   A. W. Watson, Athens
Madison Davis, Athens   John A. Stewart, Morganton
    National Committeeman—James B. Deveaux, Macon

1884

Delegates		Alternates
At Large		
A. E. Buck, Atlanta		Aaron Collins, Cartersville
W. A. Pledger, Atlanta		Smith W. Easley, Jr., Atlanta
L. M. Pleasant, Savannah		E. T. Flemming, Augusta
C. D. Forsyth, Rome		J. N. Blackshear, Macon
Districts		
A. N. Wilson, Savannah	1	James A. Sykes, Brunswick
James Blue, Brunswick		Richard Jackson, Darien
C. W. Arnold, Albany	2	W. H. Henderson, Thomasville
John C. Few, Thomasville		Carey Barnes, Cuthbert
Elbert Head, Americus	3	W. D. King, Hawkinsville
E. Seward Small, Eastman		B. C. Mitchell, Americus
W. H. Johnson, Atlanta	4	R. F. Milner, Newnan
J. C. Beall, LaGrange		E. H. Miller, Columbus
John E. Bryant, Atlanta	5	W. L. Shumate, Decatur
W. D. Moore, Atlanta		William Wilkins, Griffin
W. W. Brown, Macon	6	Richard Nelson, Gordon
P. O. Holt, Macon		W. F. Jackson, Forsyth
G. P. Burnett, Rome	7	Benjamin Duncan, Rome
J. Q. Gassett, Cartersville		T. H. Triplett, Dalton
Marcus A. Wood, Madison	8	Felix R. Rogers, Sparta
Madison Davis, Athens		Monroe B. Morton, Athens
W. T. B. Wilson, Atlanta	9	W. O. H. Shepard, Toccoa
James B. Gaston, Gainesville		John M. Allred, Jasper
W. F. Holden, Augusta	10	Jesse Wimberly, Waynesboro
R. R. Wright, Augusta		O. T. Gonder, Warrenton

    National Committeeman—Francis F. Putney, Hardaway

1888

Delegates		Alternates
At Large		
A. E. Buck, Atlanta		Milton Allen, Macon
R. D. Locke, Macon		George Wallace, Macon
W. A. Pledger, Athens		M. M. Bentley, Atlanta
W. J. White, Augusta		
Districts		
J. H. Deveaux, Savannah	1	L. M. Pleasant, Savannah
Floyd Snelson, McIntosh		L. W. Crawford, Darien
B. F. Brimberry, Camilla	2	A. E. Lippitt, Albany
C. W. Arnold, Albany		O. E. Cone, Fort Gaines
D. A. Dudley, Americus	3	Elbert Head, Americus
N. J. Taylor, Smithville		C. A. Coleman, Perry
J. C. Beall, Hamilton	4	D. W. Echols, Columbus
R. F. Milner, Newnan		Logan Heard, LaGrange
C. C. Wimbish, Atlanta	5	J. W. Smith, Monroe
Jackson McHenry, Atlanta		Taylor Slaughter, Douglasville
W. W. Brown, Macon	6	B. J. Jones, Thomaston
P. O. Holt, Macon		I. W. Wood, Forsyth
Aaron Collins, Cartersville	7	S. H. Galloway, Cartersville
A. B. Fortune, Rome		John Kimball, Marietta
Madison Davis, Athens	8	M. B. Morton, Athens
John Heard, Greensboro		J. W. Jones, Madison
S. A. Darnell, Jasper	9	L. B. Greer, Ellijay
H. D. Ingersoll, Dahlonega		Daniel Barnes, Lawrenceville
R. R. Wright, Augusta (½)	10	Noah Johnson, Sandersville
Jesse Wimberly, Waynesboro (½)		W. H. Clark, Augusta
P. H. Craig, Augusta (½)		
O. T. Gondon, Thomson (½)		

National Committeeman—W. W. Brown, Macon

- *Appendices*

1892

Delegates		Alternates
At Large		
Alfred E. Buck, Atlanta		Lewis M. Pleasant, Savannah
William A. Pledger, Athens		Thomas J. Helm, Rome
William W. Brown, Macon		Noah Johnson, Sandersville
Richard R. Wright, College		Frank J. Wimberly, McDonough
Districts		
Michael J. Doyle, Savannah	1	William H. Styles, McIntosh
Samuel B. Morse, Savannah		William E. Moore, Guyton
Benjamin F. Brimberry, Albany	2	Charles W. Arnold, Albany
Carey B. Barnes, Cuthbert		Julius Caesar Few, Thomasville
Charles E. Coleman, Macon	3	Paul C. Coley, Hawkinsville
Edward S. Richardson, Marshallville		Robert W. Everett, Hawkinsville
John T. Shepherd, Columbus	4	John D. Lovejoy, Greenville
Andrew J. Laird, LaGrange		Richard J. O'Kelly, Grantville
Christopher C. Wimbish, Atlanta	5	Henry W. Walker, Atlanta
Edgar A. Angier, Atlanta		Jackson McHenry, Atlanta
Richard D. Locke, Macon	6	Robert M. Logan, Macon
Frank Disroon, Macon		Isaac W. Wood, Forsyth
W. T. Blackford, Grayville	7	James H. Rinard, Tallapoosa
John Q. Gassett, Cartersville		D. C. Warren, Acworth
Madison Davis, Athens	8	George W. Gantt, Eatonton
Joseph W. Jones, Madison		Harrison Harris, Madison
Sion A. Darnell, Atlanta	9	Christopher C. Haley, Jasper
Andrew J. Spence, Cornelia		M. C. Wilcox, Demorest
Judson W. Lyons, Augusta	10	William Yancey, Beasley
John M. Barnes, Thomson		Andrew M. Brown, Sandersville
John H. Deveaux, Brunswick	11	Abraham L. Tucker, Waycross
William H. Matthews, Brunswick		William Jones, Valdosta

National Committeeman—W. W. Brown, Macon

1896

Delegates		Alternates
At Large		
A. E. Buck, Atlanta		R. D. Locke, Macon
H. L. Johnson, Atlanta		L. M. Pleasant, Savannah
Henry A. Rucker, Atlanta		B. J. Davis, Dawson
John H. Deveaux, Macon		R. R. Wright, College
Districts		
M. J. Doyle, Savannah	1	F. N. Sims, Thebes
S. B. Morse, Savannah		P. J. Majors, Waynesboro
B. F. Brimberry, Albany	2	J. J. Mitchell, Mercer's Mill
J. C. Styles, Dawson		A. E. Dippett, Albany
W. P. Pierce, Leesburg	3	Augustus Pate, Hawkinsville
E. S. Richardson, Marshallville		F. M. Harkless, Delegal
W. H. Johnson, Columbus	4	Samuel Lovejoy, Greenville
D. V. Norwood, Newnan		J. H. Grant, Forsyth
C. C. Wimbish, Atlanta	5	J. M. Smith, Monroe
L. J. Price, Atlanta		W. R. Gray, Campbellton
F. J. Wimberly, Atlanta	6	P. S. Arnold, Fayetteville
I. W. Wood, Forsyth		Richard Carey, Griffin
Charles Adamson, Cedartown	7	Frank Lynch, Dallas
T. M. Dent, Rome		Eli H. Chandler, Marietta
W. A. Pledger, Atlanta	8	H. Carter, Lexington
M. B. Morton, Athens		T. L. Kennedy, Elberton
A. J. Spence, Nelson	9	H. M. Ellington, Ellijay
J. B. Gaston, Gainesville		H. D. Ingersoll, Dahlonega
Judson W. Lyons, Augusta	10	William A. McCloud, Wadley
J. M. Barnes, Thomson		A. E. Williams, Gordon
William Jones, Valdosta	11	J. M. Holzendorf, Sheffield
S. M. Scarlett, Waycross		Giles McLendon, Dublin

National Committeeman—Judson W. Lyons, Augusta

1900

Delegates		Alternates
At Large		
W. H. Johnson, Columbus		Alex Akerman, Dublin
H. A. Rucker, Atlanta		L. M. Pleasant, Savannah
J. W. Lyons, Augusta		A. Graves, Atlanta
H. L. Johnson, Atlanta		T. M. Dent, Rome
Districts		
John H. Deveaux, Savannah	1	S. O. Cherry, Waynesboro
W. R. Leaken, Savannah		S. B. Morse, Savannah
W. H. Satterwhite, Albany	2	S. S. Broadnax, Thomasville
James L. Reddick, Dawson		E. B. Brown, Tifton
M. G. Hall, Cordele	3	C. H. Moore, Jeffersonville
J. T. Noble, Perry		P. C. Cooley, Hawkinsville
E. N. Clemence, Columbus	4	H. A. Poer, Hamilton
Samuel Lovejoy, Bullochville		J. B. Richardson, Hogansville
E. F. Blodgett, Atlanta	5	L. L. Lee, Atlanta
C. C. Wimbish, Atlanta		N. H. Sims, Conyers
R. D. Locke, Macon	6	J. A. Smith, Forsyth
I. W. Wood, Forsyth		W. E. Harp, Jackson
J. J. Hamilton, Rome	7	D. C. Cole, Marietta
M. C. Parker, Rome		J. W. Leigh, Etna
W. A. Pledger, Athens	8	E. W. Howell, Eatonton
M. B. Morton, Athens		W. M. Matthews, Lexington
J. R. Allen, Talking Rock	9	C. E. Williams, Winder
H. D. Ingersoll, Dahlonega		M. C. Wilcox, Mount Airy
A. E. Williams, Gordon	10	John T. White, Augusta
P. H. Craig, Augusta		A. G. Floyd, Sandersville
W. H. Matthews, Brunswick	11	J. M. Milton, Waycross
Clarke Grier, Dublin		S. S. Mincey, Ailey

National Committeeman—Judson W. Lyons, Augusta

APPENDIX D
STATE CENTRAL COMMITTEE HEADS

1867—Foster Blodgett
1872—Henry P. Farrow
1876—John E. Bryant
1880—William A. Pledger
1882—Alfred E. Buck
1898—Walter H. Johnson

Notes

CHAPTER I

1. Official documents relating to the presidential reconstruction, the provisional governorship of James Johnson, the constitutional convention of 1865, and the subsequent election, inauguration, and administration of Governor Jenkins are found in Allen D. Candler, ed., *The Confederate Records of the State of Georgia* (Atlanta, 1910), IV. Among the most comprehensive accounts of Reconstruction in secondary sources are those in Isaac Avery, *The History of the State of Georgia from 1850 to 1881* (New York, 1881) and C. Mildred Thompson, *Reconstruction in Georgia, Economic, Social, Political, 1865-1872* (New York, 1915).
2. Thompson, *Reconstruction in Georgia,* Chapter 6; Olive H. Shadgett, "The Public Life of Charles J. Jenkins, 1830-1865," unpublished thesis, University of Georgia, 1952.
3. Avery, *History of Georgia,* 358, 363; Atlanta *Daily New Era,* February 26, 1867, a clipping in the Joseph Emerson and Elizabeth Grisham Brown Collection, University of Georgia Library, Scrapbook 1866-1867. Atlanta *Daily Opinion,* February 26, 1867, a clipping in the Henry P. Farrow Collection, University of Georgia Library, Scrapbook 3, 1867-1868. Also in the Farrow Collection is an undated manuscript letter addressed to Brown and signed by a group of eleven men, asking for his views on the situation. Identified in Farrow's handwriting as the "original letter" which evoked Brown's public response, the document is the same as that printed in the *Daily Opinion* but the signatures are not identical.
4. From a speech delivered in Milledgeville, as reported in the Atlanta *Daily New Era,* June 12, 1867.
5. January 19, 1872.
6. E. Merton Coulter, *A Short History of Georgia* (Chapel Hill, 1947), 371; Walter L. Fleming, *The Sequel of Appomattox* (New Haven, 1919), 115; Thompson, *Reconstruction in Georgia,* 386-87; Walter Henry Cook, *Secret Political Societies in South during the Period of Reconstruction* (Cleveland, no date), 17-20.
7. *Proceedings of the National Union Republican Convention Held at Chicago, May 20 and 21, 1868* (Chicago, 1868), 66.
8. Henry P. Farrow, President Grand Council, U.L.A. in Georgia to the Subordinate Councils, U.L.A. in

Georgia, February 5, 1868, a printed circular in the Farrow Collection.
9. May 11, 1867, a clipping in the Farrow Collection, Scrapbook 1, 1867-1868.
10. Henry P. Farrow, Grand Secretary Grand Council, U.L.A. of Georgia to the Subordinate Councils, U.L.A. in State of Georgia, November 6, 1867, a printed circular in the Farrow Collection.
11. Thompson, *Reconstruction in Georgia*, 189-90. Allen D. Candler, ed., *The Confederate Records of the State of Georgia* (Atlanta, 1911), VI, 1020-27, includes 172 names in the list of delegates, but the designated membership of the convention was 169. The larger number may include replacements for some delegates who withdrew. According to the official list, twenty-seven delegates were born in the North, but most of these had been in Georgia before the war, some for many years, and thus were not classified as carpetbaggers. Bullock, Conley, Amos Akerman, and other leaders of the Republican party in Georgia were in this category.
12. Foster Blodgett, *The Campaign Speech of Hon. Foster Blodgett on the Issues Involved in the Georgia Campaign, at Augusta, November 3, 1870* (Atlanta, 1870), 5; Foster Blodgett, *Statement of Foster Blodgett and Evidence in Reply to the Charges of Joshua Hill, Made in the United States Senate, April 10, 1871* (Washington, 1871), 17.
13. Unidentified clipping in the Farrow Collection, Scrapbook 2, 1867-1868. A public announcement of the meeting had already been made by Farrow, on May 20. Atlanta *Daily Opinion*, May 21, 1867, a clipping in the Farrow Collection, Scrapbook 2, 1867-1868. An eight-page leaflet in the Farrow Collection, entitled "The Policy of Congress in Reference to the Restoration of the Union," published by the Executive Committee of the Union Republican Party in Georgia, includes a notice of the convention.
14. Clippings in the Farrow Collection, especially in Scrapbook 1, 1856-1867, with marginal notes in Farrow's handwriting, give an excellent picture of his background and philosophy. The collection also includes numerous letters, printed broadsides, and documents relating to Farrow's activities both before and immediately after the war.
15. Obituary, *Atlanta Constitution*, November 10, 1890.
16. Atlanta *Daily Opinion*, July 5, 1867, a clipping in the Farrow Collection, Scrapbook 2, 1867-1868.
17. Scrapbook 2, 1867-1868, in the Farrow Collection includes newspaper clippings for August, 1867, reporting meetings at Marietta, Jonesboro, Campbellton, Calhoun, Cartersville, Dalton, Ringgold, Trenton, and Lafayette.
18. Avery, *History of Georgia*, 375-76.
19. The official journal of the constitutional convention of 1867-68, together with general orders and acts relating to Reconstruction in Georgia during 1867 and 1868, and other pertinent information is found in Candler, ed., *Confederate Records*, VI.
20. R. P. Lester *et al.* to Henry P. Farrow, November 10, 1867; E. McBarron Timony, Secretary of the Grand Council U.L. of Georgia to Subordinate Councils, published in an unidentified clipping in Scrapbook 2, 1867-1868; Griffin *American Union*, January 24, 1868, a clipping in Scrapbook 2, 1867-1868; Atlanta *Daily Opinion*, February 19, 1868, a clipping in Scrapbook 2, 1867-1868; all in the Farrow Collection. Numerous other clippings in Scrapbook 2 report meetings endorsing Farrow's candidacy.
21. J. R. Parrott *et al.* to Henry P. Farrow, January 16, 1868, in the Farrow Collection.
22. Atlanta *Daily New Era*, January 22, February 2, March 6, 1868. Atlanta *Daily Opinion*, January 22, 31, February 19, 1868. The clippings from the *Daily Opinion* and other

- *Notes*

unidentified clippings on the same subject are found in the Farrow Collection, Scrapbook 2, 1867-1868. In the Farrow Collection also is a printed broadside of the convention call dated January 22.
23. Athens *Southern Watchman*, March 11, 1868.
24. *Ibid.*; Atlanta *Daily Opinion*, March 9, 1868.
25. Athens *Southern Watchman*, March 11, 1868.
26. Atlanta *Daily New Era*, March 11, 1868, a clipping in the Brown Collection, Scrapbook, 1868-1872.
27. Broadside and also unidentified newspaper clipping in the Farrow Collection, Scrapbook 2, 1867-1868.
28. Report of the Comptroller General, 1869, Table A, as given in Thompson, *Reconstruction in Georgia*, 201. The new constitution was ratified by a majority of 17,972 votes.
29. Avery, *History of Georgia*, 384 and *passim;* Thompson, *Reconstruction in Georgia*, 217; Allen D. Candler and Clement A. Evans, *Cyclopedia of Georgia* (Atlanta, 1906), I, 268; Atlanta *Daily New Era*, April 14, 1868, a clipping in the Brown Collection, Scrapbook, 1868-1872.
30. Atlanta *Constitution*, June 22, 1868; Avery, *History of Georgia*, 395.
31. Thompson, *Reconstruction in Georgia*, 207-209.
32. Albany, *Tri-Weekly News*, February 4, 1868, a clipping in the Farrow Collection, Scrapbook 3, 1867-1868.
33. Athens *Southern Watchman*, July 29, August 5, 1868. Ulrich Bonnell Phillips, ed., *The Correspondence of Robert Toombs, Alexander Stephens and Howell Cobb* (Washington, 1913), 703.
34. William J. Northen, ed., *Men of Mark in Georgia* (Atlanta, 1911), III, 71-76; Thompson, *Reconstruction in Georgia*, 146-47.
35. Names of congressmen, dates of admission, and biographical information are from *Biographical Directory of the American Congress, 1774-1961* (Washington, 1961), 187, 708, 1483, 963, 850. Names of all Georgia Republican members of Congress will be found in Appendix A.
36. Probably the best account of the proceedings of the Bullock legislature is found in Thompson, *Reconstruction in Georgia*, Chapters 8 and 10.
37. White v. Clements, 39 Georgia *Reports* 232 (1869); Northen, *Men of Mark*, III, 432-34.
38. *Journal of the Senate of the State of Georgia, . . . 1869* (Atlanta, 1869), 652-59, 688, 794, 805-806.
39. Grant carried 18 counties in Georgia and Seymour 114. The exact figures of the popular vote vary in different sources. W. Dean Burnham, *Presidential Elections, 1832-1892* (Baltimore, 1955), 333, gives Seymour 102,707 and Grant, 57,129. Avery, *History of Georgia*, 406, has it 101,786 to 57,195, while the Atlanta *Constitution*, November 21, 1868, allowed the Democratic electors a majority of 44,604.
40. Coulter, *A Short History*, 372; Burnham, *Presidential Elections*, 333-63.
41. Coulter, *A Short History*, 373.
42. A full list of Georgia delegates to this and other Republican national conventions, from 1868 through 1900, will be found in Appendix C.
43. *Proceedings of the National Republican Convention, 1868*, 32-35.
44. Atlanta *Daily New Era*, June 17, 1868; Rebecca Latimer Felton, *My Memoirs of Georgia Politics* (Atlanta, 1911), 51.
45. Atlanta *Daily New Era*, August 26, 1868, a clipping in the Farrow Collection, Scrapbook 3, 1867-1868.
46. Republican electors for all elections from 1868 through 1900 are listed in Appendix B.
47. In the Farrow Collection are a number of certified records, printed circulars, and newspaper clippings showing Farrow's speaking appointments during the campaign and the Republican vote in the counties canvassed as compared with that in the remainder of the state. In later years Farrow took great pride in

pointing out his record in this campaign and in that of 1872, when he was serving as state party chairman.
48. November 12, 1868.
49. Candler, ed., *Confederate Records*, VI, 1017; *Congressional Globe, 41st Congress, 1 S* (Washington, 1869), 16-18; *Ibid.*, *2 S* (Washington, 1870), 853-54.
50. Athens *Southern Watchman*, March 10, 1868; Avery, *History of Georgia*, 420.
51. New York *Times*, December 4, 1869, a clipping in the Brown Collection, Scrapbook, 1868-1872.
52. Avery, *History of Georgia*, 423.
53. Harris, a native of Vermont and later a resident of Ohio, was one of the more capable of Bullock's carpetbag henchmen. He appears in many different roles during the period of Republican ascendancy. His nickname, "Fatty," was obviously appropriate, as he weighed more than three hundred pounds.
54. Thompson, *Reconstruction in Georgia*, 262-64.
55. *Ibid.*, 266.
56. *Ibid.*, 267-68.
57. August 2, 1870.

CHAPTER II

1. Avery, *History of Georgia*, 439, 440. Farrow's letter, written during the time when he was contesting for a seat in the United States Senate, was widely circulated by him as part of his campaign for recognition. In the correspondence folders of the Farrow Collection are a number of letters from members of Congress acknowledging receipt of the letter and commending his stand. A printed handbill publicizing the Akerman letter is also in the collection.
2. Northen, *Men of Mark*, III, 21-27.
3. Atlanta *True Georgian*, August 11, 1870, republished in the Milledgeville *Federal Union*, August 16, 1870.
4. *Georgia House Journal, 1870*, 342-43; Avery, *History of Georgia*, 440.
5. Article II, Section XI; Article III, Section III. Candler, ed., *Confederate Records*, VI, 897, 898.
6. *Acts and Resolutions of the General Assembly of the State of Georgia ... Session of 1870* (Atlanta, 1870), 62-66; Milledgeville *Federal Union*, September 27, 1870.
7. Letter from Linton Stephens to Bullock, published in the Milledgeville *Federal Union*, January 24, 1871.
8. October 11, 1870.
9. Thompson, *Reconstruction in Georgia*, 269.
10. *Biographical Directory of Congress*, 1808, 549, 1232; Samuel Denny Smith, *The Negro in Congress, 1870-1901* (Chapel Hill, 1940), 7, 72-74.
11. Athens *Southern Watchman*, August 28, 1872; *Biographical Directory of Congress*, 1636.
12. *Ibid.*, 552.
13. Willard Range, "Hannibal I. Kimball," *The Georgia Historical Quarterly*, XXIX, (June, 1945), 47-70.
14. Atlanta *Constitution*, August 7, 1868; Alexander St. Clair-Abrams, *Manual and Biographical Register of the State of Georgia for 1871-2* (Atlanta, 1872), 3-6; Candler, ed., *Confederate Records*, VI, 1020-21; *Proceedings of National Republican Convention, 1868*, 40.
15. Atlanta *Constitution*, January 29, 1869; *Georgia House Journal, 1870*, 608.
16. Northen, *Men of Mark*, III, 205. Judging from accounts of party activities, Lochrane took little part in its organization. He was a native of Ireland.
17. St. Clair-Abrams, *Manual and Register*, 1-2.
18. *Journal of the House of Representatives of the State of Georgia, ... 1871* (Atlanta, 1872), 26.
19. St. Clair-Abrams, *Manual and Register*, 111-12. These figures, presumably accurate at the time of the publication of the *Manual*, differ somewhat from earlier estimates made in the press at the time of the

election, almost a year before the legislature convened. The Milledgeville *Federal Union*, January 24, 1871, reported a larger number of Republicans but predicted that some members elected as Republicans would work with the Democrats.
20. *Ibid.*, vi.
21. Athens, *Southern Banner*, January 5, 1872. A letter from seven Democratic state senators addressed to the people of Georgia described the proceedings of the Senate in the recent session of the legislature, especially its action in overriding the veto of the Acting Governor on certain measures.
22. *Ibid.*, December 15, 1871.
23. Atlanta *Daily New Era*, December 12, 1871.
24. December 13, 16, 18, 1871.
25. The official vote was: Smith, 39,705; Scattering, 100. *Journal of the House of Representatives of the State of Georgia, . . . 1872* (Atlanta, 1872), 25.
26. December 21, 1871.
27. Farrow's letter, published in the *Constitution*, December 23, 1871, is presented here at some length to show the thinking of what must have been a large portion of the Republican party of Georgia at that time.
28. Georgia House *Journal, 1868*, passim; Georgia House *Journal, 1870*, 357, 510-25, 549-51. Atlanta *Constitution*, July 25, August 4, 1882, October 9, 1890. Numerous letters from Atkins are found in the Farrow Collection.
29. Avery, *History of Georgia*, 467.
30. *Ibid.;* Milledgeville *Federal Union*, January 17, 1872.
31. Georgia Senate *Journal, 1870*, 27.
32. *Journal of the Senate of the State of Georgia, . . . 1872* (Atlanta, 1872), 14-15.
33. January 17, 1872; Georgia House *Journal, 1872*, 31.

CHAPTER III

1. The Farrow Collection includes almost nothing about the Republican party or about Farrow's party activities during the period of his chairmanship (1872-76). This unfortunate omission suggests that these records were kept separate from his personal files and have either been destroyed or have not yet come to light.
2. Atlanta *Constitution*, January 20, 1872; Milledgeville *Federal Union*, January 24, 1872; Savannah *Morning News*, January 23, 1872. The list of delegates appointed in January was not the final slate, as another delegation was subsequently chosen at a state convention in May. The delegates who actually attended the national convention in June were in some instances still different. Farrow was not included in any of the three versions. The lists of delegates given below, in Appendix C, are taken from the official proceedings of the Republican national conventions and do not coincide in every instance with lists published earlier in local newspapers.
3. Atlanta *Constitution*, January 20, 1872; Athens *Southern Watchman*, January 31, 1872. The proceedings at Albany are recorded in a printed broadside in the Farrow Collection.
4. The account of the Macon convention is taken from the Athens *Southern Watchman*, May 14, 1872; Atlanta *Constitution*, May 11, 1872; Milledgeville *Federal Union*, May 15, 1872; *Georgia Weekly Telegraph and Georgia Journal and Messenger* (Macon), May 14, 1872.
5. Atlanta *Constitution*, May 4, 1872; Derrell Clayton Roberts, "Joseph E. Brown and the New South," unpublished dissertation, University of Georgia, 1958, p. 99.
6. According to the story, the Georgia delegation had planned to switch its support to Adams on the seventh ballot, but Greeley was nominated on the sixth. Atlanta *Constitution*, May 9, 1872.

7. *Proceedings of the National Union Republican Convention Held at Philadelphia, June 5 and 6, 1872* (Washington, 1872), passim.
8. Atlanta *Constitution*, June 13, 1872.
9. Milledgeville *Federal Union*, July 24, 1872; Atlanta *Constitution*, July 24, 1872. One group met in the Senate chamber; the other, in the House of Representatives.
10. Atlanta *Constitution*, July 24, 25, 1872. Milledgeville *Federal Union*, July 31, 1872. James Gardner, chief Democratic negotiator in the consultation with the Liberal Republicans, was evidently a close personal friend of former Governor Brown, as, only a few weeks before, he had been chosen by Brown as his second in his proposed duel with Robert Toombs. Avery, *History of Georgia*, 476ff.
11. Atlanta *Constitution*, August 1, 1872, July 24, 1872. The editor of the *Constitution* at this time was Isaac Avery, who later became the author of one of the most-quoted histories of Georgia for the period. While highly partisan, Avery was a keen political observer, and his comments, though biased, offer an insight into the situation better than do most other sources.
12. July 31, 1872.
13. Athens *Southern Watchman*, August 28, 1872; Atlanta *Constitution*, August 22, 1872.
14. Akerman's forced resignation from the cabinet was hailed by most Southern papers as evidence of incompetence or worse. It was later attributed to his refusal to sanction the corrupt schemes of the powerful railroad interests. Northen, *Men of Mark*, III, 21-27. Atlanta *Daily New Era*, December 19, 1871, eulogizes Akerman.
15. Farrow succeeded Republican John D. Pope, who resigned, it was said, because he was unwilling to discharge the duties required of him under the Ku Klux Acts. Pope soon afterward joined the forces of the Liberal Republicans. Athens *Southern Watchman*, March 6, 1872; Milledgeville *Federal Union*, May 1, 1872; Minutes of the Executive Department of the State of Georgia, 1870-1874, MS book in the Georgia Department of Archives and History. A copy of Farrow's letter of resignation and its acceptance by the governor's office are in the Farrow Collection.
16. The editor of the Milledgeville *Federal Union*, always critical of the "Radicals," was not impressed by Farrow's eleventh-hour washing of hands. He pointed out that Farrow as attorney general had been paid by the people to advise the Governor and certainly shared the responsibility for his actions. Moreover, said he, Farrow did not expose any of Bullock's "shameful doings" until the latter had left the state and "did not have any more fat offices to bestow." December 27, 1871.
17. Avery, *History of Georgia*, 125, 356; Candler and Evans, ed., *Cyclopedia of Georgia*, III, 505; Warren Grice, *The Georgia Bench and Bar* (Macon, 1931), I, 173, 272, 342; Milledgeville *Federal Union*, January 30, 1866.
18. Avery, *History of Georgia*, 366; Augusta *National Republican*, September 3, 1867, a clipping in the Brown Collection, Scrapbook, 1866-1867.
19. Atlanta *Daily New Era*, March 11, 1868, a clipping in the Brown Collection, Scrapbook, 1868-1872.
20. August 23, 1872.
21. September 10, 24, 1872.
22. Milledgeville *Federal Union*, September 18, 1872; Athens *Southern Watchman*, October 9, 1872.
23. Atlanta *Constitution*, September 10, 1872.
24. *Ibid.*, September 24, 1872.
25. *Ibid.*, December 19, 1871. Brown's letter was addressed to Isaac Seeley in Washington, D.C. Seeley, a carpetbag member of the constitutional convention of 1867-68, had suggested that, if necessary to secure evidence, Republicans should challenge each other. Brown minced no words in denouncing the proposal

• *Notes*

and its author. Avery, *History of Georgia*, 475.
26. Avery gives the figure as 58,444. Some other sources give slightly different totals. Avery, *History of Georgia*, 502.
27. October 9, 1872.
28. Fielder, *Life and Times of Joseph E. Brown*, 465, 454.
29. Atlanta *Constitution*, October 4, 1872.
30. Athens *Southern Watchman*, October 9, 1872; Athens *North-East Georgian*, October 4, 1872; Milledgeville *Federal Union*, October 9, 1872.
31. Atlanta *Constitution*, October 6, 1872.
32. Athens *North-East Georgian*, October 4, 1872.
33. Atlanta *Constitution*, October 7, 8, 11, 1872; Milledgeville *Federal Union*, October 30, 1872. The Democratic newspapers were filled for weeks with denunciations of the "high-handed outrages."
34. Atlanta *Whig*, September 12, 1872.
35. Atlanta *Constitution*, August 22, 1872.
35. Milledgeville *Federal Union*, January 18, 1870, March 27, 1872; Athens *Southern Watchman*, March 20, 1872. During Reconstruction, there were a number of Republican papers in Georgia, usually edited by carpetbaggers. Several of these are mentioned in E. Merton Coulter, *The South During Reconstruction* (Baton Rouge, 1947), 286-87.
37. Burnham, *Presidential Elections*, 113, 172-75, 238, 333.
38. *Biographical Directory of Congress*, 914, 1610.
39. Milledgeville *Federal Union*, January 15, 1873.

CHAPTER IV

1. J. Mason Rice to Benjamin M. Conley, August 19, 1872, in Benjamin Conley MS Collection, Atlanta Historical Society, Atlanta, Georgia.
2. J. Clark Swayze to Benjamin Conley, March 8, 1872, in Conley MS Collection.
3. A large percentage of the letters in the Conley MS Collection at the Atlanta Historical Society pertain directly or indirectly to the matter of patronage and are filled with references to factional rivalries and intrigue within the party. The same thing is true of the Farrow Collection.
4. John S. Bigby to Benjamin Conley, January 20, 1874; Wesley Prettyman to Benjamin Conley, February 17, 1874; Henry P. Farrow to Benjamin Conley, January 15, 1874, in the Conley MS Collection.
5. John Conley to Benjamin Conley, January 19, 1873 [sic], in Conley MS Collection. From the context the date should obviously be 1874.
6. *Ibid*., January 20, 1874. Italics added.
7. Rufus B. Bullock to Conley, February 2, 1874, in Conley MS Collection. Bullock suggested a rather remarkable strategy by which Conley might kill off the candidacy of Prince but apparently nothing came of his proposal.
8. David Porter to Benjamin Conley, April 2, 1875; A. D. Rockafellow to Benjamin Conley, April 6, 1875, in Conley MS Collection.
9. Atlanta *Constitution*, February 11, 1876.
10. *Ibid*., April 23, 1874.
11. John Conley to Benjamin Conley, June 28, 1874, in Conley MS Collection.
12. Atlanta *Constitution*, October 8, 17, 1874. Edward Barham, "The Negro in Georgia Politics, 1867-1877," unpublished thesis, Emory University, 1955, p. 116, gives slightly different figures.
13. Atlanta *Constitution*, October 10, 9, 1874.
14. *Ibid*., October 3, November 10, December 24, 1874.
15. *Ibid*., November 10, December 24, 1874.
16. *Ibid*., January 8, 11, April 11, 1876.
17. September 12, 1872.

18. Atlanta *Constitution*, May 4, 5, 1876.
19. Avery, *History of Georgia, passim;* Thompson, *Reconstruction in Georgia*, 264-66 and *passim;* various public documents in the DeRenne Collection at the University of Georgia; contemporary newspapers; numerous items in the Farrow Collection. A six-page leaflet in the Farrow Collection, dated April 26, 1877, contains communications to President Hayes regarding "the character and antecedents of John E. Bryant." This includes a letter from General Tillson corroborating charges against Bryant and denouncing him in vehement terms.
20. John E. Bryant to Henry P. Farrow, July 26, 1876, in the Farrow Collection.
21. Macon *Georgia Weekly Telegraph and Georgia Journal and Messenger*, August 22, 1876; Atlanta *Constitution*, August 17, 1876.
22. Among the best sources of material about Norcross are his obituary in the Atlanta *Constitution*, December 19, 1898, and the various histories of the city of Atlanta, especially Thomas H. Martin, *Atlanta and Its Builders* (Atlanta, 1902) and Wallace P. Reed, *History of Atlanta, Georgia* (Syracuse, N.Y., 1889). His career is dealt with in some detail by these books, especially incidents relating to his mayoralty and his business acumen. It is significant that the various accounts hardly mention his participation in Republican politics. A copy of his *Democracy Examined* is in the DeRenne Collection, University of Georgia.
23. Avery, *History of Georgia*, 519.
24. Atlanta *Constitution*, August 23, 1876.
25. September 19, 1876.
26. September 21, 26, October 4, 1876.
27. September 19, 1876.
28. Atlanta *Constitution*, October 4, May 5, April 8, August 23, 1876.
29. Avery, *History of Georgia*, 519.

CHAPTER V

1. An excellent account of the Independent Movement in the Seventh District is found in John E. Talmadge, *Rebecca Latimer Felton, Nine Stormy Decades* (Athens, 1960).
2. Quoted in C. Vann Woodward, *Origins of the New South, 1877-1913* (Baton Rouge, 1951), 77. Woodward's chapter, "Procrustean Bedfellows," explores the question of Independentism in the South.
3. Judson C. Ward, Jr., "The Republican Party in Bourbon Georgia, 1872-1890," *Journal of Southern History*, IX (May, 1943), 198; Atlanta *Constitution*, October 13, 1874.
4. *Ibid.*, 32-41.
5. Samuel E. Crawford to W. H. Felton, September 18, 1874, R. L. Felton to Samuel Bard, September 19, 1874, Samuel Bard to R. L. Felton, September 21, 1874, in Dr. William Harrell Felton—Mrs. Rebecca Latimer Felton MS Collection, University of Georgia.
6. Atlanta *Constitution*, November 1, 1874.
7. *Ibid.*, November 7, 1874.
8. B. H. Hill to W. H. Felton, September 20, 1876, in the Felton Collection, one of the numerous letters from Hill to Felton in the collection.
9. George C. Gorham to W. H. Felton, February 19, 1879, in the Felton Collection.
10. Two months after the election Long wrote to Felton asking for a balance of twenty dollars that had not been paid to him. J. F. Long to W. H. Felton, January 2, 1879, in the Felton Collection. Felton arranged for the payment of the money but requested and received a statement from Long that the original arrangement had been made without Felton's knowledge.
11. James Longstreet to R. L. Felton, May 6, 1879, in the Felton Collection.

- *Notes*

12. Hargrove declined to accept the terms and later reported the incident to Felton. Z. B. Hargrove to W. H. Felton, May 19, 1880, in the Felton Collection.
13. Ward, "The Republican Party in Bourbon Georgia," *loc.cit.*, 199.
14. A good analysis of the alleged deterioration of the Republican party in the Seventh District after the beginning of cooperation with the Independents is found in a letter from C. D. Forsyth to Henry P. Farrow, June 26, 1882, in the Farrow Collection.
15. I. R. Gibbons to W. H. Felton, November 3, 1880, Z. B. Hargrove to W. H. Felton, November 4, 25, 1880, in the Felton Collection.
16. J. R. Wikle to R. L. Felton, December 22, 1879, in the Felton Collection.
17. Donald Bridgeman Sanger and Thomas Robson Hay, *James Longstreet: I. Soldier; II. Politician, Officeholder and Writer* (Baton Rouge, 1952), *passim*.
18. James Longstreet to Senator W. P. Kellogg, December 26, 1878, quoted *ibid.*, 383-84.
19. James Longstreet to W. H. Felton, December 3, 1881, in the Felton Collection.
20. James Longstreet to O. P. Fitzsimmons, December 17, 1881, James Longstreet to W. H. Felton, December 22, 25, 1881, in the Felton Collection.
21. H. P. Farrow to W. H. Felton, December 28, 1881, in the Felton Collection.
22. James Longstreet to Henry P. Farrow, December 29, 1881, in the Farrow Collection.
23. The story of the conference has been pieced together from the Chicago *Tribune* story, with later remarks by the *Tribune* correspondent as reported in the *Constitution*, January 3, 1882; R. L. Felton, *Memoirs*, 335, 339-41; W. H. Felton, a speech delivered in Cartersville, July 29, 1882, and published in the Atlanta *Sunday Herald*, July 30, 1882.
24. The *Tribune* interview had been reprinted in the *Constitution* for December 31, 1881, and appeared, also, in other newspapers in the state. The document issued by the committee of seven is given in full in R. L. Felton, *Memoirs*, 339-41. Good accounts of this and related events are found in Lewis Paul Rowan, "The Rise and Development of the Republican Party in Georgia," unpublished thesis, Emory University, 1948; and Ward, "The Republican Party in Bourbon Georgia," *loc. cit.*, 196-209.
25. Atlanta *Constitution*, January 3, 1882.
26. *Ibid.*, January 6, 1882.
27. *National Republican*, undated and otherwise unidentified clipping in the Felton Collection, Scrapbook No. 18.
28. Atlanta *Constitution*, January 7, 1882. The interview was dated January 2. It seems probable that Hill did not know about the Markham House conference at the time, as it was not reported in the *Constitution* until January 3. A personal letter from Hill to Felton dated January 3, 1882, in the Felton Collection, protests the *Tribune* interview but does not mention the coalition conference. Hill wrote, "I do not see how it leaves you anything but a republican, and a stalwart republican at that."
29. James Longstreet to W. H. Felton, January 23, 1882, and an undated letter from Longstreet which appears to have been written January 30, 1882, in the Felton Collection. The attitude of the national Republican party toward the South and the attempts of the various presidents to build up the party in the Southern states are dealt with in more detail below, in Chapter X.
30. Henry P. Farrow to W. H. Felton, May 8, 1882, in the Felton Collection.
31. Henry P. Farrow to James Longstreet, April 20, 1882, Letter-book 3; James Longstreet to Henry P. Farrow, May 2, 9, 1882, in the Farrow Collection.

32. Atlanta *Constitution*, May 16, 1882. The excuse of the smallpox scare had been suggested by Longstreet in a letter to Felton, May 12, 1882, in the Felton Collection. It was ridiculed by the paper as a "flimsy pretext."
33. W. H. Felton to Henry P. Farrow, May 4, 9, 1882, in the Farrow Collection.
34. W. H. Felton to Henry P. Farrow, May 25, 1882, in the Farrow Collection.
35. R. L. Felton to Henry P. Farrow, March 4, 1882, in the Farrow Collection.
36. W. P. Wright to W. H. Felton, February 22, 1882, in the Felton Collection; W. H. Felton to Henry P. Farrow, May 25, 1882, in the Farrow Collection.
37. Atlanta *Constitution*, August 4, 1882.
38. *Ibid.*, September 29, October 5, 1882.
39. C. Vann Woodward, *Origins of the New South*, 105.
40. Atlanta *Constitution*, October 3, 1882.
41. Typical examples are found *ibid.*, August 5, September 1, October 1, 2, 1882.
42. *Ibid.*, November 5, 1878. The *Constitution*, always the mouthpiece of the Democratic organization, had opposed Speer's Independent candidacy as a matter of principle, but after the election it published on its front page a two-column laudatory sketch of the new congressman, signed "H.W.G."
43. September 19, 1882. Madison Davis had served in the General Assembly representing Clarke County, 1868-1872, and was one of two Negroes not expelled from that body in 1868. He had been active in the Republican party continuously and was generally well thought of in Athens except for his political connections.
44. Athens *Banner-Watchman*, October 3, 1882.
45. *Ibid.*, October 3, 10, September 26, 1882.

CHAPTER VI

1. A well-documented discussion of this question is found in William Herman Miller, "Congressional Reconstruction as a Means of Perpetuating Radical Republicanism," unpublished thesis, Emory University, 1934.
2. Atlanta *Constitution*, October 7, 1874, May 5, 1876. Typical examples of the semi-humorous handling of Republican party news are seen *ibid.*, April 8, 22, August 8, 22, 1876.
3. *Southern Watchman*, October 12, 1870; Atlanta *Constitution*, May 4, 1876.
4. *Ibid.*, April 11, 1880. H. M. Turner, well known and respected later as a bishop in the African Methodist Church, had led one of the first movements of protest. He had organized a colored convention in Macon after the expulsion of the Negro members of the legislature in 1868, and had gone to Washington to urge a third reconstruction of Georgia.
5. Athens *Georgian*, November 7, 1876; Atlanta *Constitution*, April 24, 1880. This issue of the Atlanta paper contained sketches of several other Negroes at the convention.
6. *Ibid.*, April 30, 1880; Atlanta *Republican*, May 15, 1880.
7. Atlanta *Constitution*, July 6, 7, 1880. The account of the meeting is headed: "Uncle Jonathan Blows His Shrill Bugle Horn."
8. *Ibid.*, August 3, 1882.
9. July 28, August 1, 2, 1882.
10. Atlanta *National* (extra edition), August 2, 1882, in the Farrow Collection; Atlanta *Constitution*, August 3, 1882. After the convention, Pledger and Brown were tried in police court and both cases were dismissed. *Ibid.*, August 5, 1882.
11. This statement, dated August 22, 1882, and designed to establish the

• *Notes*   185

claims of the faction to be the duly constituted Republican party of Georgia, is found in galley-proof form in the Farrow Collection. In the collection also are copies of the handbill announcing the new time and place of the meeting.

12. Atlanta *Constitution*, August 3, 4, 1882; galley-proof statement, August 22, 1882, in the Farrow Collection.
13. Atlanta *Constitution*, August 4, 5, 1882.
14. *Ibid.*, September 1, 6, 1882; letters in the correspondence folders for August and September, 1882, in the Farrow Collection.
15. Atlanta *Constitution*, October 5, 1882. The result of the election has been described more fully above, in Chapter V.
16. *Ibid.*, November 8, 1882.
17. *Biographical Directory of the American Congress*, 619; Atlanta *Constitution*, August 29, 1882, December 5, 1902; *City of Atlanta, World's Fair Series on Great American Cities* (Louisville, 1892-93), 84-85.
18. August 4, 1882.
19. Henry P. Farrow to Chester A. Arthur, March 12, 1883, in the Farrow Collection.
20. January 12, 1884, a clipping in Scrapbook 4, 1883-1884, in the Farrow Collection.
21. Atlanta *Constitution*, April 2, 3, 9, 10, 11, 1884. The call to the convention, a circular dated April 12, 1884, in the Farrow Collection, includes the names of other members of the executive committee.
22. Atlanta *Constitution*, May 1, 2, 3, 1884.
23. Amanda Johnson, *Georgia as Colony and State* (Atlanta, 1938), 613.
24. May 2, 3, 1884. Apparently Norcross made his peace with the regular party organization, as his name heads the list of electors chosen by the state central committee in August. These electors were all white men, and their appointment was probably designed to counteract the influence of the white Republican movement. Atlanta *Constitution*, August 10, 1884.

CHAPTER VII

1. James S. Atkins to Henry P. Farrow, October 29, 1881, in the Farrow Collection.
2. Henry P. Farrow, to "My dear friend," dated December 8, 1881, in the Farrow Collection. A note in Farrow's handwriting states that it is a copy of a letter sent to several friends in November and December. The names of recipients are not included.
3. "The Georgia Cabal," a clipping from the Washington *Post*, enclosed in a letter from James Atkins to Henry P. Farrow, May 17, 1882, and Alexander N. Wilson to Henry P. Farrow, May 17, 1882, in the Farrow Collection; James Atkins, Henry P. Farrow, W. H. Johnson, C. W. Arnold, A. N. Wilson to W. H. Felton, February 10, 1882, in the Felton Collection.
4. James Atkins to Henry P. Farrow, October 29, December 29, 1881, in the Farrow Collection.
5. James Longstreet to W. H. Felton, December 3, 1881, in the Felton Collection.
6. Henry P. Farrow to W. H. Felton, December 28, 1881, in the Felton Collection.
7. James Longstreet to W. H. Felton, January 23, 1882, and James Atkins to W. H. Felton, January 26, 1882, in the Felton Collection.
8. James Atkins to Henry P. Farrow, January 16, 1882, in the Farrow Collection.
9. James Atkins *et al.* to W. H. Felton, February 10, 1882, in the Felton Collection.
10. James Atkins to Henry P. Farrow, April 12, 1882, in the Farrow Collection.
11. W. H. Felton to Henry P. Farrow, June 17, 1882, in the Farrow Collection.
12. W. A. Pledger to Henry P. Farrow, March 28, 1882, James Atkins to Henry P. Farrow, March 12, 14, 24,

1882, and Emory Speer to Henry P. Farrow, March 21, 28, 1882, in the Farrow Collection.
13. James Atkins to Henry P. Farrow, March 14, 1882.
14. James Atkins to Henry P. Farrow, August 29, 1882.
15. James Atkins to Henry P. Farrow, July 28, 1882, in the Farrow Collection.
16. James Atkins to Henry P. Farrow, August 11, 1882, in the Farrow Collection.
17. James Atkins to John Sherman, March 8, 1887, in the John Sherman Papers, Library of Congress, Washington, D.C.
18. Emory Speer to Henry P. Farrow, December 8, 1881, in the Farrow Collection.
19. Examples are Emory Speer to Henry P. Farrow, March 28, April 24, May 13, 1882, in the Farrow Collection.
20. Henry P. Farrow to A. E. Buck, January 15, 1883, in the Farrow Collection.
21. Alexander N. Wilson to Henry P. Farrow, February 21, 23, 1883, in the Farrow Collection. Letters from Wilson to Farrow at this time suggest an almost daily exchange of communications between the two.
22. A. E. Buck to Henry P. Farrow, February 25, 1883, in the Farrow Collection.
23. Emory Speer to Henry P. Farrow, March 21, 1882, in the Farrow Collection.
24. Alexander N. Wilson to Henry P. Farrow, February 21, 23, 28, 8, 1883, in the Farrow Collection.
25. Henry P. Farrow to Ulysses S. Grant, February 3, 1883, in the Farrow Collection.
26. A. E. Buck to Henry P. Farrow, February 25, 1883, in the Farrow Collection.
27. A. E. Buck to Henry P. Farrow, December 25, 1884, in the Farrow Collection.
28. Henry P. Farrow to Chester A. Arthur, March 12, 1883, in the Farrow Collection.
29. Atlanta *Constitution*, December 20, 21, 1883. Clippings and reprints of clippings on Erskine's retirement and Farrow's campaign for appointment are plentiful in the Farrow Collection, in Scrapbook 3, 1883-1884, and in the folders of broadsides. The correspondence folders for 1883 and 1884 are filled with letters of endorsement, resolutions, and other correspondence regarding the appointment.
30. A. E. Buck *et al.* to Chester P. Arthur, December 1, 1884, and A. E. Buck to Chester A. Arthur, December 13, 1884, in the Farrow Collection.
31. J. E. Bryant to Henry P. Farrow, December 15, 16, 17, 22, 1884, and James Atkins to Henry P. Farrow, December 16, 17, 18, 1884, in the Farrow Collection.
32. James Atkins to Henry P. Farrow, January 5, [1885], in the Farrow Collection. (This letter is dated "1884," obviously an error.) Atkins had already suggested that Arthur might appoint Speer, in a letter dated December 18, 1884.
33. Emory Speer to Chester A. Arthur, December 3, 1884, in the Farrow Collection.
34. Atlanta *Constitution*, January 17, 18, 1885. In the Farrow Collection, all mention of the campaign for the judgeship ceases abruptly after the first few days in January.
35. *Ibid.*, January 20, 21, 23, 1885.
36. *Ibid.*, January 27, February 11, 17, 19, 1885.

CHAPTER VIII

1. This study touches lightly upon the Populist movement itself, being concerned primarily with its effect upon the Republican party in Georgia. A standard work on Populism in the United States is John D. Hicks, *The Populist Revolt* (Minneapolis, 1931), while the best study of the movement in Georgia is A. M. Arnett, *The Populist Movement in*

- *Notes*

Georgia (New York, 1922). A good brief discussion is found in John D. Hicks, *The American Nation*, 2nd ed. (Boston, 1949), Chapter XI, "The Populist Revolt," 245-59.
2. Atlanta *Constitution*, October 4, 1888.
3. Albert B. Saye, *A Constitutional History of Georgia* (Athens, 1948), 324-26.
4. *Ibid.*, 328-29.
5. Atlanta *Constitution*, November 4, 5, October 2, 3, 1890.
6. In 1888 the Republican state central committee had urged party members to support Independent candidates for the legislature who advocated such measures as liberal appropriations for public schools, repeal of the chaingang system, and temperance legislation. *Ibid.*, September 5, 1888.
7. Alexander Heard, *A Two Party South?* (Chapel Hill, 1952), 48.
8. V. O. Key, Jr., *Southern Politics in State and Nation* (New York, 1950), 284.
9. Atlanta *Constitution*, July 15, 1892.
10. *Ibid.*, August 11, 12, 1892.
11. Arnett, *Populist Movement*, 1953.
12. *Ibid.;* Atlanta *Constitution*, July 18, 1890.
13. C. Vann Woodward, *Origins of the New South* (Baton Rouge, 1951), 192, 256, n. 63.
14. *Ibid.*, 257. The Watson article, "The Negro Question in the South," was published originally in *Arena*, VI (1892), 541-48.
15. Atlanta *Constitution*, September 23, 1892.
16. *Ibid.*, September 29, 27, 1892.
17. *Ibid.*, October 1, 1892.
18. September 30, October 1, 1892.
19. October 4, 1892.
20. Quoted in Atlanta *Constitution*, October 2, 1892.
21. Atlanta *Constitution*, October 1, 1892.
22. *Ibid.*, October 7, 1892. Some writers, including Arnett, *Populist Movement*, 153, and Hicks, *Populist Revolt*, 246, state that Peek's name was placed on the Republican ticket as gubernatorial candidate although separate nominations were made for other state officers. Nothing has been found in contemporary sources to substantiate this and it seems highly improbable in light of the developments described above. No Republican nominations were made for other state offices unless reference is made to candidates for the legislature from the various counties. Some Republicans did run for the General Assembly and four were elected. Atlanta *Constitution*, October 7, 1892.
23. *Ibid.*, October 1, 7, 9, 1892. Hicks says that the Republicans apparently favored fusion but that the Populists, fearing the loss of caste that such action on their part would entail, were unwilling to go the full length. *Populist Revolt*, 251. Sion Darnell's diagnosis of the situation was probably accurate. The Populists, like the Independents before them, wanted Republican votes but most of them did not want to associate with or to *be* associated with the Republicans, especially the colored Republicans.
24. Atlanta *Constitution*, October 13, 1892.
25. Arnett, *Populist Movement*, 182-84.
26. Atlanta *Constitution*, August 29, 30, 1894.
27. The Atlanta *Constitution*, which was not always kind in its appraisal of Republican leaders, characterized Walter Johnson as "a man of remarkable popularity and one whose name is regarded among democrats or republicans as being synonymous with integrity and honesty." August 29, 1894.
28. *Ibid.*, August 30, 1894.
29. *Ibid.*
30. *Ibid.*, October 5, 1892.
31. Hicks, *Populist Revolt*, 330, 333.
32. An excellent account of the elections of 1894 is found in B. O. Quillian, "The Populist Challenge in Georgia in the Year 1894," unpublished thesis, University of Georgia, 1948.
33. From supposedly "official" returns as given in the Atlanta *Journal*,

October 6, 1894. The Atlanta *Constitution*, October 7, 1894, in a so-called "complete" list, says forty-seven Populists, while Arnett, *Populist Movement*, 184, reports a total of fifty-two.
34. Atlanta *Constitution*, August 6, 10, 1896.
35. *Ibid.*, August 10, 18, 1896.
36. *Ibid.*, August 16, 1896.
37. *Ibid.*, August 17, 19, 1896.
38. August 16, 1896.
39. August 17, 1896.
40. *Ibid.*, August 19, October 3, 1896.
41. *Ibid.*, October 1, 2, 1896.
42. *Ibid.*, October 2, 3, 1896. Pledger failed to mention that he himself had led the opposition to the nomination of a gubernatorial candidate in 1876, when he was a strong supporter of Alfred Colquitt. In 1892 he had campaigned for Northen and in 1896 was urging the re-election of Atkinson.
43. *Ibid.*, October 8, 18, 30, 1896.
44. *Ibid.*, October 14, 23, November 4, 1896.
45. Saye, *Constitutional History*, 329-30.
46. A letter addressed to Mark H. Blandford and B. A. Thornton, published in the Atlanta *Constitution*, May 15, 1892.
47. Hicks, *Populist Revolt*, 335-36, 377-93, *passim*. Hicks states (p. 378) that two Democrats were elected to Congress in 1896, but the *Biographical Directory of Congress* lists only one Democrat from North Carolina as serving in the Fifty-fifth Congress. One seat was contested and the Populist candidate was seated by Congress.
48. The *Constitution* sent a staff correspondent to North Carolina in August, 1898, to look over the situation and to prepare a series of feature stories for the paper. A two-page story and an editorial on August 29 presented a picture of corruption and incompetence in the government of the neighboring state and warned of threats to the safety of white women in the black-belt counties. Similar stories on September 4 and September 25, each covering almost a full page, were examples of the campaign waged by the Democrats of Georgia on the basis of the example of North Carolina.
49. Hicks, *Populist Revolt*, 393.
50. Augusta *Chronicle*, October 31, 1896, quoted in C. Vann Woodward, *Tom Watson, Agrarian Rebel* (New York, 1938), 326.

CHAPTER IX

1. August 19, 21, 1888. There is nothing in the newspaper stories to indicate that the Republican party in Georgia had anything to do with McKinley's coming, but a letter written by A. E. Buck, state chairman, about two weeks before, refers to the fact that he (Buck) had started the movement to get McKinley." A. E. Buck to D. A. Alexander, August 5, 1888, V. 37, Benjamin Harrison Papers, Library of Congress, Washington, D. C. The *Constitution*, March 12, 1895, stated that Henry W. Grady issued the invitation to McKinley.
2. William S. Myers, *The Republican Party, A History* (New York, 1928), 327 ff.; Herbert Croly, *Marcus Alonzo Hanna, His Life and Works* (New York, 1912), 173 ff.
3. Arthur W. Dunn, *Harrison to Harding* (New York, 1922), I, 171-73.
4. Perhaps the most complete secondary account of the Thomasville phase of McKinley's campaign is Edward T. Heald, *The Stark County Story* (Canton, Ohio, 1959), IV, part 3, pp. 783-89. Margaret Leech, *In the Days of McKinley* (New York, 1959), 62-63, tells the story briefly but with valuable documentation. Some Georgia newspapers carried a running account of McKinley's visit and apparently recognized its underlying purpose, but Northern papers usually concerned with Republican news seemed

strangely unaware of what was going on. The New York *Times* referred briefly and disparagingly to the Thomasville visit, March 20, April 2, 1895, but an examination of the New York *Tribune* for the entire month of March failed to turn up any mention of the visit. Croly, *Hanna*, writes of the Thomasville venture with keen insight, but Dunn, *Harrison to Harding*, and Myers, *The Republican Party*, make no reference to this part of the McKinley campaign. There are a few pertinent letters in McKinley's Letter Press Copy Book, Vol. 87, William McKinley Papers, Series 2, Library of Congress, Washington, D.C.
5. Atlanta *Constitution*, March 12, 13, 1896.
6. William McKinley to A. E. Buck, February 1, 1895, Letter Book V. 87, McKinley Papers.
7. Thomasville *Times-Enterprise*, March 16, 23, 1895, quoted in Heald, *Stark County Story*, IV, part 3, pp. 783-87.
8. Savannah *Morning News*, March 21, 22, 23, 1895; Croly, *Hanna*, 175-76.
9. Savannah *Morning News*, March 30, 31, 1895.
10. *Ibid.*, March 25, 1895.
11. *Ibid.*, March 28, 29, 1895.
12. *Ibid.*, March 14, 1895.
13. A. E. Buck to D. A. Alexander, August 5, 1888, Vol. 37, Benjamin Harrison Papers.
14. A. E. Buck to Benjamin Harrison, August 28, 1889, Vol. 85, Benjamin Harrison Papers. Buck blamed Grady's defection on his ambition for public office, which had made him take advantage of race prejudice to appeal to the passions of white Democrats.
15. D. W. W. Bowes to John Sherman, February 9, 20, 1888, Vols. 428 and 430, The Papers of John Sherman, 1846-1893, Library of Congress, Washington, D.C. Bowes identified himself as a Republican who had come to Atlanta from Toledo, Ohio, about a year and a half before, but he was apparently not active in the Georgia party.
16. March 16, 1895.
17. Atlanta *Constitution*, March 12, 1895; Atlanta *Journal*, March 12, 1895.
18. Atlanta *Constitution*, March 12, 1895.
19. *Ibid.* It is interesting to contrast the tone of the stories appearing in the *Constitution* and the *Journal*, March 12, 13, 1895, regarding McKinley's visit, the Republican club, and the protection league conference. The former paper, favorably disposed toward McKinley and protection, gives a dignified and factual version of the three occurrences. The *Journal*, staunch supporter of Cleveland, disparages the entire sequence of events and presents McKinley personally in a most unattractive light.
20. W. D. Kelly to W. H. Felton, December 15, 1881, in the Felton Collection. The sketch of Hanson in Northen, *Men of Mark*, VI, 378-83, emphasizes his prominence. After 1895 he was known especially for his work in developing the state's railroads.
21. William McKinley to J. F. Hanson, February 27, 1895, Letter Book V. 87, McKinley Papers; Atlanta *Constitution*, March 13, 1896.
22. Atlanta *Journal*, January 6, 1896.
23. Savannah *Morning News*, December 29, 1895; Atlanta *Constitution*, December 31, 1895.
24. Savannah *Morning News*, March 6, 8, 14, April 28, 1896.
25. William McKinley to J. W. Cullers, September 24, 1895, Letter Book V. 87, McKinley Papers.
26. William McKinley to E. K. Love, March 11, 1896, Letter Book V. 87, McKinley Papers.
27. William McKinley to A. E. Buck, January 8, 1896, and William McKinley to Walter H. Johnson, January 8, 1896, Letter Book V. 87, McKinley Papers.
28. Atlanta *Constitution*, April 9, 1, 2, 3, 7, 8, 1896.
29. *Ibid.*, April 28, 1896.
30. *Ibid.;* Savannah *Morning News*,

April 28, 1896. Both Deveaux and Wright had been among those who had conferred with McKinley during his visit to Georgia in March, 1895. Both men were active in arranging the meeting with the Negroes in Savannah. *Ibid.*, March 23, 31, 1895. Deveaux was editor of the Savannah *Tribune*, and Wright was president of the Georgia State Industrial College in Savannah.
31. Atlanta *Constitution*, April 28, 29, 30, 1896. As there were contesting delegations in three districts, the exact racial make-up was not yet settled, but of the twenty-eight claimants for the twenty-two district places eighteen were colored and ten white.
32. *Ibid.*, April 28, 29, 1896; Savannah *Morning News*, April 28, 29, 1896.
33. Letters from McKinley to Buck and Wright indicate that the latter had been offered a place on the delegation several months before the convention and was debating its acceptance. William McKinley to R. R. Wright, January 4, 1896, and William McKinley to A. E. Buck, January 4, 1896, Letter Book V. 87, McKinley Papers. Wright was one of the outstanding men of his race in Georgia and was one of the first graduates of Atlanta University. Many of the colored leaders were mulattoes but Wright was a full-blooded Negro. At the time of the state convention in 1880, he was characterized by the Atlanta *Constitution* as "the most cultured colored man in the convention," April 24, 1880.
34. William McKinley to A. E. Buck, May 20, 1896, Letter Book V. 87, McKinley Papers. Atlanta *Constitution*, April 30, May 1, 2, 4, 1896; Savannah *Morning News*, April 30, May 1, 1896; Macon *Telegraph*, April 30, 1896; Augusta *Chronicle*, April 30, 1896.
35. May 1, 1896.
36. Atlanta *Constitution*, June 12, 19, 1896.
37. *Ibid.*, July 26, 1896. Longstreet had dropped out of active participation in party politics after his removal as marshal in 1884 but his name was evidently still considered as influential. Eighteen members of the Love-Wright faction were on the committee and they participated in the meeting, although neither Love nor Wright was a member and neither was in Macon.
38. *Ibid.*, October 3, 1896. This was not the first time that an all-white slate of electors had been chosen, but ordinarily some Negroes were included as a matter of policy.
39. *Ibid.*, August 15, 1896. (The story of Republican politics on the state level in 1896 is told above, in Chapter VIII.)
40. *Ibid.*, August 6, 1896.
41. *Ibid.*, October 9, 10, 1896.
42. Stanwood, *History of the Presidency*, 567, gives these figures: McKinley 60,091; Bryan, 94,672; Others, 8,864. The comparative figures may not present an accurate picture of Republican strength, however, as many Populists, disappointed at the failure to effect a fusion ticket with the Democrats, either refrained from voting or voted for McKinley as a protest.
43. Atlanta *Constitution*, November 5, 1896.

CHAPTER X

1. Vincent P. DeSantis, *Republicans Face the Southern Question—The New Departure Years, 1877-1897* (Baltimore, 1959) elaborates this thesis. To clear up misconceptions regarding the relationship of the national Republican party and the South, the author makes extensive use of papers of the Republican presidents of the period and of other party leaders, as well as contemporary newspapers and periodicals. For the most part, political developments in Georgia seem to bear out

- *Notes*

DeSantis's contentions, although the book includes a number of errors regarding the situation in Georgia.
2. In spite of this, Grant polled a larger total in Georgia in 1872 than in 1868. This was due not so much to Republican strength as to the combination of circumstances described above, in Chapter III.
3. Jack B. Scroggs, "Southern Reconstruction: A Radical View," *Journal of Southern History*, XXIV (November, 1958), 407-29, includes a discussion of the situation in Georgia, documented by letters from Georgia Republicans to heads of the national party.
4. Charles R. Williams, *Rutherford Birchard Hayes* (Columbus, Ohio, 1914), I, 462, 464-65, II, 7-8; Charles R. Williams, ed., *Diary and Letters of Rutherford Birchard Hayes* (Columbus, Ohio, 1924), III, 421, 429.
5. C. Vann Woodward, *Reunion and Reaction, The Compromise of 1877 and the End of Reconstruction* (Boston, 1951), 11-12, 35; Malcolm Moos, *The Republicans, A History of Their Party* (New York, 1956), 154.
6. DeSantis, *Republicans Face the Southern Question*, 66-67; Woodward, *Reunion and Reaction*, 11-12 and *passim*. Woodward presents the Hayes strategy as part of the Compromise of 1877. DeSantis cites many sources to emphasize Hayes's deep personal conviction in the matter, quite aside from any consideration of expediency.
7. Albert V. House, Jr., "President Hayes' Selection of David M. Key for Postmaster General," *The Journal of Southern History*, IV (February, 1938), 91.
8. Interview with John M. Carson, New York *Times*, March 12, 1877, quoted *ibid.*, 90.
9. Many letters in the Felton Collection pertain to appointments made during the Hayes administration. Dr. Felton was often consulted even in the appointment of Republicans, although in Congress he was always classed as a Democrat. D. M. Key to W. H. Felton, December 13, 1879, and other letters in the Felton Collection.
10. Cincinnati *Commercial*, quoted in Atlanta *Constitution*, September 27, 1877.
11. New York *Tribune*, quoted in Williams, *Life of Hayes*, II, 253.
12. Atlanta *Constitution*, September 27, 1877. Hayes's Southern tour, including his Atlanta speech, is reported in Williams, *Life of Hayes*, II, 248-54.
13. *Proceedings of the Republican National Convention Held at Cincinnati, Ohio, Wednesday, Thursday, and Friday, June 14, 15, and 16, 1876* (Concord, N.H., 1876), 84-108.
14. Edwin Belcher to John Sherman, October 7, 1879, in the John Sherman Papers, Library of Congress, Washington, D.C. Belcher was one of the two colored men not expelled from the Georgia legislature in 1868, when most of the Negroes were excluded from that body.
15. Edwin Belcher to John Sherman, June 29, 1880, in the John Sherman Papers.
16. W. L. Clark to John Sherman, June 23, 1880, in the John Sherman Papers. The Sherman Papers for this period include a number of letters from Georgia Republicans regarding patronage, some protesting the appointment of Democrats and "alleged" Republicans.
17. Atlanta *Constitution*, August 4, 1882. For a while Bryant edited the Georgia *Republican*, in competition with Clark's Atlanta *Republican*.
18. DeSantis, *Republicans Face the Southern Question*, 99-100.
19. *Ibid.*, 94-97.
20. Theodore C. Smith, *The Life and Letters of James Abram Garfield* (New Haven, 1925), II, 1066; George F. Howe, *Chester A. Arthur, A Quarter-Century of Machine Politics* (New York, 1934), 135-37.
21. Smith, *Life and Letters of Garfield*, II, 1065-66, 1116-17.

22. Howe, *Chester Arthur*, 215-16; DeSantis, *Republicans Face the Southern Question*, 152ff.
23. James Longstreet to W. H. Felton, December 22, 1881, in the Felton Collection.
24. James Longstreet to W.H. Felton, January 23, 1882, in the Felton Collection.
25. James Atkins to W. H. Felton, January 26, 1882, in the Felton Collection.
26. James Atkins to Henry P. Farrow, January 16, 1882, in the Farrow Collection.
27. James Longstreet to Chester Arthur, May 1, 1882, in the Chester A. Arthur Papers, Library of Congress, Washington, D.C.
28. Emory Speer to Henry P. Farrow, May 13, 1882, in the Farrow Collection.
29. B. H. Hill to W. H. Felton, January 3, 1882, in the Felton Collection. This letter was written the day before Hill's famous interview with Henry Grady in which he charged that the Republican party was making its second attempt to Africanize the South, a charge made also in the letter quoted above.
30. A. H. Stephens to W. H. Felton, January 10, 1882, in the Felton Collection.
31. May 2, July 25, 26, 1882.
32. Vincent P. DeSantis, "Negro Dissatisfaction with Republican Policy in the South, 1882-1884," *Journal of Negro History*, XXXVI (April, 1951), 148-59; DeSantis, *Republicans Face the Southern Question*, 172-73.
33. *Ibid.*, 178-80
34. Stanwood, *History of the Presidency*, 483. Harrison's total popular vote throughout the nation was smaller than that of Grover Cleveland, his defeated rival.
35. Benjamin Harrison, "The South, and Suppression of the Republican Vote," from a speech delivered in Detroit, February 22, 1888, quoted in Lew Wallace, *Life of Gen. Ben Harrison* (Indianapolis, 1888), 307-308; Paul H. Buck, *The Road to Reunion, 1865-1900* (Boston, 1937), 278-81.
36. March 17, 19, July 4, 1890.
37. DeSantis, *Republicans Face the Southern Question*, 228-30.
38. Atlanta *Constitution*, September 23, 24, 1892.
39. *Ibid.*, October 19, 1892. Fifteen Populists were elected to the legislature but only three Republicans, two of them colored.
40. *Ibid.*, October 10, 1892.
41. *Ibid.*
42. DeSantis, *Republicans Face the Southern Question*, 191, 261-62.

CHAPTER XI

1. Lynwood M. Holland, *The Direct Primary in Georgia* (Urbana, Illinois, 1949), 17-25, 35. This book is the most complete source available regarding the growth of the primary system in Georgia. Much of the same material is included in John M. Graybeal, "The Georgia Primary Election System," unpublished thesis, Emory University, 1932.
2. Holland, *The Direct Primary*, 49-54.
3. *Ibid.*, 28, 31.
4. The Democratic white primary was probably the most effective single device developed in the Southern states to control Negro voting. It was finally outlawed by the Supreme Court in *Smith v. Allwright*, 321 U.S. 649 (1944).
5. Quoted in Athens *Georgian*, September 12, 1876.
6. Athens *Weekly Banner-Watchman*, July 3, 1888. At the general election in Clarke County in 1888, William A. Pledger, Negro Republican leader, was a candidate for the legislature. His candidacy was hardly mentioned in the Athens paper except for a humorous account of his defeat by the Democratic candidate, *ibid.*, October 9, 1888. The

• *Notes* 193

publicity ordinarily given to the general election had been given to the Democratic primary and the campaign which preceded it.
7. Atlanta *Constitution,* October 18, 1892. Among those signing the petition was C. C. Wimbish, a leading Negro Republican of Fulton County. Wimbish was a delegate to the Republican national convention in 1888 and again in 1896 and 1900, served as chairman of the Fifth District Republican committee, and had been appointed to federal office as a Republican. His signature on the petition to allow Negroes to vote in the Democratic primary seems somewhat incongruous.
8. Holland, *The Direct Primary,* 50, 54.
9. May 15, 1900.
10. May 3, 1900.
11. Savannah *Morning News,* January 19, 1872.
12. "Studies in the South," *Atlantic Monthly,* L (July, 1882), 109. These articles regarding conditions in the South appeared in eleven installments from January, 1882, through January, 1883. A number of them include comments on the political situation. The name of the author is not given.
13. Statement of Benjamin H. Hill in the *Ku Klux Report,* 1871, quoted in Walter L. Fleming, *Documentary History of Reconstruction* (New York, 1950), II, 91-92.
14. Theodore Roosevelt to Julian Harris, August 1, 1912, quoted in Heard, *A Two-Party South,* 223.
15. Heard, *A Two-Party South,* 221.
16. This phase of the party's history has been told in Chapter VI.
17. Atlanta *Constitution,* March 7, 8, July 6, 1900.
18. Atlanta *Constitution* March 16, 18, 1890. When Buck made a similar report to national Republican leaders regarding the "host of protectionists" who voted Democratic, he termed as "negrophobia" the influence that kept them from voting their principles. A. E. Buck to D. A. Alexander, August 5, 1888, and A. E. Buck to Benjamin Harrison, August 28, 1889, in the Benjamin Harrison Papers.
19. March 20, 1890.
20. Quoted, *ibid.,* November 3, 1895.
21. *Ibid.,* May 1, 2, 1896.
22. *Ibid.,* November 3, 1895. After Buck's departure for Tokyo, Bullock attended the state convention in 1900 and served on a committee to make recommendations regarding the advisability of putting out a state ticket. He advised against such a move.
23. Atlanta *Constitution,* March 20, 1890.

Bibliography

PRIMARY SOURCES

Newspapers

Athens *Banner*, 1880.
Athens *Banner-Watchman*, 1882.
Athens *Georgian*, 1876, 1877.
Athens *North-East Georgian*, 1872.
Athens *Southern Banner*, 1869-1872.
Athens *Southern Watchman*, 1868-1873.
Athens *Weekly Banner-Watchman*, 1888.
Atlanta *Constitution*, 1868-1904.
Atlanta *Daily New Era*, 1867-1871.
Atlanta *Daily Opinion*, 1868.
Atlanta *Journal*, 1892, 1895, 1896, 1900.
Atlanta *Republican*, 1880.
Atlanta *Sunday Herald*, 1884.
Atlanta *Whig*, 1872.
Macon *Georgia Weekly Telegraph and Georgia Journal and Messenger*, 1871, 1872.
Macon *Telegraph*, 1896.
Milledgeville *Federal Union*, 1866-1874.
Negro Newspapers, miscellaneous collection on microfilm in Library of Congress.
New York *Times*, 1895.
New York *Tribune*, 1895.
Savannah *Morning News*, 1871, 1872, 1895, 1896.

Special Collections

Arthur, Chester A., Papers. In the Library of Congress.
Brown, Joseph Emerson and Elizabeth Grisham Brown Collection. In

• *Bibliography* 195

the Library of the University of Georgia.
Chandler, William E., The Papers of. In the Library of Congress.
Chandler, Zachariah, Papers of. In the Library of Congress.
Conley, Benjamin, Letters—Papers, 1826-1874. In the Library of the Atlanta Historical Society.
Farrow, Henry P., Collection. In the Library of the University of Georgia.
Felton, Dr. William Harrell and Mrs. Rebecca A. Latimer Felton MS Collection. In the Library of the University of Georgia.
Harrison, Benjamin, Papers. In the Library of Congress.
McKinley, William, Papers, Series 2. In the Library of Congress.
Sherman, John, The Papers of. In the Library of Congress.

General

Acts and Resolutions of the General Assembly of the State of Georgia . . . Session of 1870. Atlanta: Public Printer, 1870.
"Atlanta's Oldest Citizen," *The Atlanta Historical Bulletin No. 10*, July, 1937. Letter from Jonathan Norcross reprinted from the Atlanta *Constitution*, February 5, 1896.
Blodgett, Foster, *The Campaign Speech of Hon. Foster Blodgett on the Issues Involved in the Georgia Campaign, at Augusta, November 3, 1870*. Atlanta: *New Era* Printing Establishment, 1870.
Blodgett, Foster, *Statement of Foster Blodgett and Evidence in Reply to the Charges of Joshua Hill, Made in the United States Senate, April 10, 1871*. Washington, 1871. In the DeRenne Collection, University of Georgia.
Bryant, John E., *An Appeal to Republican Senators by Wealthy and Influential Republican Leaders of Georgia*. Washington: Gibson Brothers, Printers, 1870. In the DeRenne Collection, University of Georgia.
Bryant, John E., *Col. J. E. Bryant of Georgia and The Washington Chronicle*. Washington, 1870. In the DeRenne Collection, University of Georgia.
──────────, *A Letter to Hon. Charles Sumner of the United States Senate, Exposing the Bullock-Blodgett Ring in their Attempt to Defeat the Bingham Amendment*. Washington: Gibson Brothers, Printers, 1870. In the DeRenne Collection, University of Georgia.
──────────, *Memorial of John E. Bryant Protesting Against the Admission of Foster Blodgett to a Seat in the Senate*. 42nd Congress, 1 S, Senate Miscellaneous Document No. 30. Washington, 1871. In the DeRenne Collection, University of Georgia.
──────────, *Republicanism in the South*. Speech delivered April 2, 1879, by Chairman of Republican State Central Committee at

Organization of State Council of the Union League of America at Atlanta. Folio broadcast, in the DeRenne Collection, University of Georgia.

Caldwell, John H. and J. E. Bryant, *The Georgia Question before the Judiciary Committee of the United States Senate.* Washington: Gibson Brothers, Printers, 1870. In the DeRenne Collection, University of Georgia.

Candler, Allen D., ed., *The Confederate Records of the State of Georgia,* IV, VI. Atlanta: Charles P. Byrd, 1910, 1911. 5 vols.

Congressional Globe, 41st Congress, 1st Session, 2nd Session. Washington: Office of Congressional Globe, 1868, 1870.

Echols, Samuel A., *Georgia's General Assembly of 1878—Biographical Sketches of Senators, Representatives, the Governor and Heads of Departments.* Atlanta: James P. Harrison and Company, 1878.

Farrow, Henry Pattillo, *Letter to the Hon. Charles Devens, Attorney General of the United States,* January 26, 1880. [No place, 1880]. In the DeRenne Collection, University of Georgia.

Fleming, Walter L., *Documentary History of Reconstruction.* I, II. New York: Peter Smith, 1950. 2 vols.

Georgia Convention Sketches, Brief Biographies of the Members of the Constitutional Convention, July 11, 1877. Atlanta: The Constitution Publishing Company, 1877.

Georgia State Directory, 1876-'77. Nashville: Wheeler, Marshall & Bruce, 1876. In the DeRenne Collection, University of Georgia.

Hinsdale, Burke A., ed., *The Works of James Abram Garfield,* II. Boston: James R. Osgood & Company, 1882. 2 vols.

Journal of the House of Representatives of the State of Georgia, . . . 1868, 1869, 1870, 1871, 1872. Published contemporaneously by the State Printer.

Journal of the Senate of the State of Georgia, . . . 1868, 1869, 1870, 1871, 1872. Published contemporaneously by the State Printer.

Minutes of the Executive Department of the State of Georgia, 1870-1874. MS Book in the Georgia Department of Archives and History.

Norcross, Jonathan, *Democracy Examined: or, A Conversation Between a Republican and a Moderate Democrat.* Atlanta: James P. Harrison & Company, 1880. In the DeRenne Collection, University of Georgia.

Norwood, Thomas Manson, *Civil Rights.* Speech delivered in the United States Senate, April 30 and May 4, 1874. Washington: Government Printing Office, 1874. In the DeRenne Collection, University of Georgia.

Phillips, Ulrich Bonnell, ed., *The Correspondence of Robert Toombs, Alexander Stephens and Howell Cobb.* Vol. II of American Historical Association *Annual Report, 1911.* Washington, 1913.

• *Bibliography* 197

Proceedings of the Republican National Convention, 1868, 1872, 1876, 1880, 1884, 1888, 1892, 1896, 1900. Published contemporaneously. On microfilm in the Library of the University of Georgia.

St. Clair-Abrams, Alexander, *Manual and Biographical Register of the State of Georgia for 1871-72.* Atlanta: Plantation Publishing Company, 1872.

Thomas, E. B., *A Complete Directory of the Legislature of the State of Georgia for 1890-91.* Atlanta: C. P. Byrd, 1890.

Williams, Charles R., ed., *Diary and Letters of Rutherford Birchard Hayes,* III. Columbus, Ohio: The Ohio State Archaeological and Historical Society, 1924. 5 vols.

SECONDARY WORKS

Periodicals

Bacote, Clarence A., "Negro Proscriptions, Protests, and Proposed Solutions in Georgia, 1880-1908," *The Journal of Southern History,* XXV (November, 1959), 471-498.

Cason, Roberta F., "The Loyal League in Georgia," *The Georgia Historical Quarterly,* XX (June, 1936), 125-153.

DeSantis, Vincent P., "Negro Dissatisfaction with Republican Policy in the South, 1882-1884," *Journal of Negro History,* XXXVI (April, 1951), 148-159.

―――――, "President Garfield and the Solid South," *North Carolina Historical Review,* XXXVI (October, 1959), 442-465.

―――――, "President Hayes' Southern Policy," *The Journal of Southern History,* XXI (November, 1955), 476-494.

House, Albert V., Jr., "President Hayes' Selection of David M. Key for Postmaster General," *The Journal of Southern History,* IV (February, 1938), 87-93.

Kurtz, Annie Laurie Fuller, "Atlanta's Pioneer Merchants," *The Atlanta Journal Magazine,* September 15, 1935.

Range, Willard, "Hannibal I. Kimball," *The Georgia Historical Quarterly,* XXIX (June, 1945), 47-70.

Roberts, Lucien E., "The Political Career of Joshua Hill, Georgia Unionist," *The Georgia Historical Quarterly,* XXI (March, 1937), 50-72.

Scroggs, Jack B., "Southern Reconstruction: A Radical View," *The Journal of Southern History,* XXIV (November, 1958), 407-429.

Shadgett, Olive H., "A History of the Republican Party in Georgia," *The Georgia Review,* VII (Winter, 1953), 428-442.

―――――, "James Johnson, Provisional Governor of Georgia," *The Georgia Historical Quarterly,* XXXVI (March, 1952), 1-21.

"Studies in the South," *The Atlantic Monthly,* XLIX-LI (January,

1882-January, 1883). Published in eleven installments; no author given.

Talmadge, John E., "The Death Blow to Independentism in Georgia," *The Georgia Historical Quarterly*, XXXIX (December, 1955), 37-47.

Ward, Judson C., Jr., "The Republican Party in Bourbon Georgia, 1872-1890," *The Journal of Southern History*, IX (May, 1943), 196-209.

Woodward, C. Vann, "The Antislavery Myth," The American Scholar, XXXI (Spring, 1962), 312-320.

Unpublished Theses

Coleman, Kenneth, "The Administration of Alfred H. Colquitt as Governor of Georgia." Unpublished M.A. thesis, University of Georgia, 1940.

Cooper, Fleeta, "The Triumvirate of Colquitt, Gordon, and Brown." Unpublished M.A. thesis, Emory University, 1931.

Drake, Richard Bryant, "The American Missionary Association and the Southern Negro, 1861-1888." Unpublished Ph.D. dissertation, Emory University, 1957.

Graybeal, John M., "The Georgia Primary Election System." Unpublished M.A. thesis, Emory University, 1932.

Martin, Tommie, "Benjamin Harvey Hill in Georgia Reconstruction." Unpublished M.A. thesis, Emory University, 1928.

Meador, John Allen, Jr., "The Decline of the Two-Party System in Georgia." Unpublished M.A. thesis, Emory University, 1959.

Miller, William Herman, "Congressional Reconstruction as a Means of Perpetuating Radical Republicanism." Unpublished M.A. thesis, Emory University, 1934.

Quillian, Bascom Osborne, Jr., "The Populist Challenge in Georgia in the Year 1894." Unpublished M.A. thesis, University of Georgia, 1948.

Rice, Jessie Pearl, "Governor Rufus B. Bullock and Reconstruction in Georgia, 1867-1871." Unpublished M.A. thesis, Emory University, 1931.

Roberts, Derrell Clayton, "Joseph E. Brown and the New South." Unpublished Ph.D. dissertation, University of Georgia, 1958.

Rowan, Lewis Paul, "The Rise and Development of the Republican Party in Georgia." Unpublished M.A. thesis, Emory University, 1948.

Shadgett, Olive H., "The Public Life of Charles J. Jenkins, 1830-1865." Unpublished M.A. thesis, University of Georgia, 1952.

Towery, James Gaston, "The Georgia Gubernatorial Campaign of 1886." Unpublished M.A. thesis, Emory University, 1945.
Ward, Judson C., Jr., "Georgia under the Bourbon Democrats, 1872-1890." Unpublished Ph.D. dissertation, University of North Carolina, 1948.
Young, Edward Barham, "The Negro in Georgia Politics, 1867-1877." Unpublished M.A. thesis, Emory University, 1955.
Zuber, Richard Lee, "The Role of Rufus Brown Bullock in Georgia Politics." Unpublished M.A. thesis, Emory University, 1959.

General

Avery, Isaac W., *The History of the State of Georgia from 1850 to 1881.* New York: Brown and Derby, 1881.
Arnett, Alex Mathews, *The Populist Movement in Georgia, a View of the "Agrarian Crusade" in the Light of Solid-South Politics.* New York: Columbia University, 1922. Vol. CIV, No. 1, Studies in History, Economics and Public Law, edited by the Faculty of Political Science of Columbia University.
Barnard, Harry, *Rutherford B. Hayes and His America.* Indianapolis: Bobbs-Merrill Company, Inc., 1954.
Biographical Directory of the American Congress, 1774-1961. Washington: United States Government Printing Office, 1961.
Buck, Paul H., *The Road to Reunion, 1865-1900.* Boston: Little, Brown and Company, 1937.
Burnham, W. Dean, *Presidential Elections, 1836-1892.* Baltimore: The Johns Hopkins Press, 1955.
Candler, Allen D. and Clement A. Evans, *Cyclopedia of Georgia,* II, III. Atlanta: State Historical Association, 1906. 3 vols.
City of Atlanta, World's Fair Edition on Great American Cities. Louisville: The Inter-State Publishing Company, 1892-93.
Cook, Walter Henry, *Secret Political Societies in the South during the Period of Reconstruction.* Cleveland: Evangelical Publishing House, n.d.
Coulter, E. Merton, *A Short History of Georgia.* Chapel Hill: University of North Carolina Press, 1947.
—————————, *The South During Reconstruction.* Baton Rouge: Louisiana State University Press, 1947. Vol. VIII in the *History of the South* Series, Wendell Holmes Stephenson and E. Merton Coulter, eds.
Croly, Herbert, *Marcus Alonzo Hanna, His Life and Works.* New York: The Macmillan Company, 1912.
DeSantis, Vincent P., *Republicans Face the Southern Question—The New Departure Years, 1877-1897.* Baltimore: The Johns Hopkins Press, 1959.

Dunn, Arthur W., *Harrison to Harding,* I. New York: T. P. Putnam's Sons, 1922. 2 vols.

Eckenrode, H. J. *Rutherford B. Hayes, Statesman of Reunion.* New York: Dodd, Mead & Company, 1930.

Felton, Rebecca Latimer, *My Memoirs of Georgia Politics.* Atlanta: The Index Printing Company, 1911.

Fielder, Herbert, *A Sketch of the Life and Times and Speeches of Joseph E. Brown.* Springfield, Mass.: Press of Springfield Printing Company, 1883.

Fleming, Walter Lynwood, *The Sequel of Appomattox.* New Haven: Yale University Press, 1919. Vol. 32 of *The Chronicles of America* Series, Allen Johnson, ed.

Garrett, Franklin M., *Atlanta and Environs.* New York: Lewis Historical Publishing Company, Inc., 1954. 3 vols.

Grice, Warren, *The Georgia Bench and Bar,* I. Macon: The J. W. Burke Company, 1931. 1 vol.

Heald, Edward T., *The Stark County Story,* IV, part 3. Canton, Ohio: The Stark County Historical Society, 1959. 7 vols.

Heard, Alexander, *A Two-Party South?* Chapel Hill: The University of North Carolina Press, 1952.

Herbert, Hilary A. et al., *Why the Solid South?* Baltimore: R. H. Woodward & Company, 1890.

Hicks, John D., *The American Nation.* Boston: Houghton Mifflin Company, 1949.

————, *The Populist Revolt.* Minneapolis: The University of Minnesota Press, 1931.

Holland, Lynwood M., *The Direct Primary in Georgia.* Urbana: University of Illinois Press, 1949.

Hornady, John R., *Atlanta, Yesterday, Today, and Tomorrow.* Atlanta: American Cities Book Company, 1922.

Howe, George F., *Chester A. Arthur, A Quarter-Century of Machine Politics.* New York: Dodd, Mead & Company, 1934.

Howell, Clark, *History of Georgia,* I. Chicago: The S. J. Clarke Publishing Company, 1926. 3 vols.

Hull, Augustus Longstreet, *Annals of Athens, Georgia, 1801-1901.* Athens: Banner Job Office, 1906.

Johnson, Amanda, *Georgia as Colony and State.* Atlanta: Walter W. Brown Publishing Company, 1938.

Key, V. O., Jr., *Southern Politics in State and Nation.* New York: Alfred A. Knopf, 1950.

Knight, Lucian Lamar, *Georgia's Bi-Centennial Memoirs and Memories,* III. Published by the author for private distribution, 1932. 4 vols.

Leech, Margaret, *In the Days of McKinley.* New York: Harper & Brothers, 1959.

Martin, Thomas H., *Atlanta and Its Builders,* I, II. Atlanta: Century Memorial Publishing Company, 1902. 2 vols.
Memoirs of Georgia, I. Atlanta: The Southern Historical Association, 1895. 2 vols.
Miller, Paul W., *Atlanta, Capital of the South.* New York: Oliver Durrell, Inc., 1949. American Guide Series.
Moos, Malcolm, *The Republicans, A History of Their Party.* New York: Random House, 1956.
Myers, William Storr, *The Republican Party, A History.* New York: The Century Company, 1928.
Northen, William J., ed., *Men of Mark in Georgia,* III, VII. Atlanta: A. B. Caldwell, 1911. 7 vols.
Pioneer Citizens' History of Atlanta, 1833-1902. Atlanta: Pioneer Citizens Society of Atlanta, 1902.
Reed, Wallace P., *History of Atlanta, Georgia.* Syracuse: D. Mason & Company, 1889.
Sanger, Donald Bridgeman and Thomas Robson Hay, *James Longstreet: I. Soldier; II. Politician, Officeholder, and Writer.* Baton Rouge: Louisiana State University Press, 1952.
Saye, Albert B., *A Constitutional History of Georgia.* Athens: University of Georgia Press, 1948.
Smith, Samuel Denny, *The Negro in Congress, 1870-1901.* Chapel Hill: University of North Carolina Press, 1940.
Smith, Theodore C., *The Life and Letters of James Abram Garfield,* II. New Haven: Yale University Press, 1925. 2 vols.
Stanwood, Edward, *A History of the Presidency from 1788 to 1897.* Boston: Houghton Mifflin Company, 1898.
Thompson, C. Mildred, *Reconstruction in Georgia, Economic, Social, Political, 1865-1872.* New York: The Columbia University Press, 1915. No. 154 in the Columbia University Studies.
Van Noppen, Ina Woestemeyer, *The South, A Documentary History.* Princeton: D. Van Nostrand Company, Inc., 1958.
Wallace, Lew, *Life of Gen. Ben Harrison.* Indianapolis: Union Book Company, 1888.
Ward, George G., Susan Mauney, and one other not identified, "Biographical Sketches of Jonathan Norcross." Unpublished sketches in the Library of the University of Georgia.
Williams, Charles R., *The Life of Rutherford Birchard Hayes,* I, II. Boston: Houghton Mifflin Company, 1914. 2 vols.
Woodward, C. Vann, *Origins of the New South.* Baton Rouge: Louisiana State University Press, 1951. Vol. IX in the *History of the South Series,* Wendell Holmes Stephenson and Merton Coulter, eds.

―――――, *Reunion and Reaction, The Compromise of 1877 and the End of Reconstruction.* Boston: Little, Brown and Company, 1951.

―――――, *Tom Watson, Agrarian Rebel.* New York: Rinehart and Company, Inc., 1938.

Index

Adams, Charles Francis, 36
Adkins, Joseph, 31n
Akerman, Amos T., 16, 22, 28, 35, 39, 57; opposes prolongation, 21; attorney general under Grant, 21, 39, 180 (n14); campaign of 1872, 41-42, 46
Akerman Election Law, 22
Allison, W. B., 130, 131
American party (Know-Nothing), 10
Angier, Nedom L., 25, 48; conflict with Bullock, 25
Arnold, Charles W., member of syndicate, 91, 92, 93, 97-98
Arnold, John W., 93
Arthur, President Chester A., 31, 87; cooperation with Independents, 70-71, 93, 94, 144, 145-47; relations with syndicate, 87n, 90, 91 92-93, 94, 95-96, 98, 100, 101-103, 145-46; concern about re-nomination, 94, 95-96, 100; subordination of Negro, 147; failure of Southern policy, 147
Athens *Banner,* on Negro vote, 111
Athens *Banner-Watchman,* feud with Emory Speer, 74-75
Athens *Blade,* Pledger editor, 56, 79
Athens *Georgian,* on Pledger, 79-80
Athens *North-East Georgian,* on 1872 election in Clarke County, 44
Athens *Southern Watchman,* on inauguration of Smith, 32; on 1872 election, 41, 44; on Negroes in party, 77
Atkins, James S., 30-31, 50, 53, 54, 57, 68, 87n; alleged candidate for governor, 29, 30; formation of syndicate, 90-91; Washington representative of syndicate, 91, 92, 93, 98, 145, 146; advocates white Republican party 94-95; attempts to control 1882 convention, 95-96; rejection for judgeship, 31, 96-97; exasperation with Longstreet, 92, 99; aids Farrow's try for judgeship, 101, 102, 103
Atkinson, R. H., 26
Atkinson, Governor W. Y., 112, 116
Atlanta and West Point Railroad, 25
Atlanta *Constitution,* on 1868 election, 17; on Atkins, "secret candidate," 29; on 1872 delegation, 34; delegates to Liberal-Republican convention, 36n; on Saffold, 38; on Walker and the 1872 election, 41; on Benjamin Conley, 51-52; on election of 1874, 52-53; takes issue with Norcross, 59; on first Markham House conference, 68; on coalition, 69-70; letter from Stephens, 72; on Negroes in party, handling of news, 77; on Pledger, 80; predictions on 1882 convention, 82; on position of Negroes, 87; on Longstreet, 87; Norcross statement on white Republican party, 89; on fusion, 111, 116, 120; welcomes McKinley, 123-24; views on protection, 128; on businessmen's leaning toward Republicanism, 129; cartoon on Hanna, 135; sees

Arthur behind coalition, 147; opposes "Force Bill," 149; meaning of white primary, 154-55
Atlanta *Daily New Era,* suspends publication, 46; Bard, former editor, 51
Atlanta Dixie Band, 132
Atlanta *Journal,* on Negro support of Northen, 111
Atlanta *Republican,* urges support of Felton, 64; "Republican Address," 80-81; W. L. Clarke, editor, 81; supports Hayes, 142-43
"Atlanta Ring," 63
Atlanta *Weekly Defiance,* scene of Pledger caucus, 83
Atlanta *Whig,* official party organ, 46; criticizes party leaders, 54
Atlantic Monthly, series of articles on South, 156
Auburn-Athens football game, 136
Augusta *Constitutionalist,* Gardner, editor, 38; on white primary in Augusta, 154
Augusta *Daily Chronicle,* on Union Republican club parade, 4
"Augusta Ring," 5, 7
Avery, Isaac, 6, 9, 31, 180 (n11); comments on Norcross, 58, 59n, 89

Baldwin County, small vote for Walker, 43; defeat of Negro incumbent, 44
Bard, Samuel, 46, 51, 63
Belcher, Edwin, 13n, 78, 142; connection with syndicate, 95
Bell, Madison, 25, 30, 48
Bell, Dr. W. R., 36n
Bethany College, 30, 48
Bethune, Marion, 23, 24, 53
Bibb County, resolutions on Populists, 110
Bibb Manufacturing Company, 129
Bigby, John S., 24-25, 30, 36, 67, 69
Blaine, James G., 55, 79n, 91, 95n, 100, 141, 147
Blodgett, Foster, 5, 7, 17, 81; named party chairman, 6, 8; candidate for U.S. Senate, 10, 19, 56; charges regarding state railroad, 25, 31; resignation as party chairman, 30, 34
Bourbons, 61, 65, 70, 71, 73, 107, 127, 128; defined, 61n
Bowers, William F., 36n, 85
Bradley, Aaron Alpeoria, 13n, 78
Bristow, Benjamin H., 55, 141

Brown, B. Gratz, 36, 37, 38, 42, 46
Brown, J. H., 83
Brown, Governor Joseph E., 2, 3, 13, 28, 30, 40, 104, 124; views on Reconstruction, 2-3; nomination of Bullock, 8, 9; defeated for U.S. Senate, 10; at Republican national convention, 1868, 15-16; active in Grant-Colfax campaign, 16; opposes Radical policies, 21, 22, 25, 43, 55n; takes part in Liberal-Republican movement, 34, 36, 37-38; returns to Democratic party, 34, 42-43, 44; warns of splitting vote, 63, 119-20; power over patronage, 104n
Bryan County, election disorders, 45
Bryan, William J., 115n, 118
Bryant, John E., 5, 45, 50, 51, 52, 53, 55-56, 65, 66, 81, 86, 102, 103; state party secretary, 5, 7; state party chairman, 54-55, 56, 78-79; supports Pledger faction in 1882 split, 83, 95; secretary of compromise slate, 85, 97; thought Blaine supporter, 91, 95n; member of syndicate, 98; replaces Longstreet as marshal, 87n, 99, 100; conflict with Hayes, 142, 143
Buck, Alfred E., 70, 82, 86, 109, 113; supports Pledger faction in 1882 split, 83, 84, 85, 95; becomes state party chairman, 85-86; thought Blaine supporter, 91, 95n, 96; member of syndicate, 98; takes hand in patronage, 99-100, 101, 102, 103; undisputed leader of party, 104; shifts position on fusion, 108, 110, 111, 112, 115, 116, 117-18, 149-50; goes to Tokyo as minister, 119, 158; welcomes McKinley to Atlanta, 124, 125; on protectionists in Georgia, 127-28; manages McKinley campaign, 131-35; opposes Hayes's Southern policy, 143; conduct of party criticized, 158, 159
Bullock, Governor Rufus B., 5, 9, 14, 16, 28, 29, 31, 40, 42, 44, 46, 51, 81, 124, 155; excesses of administration, vii, 19, 33, 38, 39, 43, 48, 77; election as governor, 7, 8-9; takes office, 10; opposed by Moderate Republicans, 9, 10, 12-13, 14, 15, 21, 55; return to military rule, 17-18; pushes prolongation plot, 21-22; resigns and leaves state, 25-26; repudiated by Farrow, 30, 39-40; acquitted of charges, 159;

Index 205

later position in party, 159-60, 193 (n22)
"Bullock-Blodgett Ring," 56
Butler, General Benjamin F., 19

Campbell, Tunis G., 78
Candler, Governor Allen D., 75, 119
Carpetbaggers, 1, 4, 9, 11, 26, 54, 112, 137, 158; preference given under Grant, 50, 51, 138, 156; Bryant termed "most obnoxious," 56; opposed by syndicate, 91, 92; shunned by Hayes, 139, 140, 141, 142
Carroll County, "illegal" vote for Populists, 114
Chicago *Tribune*, on Markham House conference, 68; interview with Felton, 69, 70, 74, 147
Christy, John H., 11
Clark, Andrew, 92n, 93
Clark, W. L., 64-65, 80, 81, 88, 142-43
Clarke County "redeemed," 44
Clarkson, James S., 130
Clements, Judson C., 65
Cleveland, President Grover, 103, 104, 113, 122, 123
Clift, Joseph W., 11
Colfax, Schuyler, 15, 16, 37
Columbia County, drop in Republican vote, 14-15
Collins, James D., 129
Colquitt, Governor Alfred H., 56, 57, 58, 82; supported by Negroes, 60, 110; opposes Speer appointment, 103-104
Compromise of 1877, 139
Confederate army, 23, 25, 67
Confederate Nitre and Mining Bureau, 5
Conkling, Roscoe, 55, 87n, 91, 141
Conley, Governor Benjamin, 5, 17, 26, 33, 35, 37, 39, 81; president of Senate, 10, 31; succeeds Bullock as governor, 26-27, 31; views of office, 27, 29; conflict with legislature, 28, 44; transfer of office, 31-32; difficulties with patronage, 50-52, 53; appointed postmaster in Atlanta, 51-52; promotes nomination of Norcross, 56, 57; supports Farrow-Longstreet faction, 83, 84, 85
Conley, John L., 39, 45; difficulties with patronage, 50-51, 52, 53; supports Farrow-Longstreet faction, 83

Constitutional convention of 1867-68, 4, 7, 8; delegates, 4-5, 6, 11, 13, 21, 23, 24, 25, 26, 81-82, 176 (n11); proceedings, 6-7, 176 (n19); nominating session, 7-8
Convention of 1865, 24
Cotting, David G., 25, 48
Cullom, Shelby M., 130, 131
Cunningham, J. D., 85
Cunningham, John, 117
"Custom House Ring," 50, 52, 56

Darnell, Sion A., 53, 83, 85, 108; connection with syndicate, 95
Davis, B. J., 134
Davis, Madison, 13n, 44, 74-75, 184 (n43)
"Dear Mat" letter, 74-75
Decatur County "redeemed," 52-53
Decline of the party in Georgia by 1900, deterioration from within, 155, 160; outside forces, 155-56; problem of the Negro, 156-57, conditions in 1900, 157-58
Delegates to Republican national conventions, 1868-100, Appendix C, 166-73; some mentioned individually, *passim*; basis for apportionment, 34; usual method of selection, 34, 54; controversy over selection, 34-35, 54-55, 78-79, 131-32, 133-34
Democracy Examined, by Norcross, 58
Desire for second party, vii, 156
Deveaux, James B., 147
Deveaux, John H., 131, 132, 133, 134, 159
Disorders on election days, 45, 65, 114, 136
Dunning, James, 29

Edwards, William Posey, 11
Election of U.S. Senators, 10, 19, 30
Elections in Georgia (state elections in October, national elections in November, unless otherwise specified), for constitutional convention, October-November, 1867, 4; state election, April, 1868, 8-9, 14-15; national election, 1868, 14-15, 16-17, 46-47, 76, 137; state and national elections, December, 1870, 21-23; special election for governor, December, 1871, 28, 29; state election, 1872, 39, 40-45; national election, 1872, 45-47; state election, 1874, 52-53, 62; national

election, 1874, 52, 53, 63; state election, 1876, 57-60; national election, 1876, 63, 64, 141; national election, 1878, 63, 64, 74; national election, 1880, 65-66, 74 (143n); state election, 1882, 73, 85; national election, 1882, 73, 74-75, 85, 98; national election, 1888, 148; state and national elections, 1890, 106, 107; state election, 1892, 107, 108, 110, 112; state and national elections, 1894, 112, 114-15, 120; state election, 1896, 116, 117-18; national election, 1896, 115, 118, 122-36, 150; state and national elections, 1898, 119; state election, 1900, 119.
Emory College at Oxford, 24
Erskine, John J., 100, 101, 102
Evans, Dr. Charles, 29

Fain, John S., 36n
Farmers' Alliances, 105-106; in Georgia, 106, 107; Colored Alliance, 109
Farrow, Henry P., 5-6, 16, 19, 23, 29, 50, 56, 81; officer of Union League, 4, 5, 81-82; candidate for nomination for governor, 7, 8; attorney general under Bullock, 21, 25; opposes some Bullock policies, 21, 22, 25, 29-30; state party chairman, 34, 35, 39, 40, 54, 55, 179 (n1); U.S. attorney for Georgia, 25, 39, 45, 53; cooperation with Independents, 68-73, 75, 93, 94, 146; opposition to Longstreet, 68, 87, 92, 93, 99; party split in 1882, 83-85; recognition of Negro problem, 87; the syndicate, 90-99; collector of customs at Brunswick, 93, 97, 104n, 146; campaign for judgeship, 100-103; later position in party, 104
Federal patronage, 40, 57, 70, 78; preoccupation of party with, viii, 49-50, 53-54, 93, 158; officeholders control party, 35, 40, 50, 78, 81, 82, 87; divisive force, 49, 53, 77, 94, 157; experience of Benjamin Conley, 50-52; postoffice Republicans, 160. See also Syndicate
Felton, Rebecca L., 62-63, 65-66, 68, 72
Felton, Dr. William H., 62-63, 73, 75, 101n, 105, 129; elected to Congress as Independent, 63; Republican support in campaigns, 63-66, 73-74, 144, 145; defeated for Congress, 65, 73; coalition with Republicans, 66, 67-73; denounced by Benjamin Hill, 70, 183; patronage activities of syndicate, 92, 93, 94; warning by Hill and Stephens, 146-47
Fielder, Herbert, 43-44
Fifteenth Amendment, 14, 18, 19, 148; circumvented by white primary, 153
Finch, William, 35
Fitzsimmons, O. P., 142
"Force Bill" of 1890, 148, 149
Forsyth, C. D., 85, 98
Fortune, T. Thomas, 130
Fourteenth Amendment, 2, 10, 19, 148; test of eligibility, 12, 18
Freedmen's Bureau, 3, 4; Bryant connection, 5, 55
Freeman, James C., 47, 53
Fulton County, factional strife, 53, 60
Fusion in Georgia, 105-21, 149-50, 153; contrasted with Independent movement, 105; effects on Populist and Republican parties, 111-12, 119, 120
Fusion in North Carolina, 120, 188 (n48)

Gardner, James, 38, 180 (n10)
Garfield, President James, 65, 143, 147; Southern policy, 144-45
Gartrell, General Lucius J., 73, 84, 101n
Georgia Act of July 15, 1870, 19
Georgia Platform of 1850, 1
Georgia *Republican*, backs Holtzclaw against Felton, 65
Georgia state troops, 13
Georgia Supreme Court, 2, 13, 26, 32, 39, 40; test case on Negro officeholders, 13
Georgia Volunteer Infantry, 11
Gibson, William, 36n
Gordon, General John B., 9, 48, 53; patronage power, 64, 101n, 140, 142
Gorham, George C., 64
Gove, Samuel Francis, 11, 53
Grady, Henry W., 70, 74, 128, 160n
Grant, A. P., 113
Grant, President Ulysses S., 21, 28, 39, 79n, 91; election in 1868, 8, 14-16; administration, 35, 43, 46; election in 1872, 37, 41-42, 45, 46-47; friendship with Longstreet, 67n, 92, 99; Southern policy, 137-38, 139, 142
Greeley, Horace, 36, 37; support in Georgia, 37-38, 41, 42, 44; unpopularity, 46-47

• *Index* 207

Griffin *American Union*, advocates Farrow for governor, 7
Gwinnett County, Negroes organized for Populists, 114

Hall, John I., 42
Hammond, W. M., 126
Hanna, Mark, 117, 122, 135, 150; Strategy in South, 124-26, 127, 129, 130
Hanna, Mel, 125
Hanson, James F., 129-30; active in 1896 campaign, 131, 132, 133, 134, 135, 159
Harbin, N. P., 63
Harrell, David B., 36n
Hargrove, Z. B., 64, 65, 110
Harris, A. L., 18, 178 (n53); protests conditions in party, 158-59
Harris, John, 36n, 37
Harrison, President Benjamin, 111, 115, 130, 148; attempt to pass "Force Bill," 148-49; support of fusion, 149-50; failure of Southern policies, 150
Harvard Medical School, 11
Hauck, Thomas, 52
Hayes, President Rutherford B., 56, 144, 147; conciliatory attitude toward South, 139-40; subordination of Negro, 139, 140, 141, 142, 147; visit to Atlanta, 141; unpopularity with Georgia Republicans, 141-43; failure of Southern policy, 143, 157
Hayes, Mrs. Rutherford B., 141
Hendricks, J. C., 36n, 118
Hetherington, J. H., 134
Hill, Benjamin H., 53, 74, 156; disapproves Felton policies, 64, 70, 146, 147
Hill, Joshua, 10-11, 19, 28; term in U.S. Senate, 12, 23, 24, 48
Hines, James K., 112, 113, 116
History of Democracy, by Norcross, 58
Hogan, J. R., 119
Holtzclaw, J. A., 65
Hook, James J., 69
Hooks, Charles S., 36n
Howell, Evan P., 128
Hulbert, Edward, 36n
Humphrey, R. M., 109

Independent movement in Georgia, 61-75, 93, 94, 144, 145-47; Republican support a liability, 63-65, 73-75

Jackson, Henry, 101n

Jackson, James, 101n
Jackson, Jesse W., 53, 54, 60
Jackson, General Stonewall, 13
Jenkins, Governor Charles J., 1-2, 6, 10, 58
Johnson, President Andrew, 1, 2, 11, 97, 100n, 140
Johnson, Henry Lincoln, 113, 116, 132, 133, 134; comment on Populist attitude toward Negro, 117
Johnson, Provisional Governor James, 1, 30, 36, 113
Johnson, Tomlinson F., 83, 115
Johnson, Walter H., 83, 101, 113, 116, 187 (n27); secretary of state party, 85, 97; member of syndicate, 91, 92, 93, 145; acting chairman for Buck, 113, 119, 133; position in party in 1900, 158
Jones, John, 6

Key, David M., 140
Kimball, Hannibal I., 25, 160n
Ku Klux Klan, 14, 15, 45, 56, 138, 155

Lee, General Robert E., 66
Legislature, party alignment: 1868, 9, 13, 18; 1871, 27-28; 1873, 44; 1875, 52, 62; 1891, 106; 1895, 114-15; 1897, 118
Liberal Republican movement, 33-34, 35-36; Cincinnati convention, 36; Georgia convention, 37-38; effect on Georgia state election, 1872, 42-43; reasons for failure, 46-47
Livingston, Leonidas, 118
Lochrane, O. A., 26, 178 (n16)
Locke, R. D., 83, 84, 129, 133, 134; connection with syndicate 95
Long, Jefferson F., 23, 45, 54, 57, 78, 132; only Negro congressman from Georgia, 24; campaigns for Felton, 64, 182 (n10)
Longstreet, General James, 66-67, 85, 135; cooperation with Independents, 64, 66, 67, 68, 70-72, 145, 146; position as party leader, 67n, 82, 88n, 97; friendship with Grant 67n, 92, 99; party split in 1882, 83-85; white Republican movement, 86, 87-89, 94; member of syndicate, 91, 92, 93, 95, 97; ousted as marshal, 99-100.
Love, E. K., 126, 131, 134
Loyal Leagues (Union Leagues), 3
Lumpkin, J. H., 101n

Macon, election disorders, 45
Macon *Telegraph,* on Independent candidates, 62; on 1896 convention, 134
Macon *Weekly Telegraph,* on Norcross speech, 58
Macon *Union,* on special election, 28
Magee, Chris, 149-50
Mahone, General William, 144-45
Markham House conferences, first conference, 67-69, 72, 75, 90, 92, 97, 105, 145; second conference, 71, 72, 75
Markham House Platform, 69
Markham, William, 4, 5, 6, 29, 35, 54, 60
Mayor of Atlanta, 124; Markham, 6; Norcross, 57
McCay, Henry K., 13, 96n
McKinley, President William, 86, 115, 122, 123, 130; visit to Atlanta in 1888, 123-24, 128; trip to Georgia in 1895, 125-27, 129, 130; support in Georgia, 131, 132, 133, 134, 135; election, 135-36, 150; new approach to South, 122, 127, 150
McKinley, Mrs. William, 125-26
McWhorter, J. H., 36n
McWhorter, R. L., 10, 36n, 37
Meade, General George G., 6, 9, 12, 18
Milledgeville *Federal Union,* on prolongation scheme, 20; on Liberal Republican movement, 36, 38-39; on 1872 election, 41, 43; on Negroes in party, handling of news, 77
Miller, Dr. H. V. M., U.S. Senator, 10, 12, 19, 23; Markham House conference, 69
Mills, J. T. W., 18
Moderate Republicans in Georgia, key position in legislature, 9, 10, 12-13, 14, 21; falling away from Bullock, 15, 49, 77, 156; interest in Liberal Republican movement, 36
"Moral Party," 57
Morgan County elects Democrats, 52
Morton, Levi P., 130, 131
Morton, Oliver P., 55, 141
Mott, R. L., 30, 36n, 37

Negroes, abandonment by national party: new approach by McKinley, 127, 131, 150; change of opinion in North, 138; subordination by Hayes and Arthur, 139, 140, 141, 142, 147; defeat of "Force Bill," 148-49

Negroes, expulsion from legislature, 12-13, 14
Negroes, predominance in state party: 23, 28, 39, 40, 54, 75, 108, 118, 124, 127, 132, 154, 155, 157-58; party develops from Union Leagues, 3-4; great majority of Republican voters Negroes, 40, 77, 118, 127, 154; effect on party, 76-77, 156, 157; Negroes get upper hand in 1880, 78-79; dilemma of party, 87, 157
Negroes, return to legislature, 18
Negroes, suffrage: 4, 12, 15, 76; vote reduced by intimidation, 14-15, 17, 47, 138; effect of poll tax, 44-45; white primary, 153, 154-55
"New Movement," 70
New South, 127, 128
New York *Herald,* on special election, 28; Bullock's letter criticizing party heads, 159
New York *Sun,* editor in Georgia, 130
New York *Times,* Bullock's letter on alleged irregularities, 18; interview with Key, 140
Norcross, Jonathan, 52, 57, 77; candidate for governor in 1876, 57-59; not unfriendly to Negroes, 59-60; heads white Republican movement, 80, 81, 86, 88-89
Northen, Governor W. J., 107, 109, 110, 111, 112, 116

Oglethorpe County, drop in Republican vote, 14

Paris, Robert M., 36n
Parrott, J. R., 7, 30, 36n
Peek, W. L., 106, 109, 111, 112, 118, 150; comment on Republican support, 111-12
People's party (Populist), 106, 107; bond between Republicans and Populists in Georgia, 107-108; appeal to Negro, 109-10; resentment of Negro, 117. *See also* Fusion in Georgia
People's Party Paper, published by Thomas E. Watson, 106
Piedmont Chautauqua, 123, 124
Pierce, W. P., 53
Pleasant, L. M., 95, 134; connection with syndicate, 95
Pledger, William A., 56, 57, 81, 89, 95, 135, 158n; becomes state party chairman, 79-80; deposed, 82-85, 94;

- *Index*

opposes fusion, 108-109, 110, 111, 113, 116, 118; opposes McKinley slate, 131, 132, 133, 134; tactics protested, 134; ignored by Hayes and Arthur, 142, 147; comment on Bullock, 159; runs for legislature, 192 (n6)
Poll tax, source of irritation, 44-45
Pope, General John, 11
Pope, John D., 36n, 37, 180 (n15)
Postoffice Republicans, 160
Presidential Republicans, 136, 160
Prince, Charles Henry, 11, 50, 51, 54, 91
Prolongation dispute, 20, 21, 22, 30
Protectionist views in Georgia, 122, 123, 127-29, 159, 193 (n18)
Putnam County, Negroes vote Populist, 114
Putney, F. F., 85

Quarles, J. F., 37
Quay, Matthew, 130, 131, 132, 134

Rawls, Morgan, 47
Readjuster movement, 144-45
Reconstruction in Georgia, legal phases: presidential reconstruction, 1; under Sherman Act, 2-10; under special act of December 22, 1869, 18-19
Reconstruction period, 1-32, 40, 43, 46, 137-38, 158; identification of Republican party with Radical Reconstruction, vii, viii, 33, 76, 155, 156; later echoes, viii, 44, 48, 58, 114, 120, 139, 149
Reed, H. W., 117
Reed, T. W., 111
Reed, Thomas B., 130, 131, 132, 134
Reimann, F., 80
"Republican Address," 1880, 80-81
Republican members of Congress from Georgia, 1868-75, Appendix A, 162-63. *See also* each name
Republican newspapers in Georgia, 46, 64-65, 80-81, 142-43
Republican Presidential Electors for Georgia, 1868-1900, Appendix B, 163-65; some mentioned individually, *passim*
Republican state conventions in Georgia, organization convention, July 4, 1867, 5, 6; special nominating convention, March 7, 1868, 7-8; March 5, 1869, 17; May 8-9, 1872, 35; August 21, 1872, 39; May 3, 1876, 54; August 16, 1876, 56-57; April 21, 1880, 78-79; August 2, 1882, 82-85, 94, 95-96; April, 1892, 108; August 11, 1892, 108-109; August 29, 1894, 112-14; April 29, 1896, 131-34; March, 1900, 157-58, 193 (n22)
"Revenue Clique," 50
Richardson, Alfred, 44
Richardson, Ed S., 109
Rome, election disorders in 1880, 65; duty to support Populists, 110
Roosevelt, President Theodore, 156-57
"Rowdy Party," 57
Rucker, H. A., 132, 133, 159

Saffold, Thomas P., 36, 38
St. Clair-Abrams, Alexander, 27, 28
Savannah, riot at polls, 45
Savannah *Journal,* official party organ, 46
Savannah *Morning News,* on term "Radical," 3; on financial policies of Cleveland, 128
Scalawags, 1, 5, 137
Sewall, Arthur, 115n
Sherman Act, 2, 4
Sherman, John, 79n, 97, 128, 142-43
Sherman, General William T., 11
Simms, James M., connection with syndicate, 95
Sloan, Andrew, 47-48, 53
Smith, Governor James M., 29, 31, 32, 39, 41, 42, 43, 44, 48, 58
Smith, W. E., 53
Smyth, W. H., 79n, 91, 134
Snelson, Floyd, 85
Solid South, comment by Joseph E. Brown, 119-20; cause of, 138; schemes to disrupt, 147, 148
"Southern Question," 137, 139, 148, 150
Southwest Georgian, official party organ, 46
Speer, Emory, 101n, 105, 146; elected to Congress as Independent, 63, 74; defeated, 73, 98; supported by Republicans, 74-75, 144; cooperation with syndicate, 75n, 95, 96, 98-99, 100; becomes member of syndicate, 99; appointed judge, 102-104
Speer, Thomas J., 23, 24
Stephens, Governor Alexander H., 10, 55n, 75; overtures of Independents, 67, 68, 71, 72, 94, 146; elected gov-

ernor as Democrat, 73; opposed by Republicans, 73, 84; warns Felton of Radicals, 146-47
Splits in party, viii, 84n; two organizations in 1882, 83-85; in 1896, 134, 190 (n7). *See also* white Republican movements
State central committee heads, Appendix D, 174. *See also* each name
State Medical College, 62
State railroad, 25, 31
Strickland, Solomon L., 36n
Summers, J. W. B., 36n
Syndicate, 82, 84, 90-104, 145, 146, 147; formation and objects, 90-91; original members, 91; members added, 95, 98-99; dissolution, 104

Talmadge, John E., 72n
Terrell County, Negroes solid for Populists, 114
Terry, General Alfred E., 18
Terry's Purge, 18
Thirteenth Amendment, 1
Thomasville, Negroes wrought up over fusion, 110
Thomasville phase of McKinley campaign, 125-26
Thompson, Mildred, 9
Thomas, George S., 85
Thurman, T. W., 35
Tillson, General Davis, 55
Toombs, Robert, 10, 11, 55n
Trammell, L. N., 27
Traylor, L. H., 119
Turner, H. M., 54-55, 78, 184 (n4)
Tyner, James N., 140n

Union Leagues, foundation for state Republican parties, 3-4, 5, 76; Farrow connection, 5, 6, 7, 8, 82; active in elections, 4, 15
"Union Republican Party of Georgia," 5, 6, 55
Unionists in Georgia, vii, 2, 6, 7, 58, 62, 97, 107, 156

United States Supreme Court, 2, 86
University of Georgia, 25, 62, 64
University of Virginia, 5

Walker, Dawson A., 8, 35, 40-41; candidate for governor in 1872, 39-42; defeated, 43-44
Wallace, George, 35, 44, 54
Ware County, Populists supported by Negroes, 114
Warner, Hiram, 13, 32
Waterville College, 86
Watson, Thomas E., 63n, 106, 113; Populist leader, 106, 107, 112, 114, 115n; 1892 views on Negro, 109-10; comments on fusion, 112, 115n, 121
Whig party in Georgia, vii, 3, 88, 139, 144, 156; former Whigs: Jenkins, 1, 10; Markham, 6; Joshua Hill, 10; Stephens, 10, 71; Toombs, 10; Benjamin Conley, 26; Norcross, 57, 58; Benjamin Hill, 156
"Whig Republican party," 88
White, W. J., 85
White primary in Georgia, statewide, 152; earlier development, 153-54; effect on Republican party, 154-55
White Republican movements, 59n, 157; by Norcross in 1880, 80, 81; by Norcross and Longstreet in 1884, 86, 87-89; Atkins advocates, 94-95
Whiteley, Richard H., 19, 23-24, 47, 53
Wikle, J. R., 65-66
Wilson, Alexander, 68, 69, 97, 98, 101; member of syndicate, 91, 92, 93, 95, 97, 99, 100
Wilson, Henry, 4, 37, 39, 41, 42, 45, 46
Wimbish, C. C., 113, 158, 193 (n7)
Wimpy John A., 11, 53
Wood, William B., 86
Wright, Richard R., 84, 126; rejected as delegate, 132, 133, 134, 159, 190 (n33); holds rump convention, 134
Wright, Seaborn, 116

www.ingramcontent.com/pod-product-compliance
Lightning Source LLC
Chambersburg PA
CBHW020947230426
43666CB00005B/201